The Ethics of Climate Change

The Ethics of Climate Change: An Introduction systematically and comprehensively examines the ethical issues surrounding arguably the greatest threat now facing humanity. Williston addresses important questions such as:

- Has humanity entered the Anthropocene?
- Is climate change primarily an ethical issue?
- Does climate change represent a moral wrong?
- What are the impacts of climate change?
- What are the main causes of political inaction?
- What is the argument for climate change denial?
- What are intragenerational justice and intergenerational justice?
- To what extent is climate change an economic problem?
- Is geoengineering an ethically appropriate response to climate change?

Featuring case studies throughout, this textbook provides a philosophical introduction to an immensely topical issue studied by students within the fields of applied ethics, global justice, sustainability, geography, and politics.

Byron Williston is Associate Professor of Philosophy at Wilfrid Laurier University, Canada. He is the author of *The Anthropocene Project: Virtue in the Age of Climate Change* (OUP, 2015).

THE ETHICS OF ...

When is it right to go to war? What are the causes of poverty? Are human intelligence and machine intelligence the same? What is cyber-terrorism? Do races exist? What makes a person a refugee?

Each engaging textbook from *The Ethics of...* series focuses on a significant ethical issue and provides a clear and stimulating explanation of the surrounding philosophical discussions. Focusing on moral debates at the forefront of contemporary society they have been designed for use by students studying philosophy, applied ethics, global ethics and related subjects such as politics, international relations and sociology. Features to aid study include chapter summaries, study questions, annotated further reading and glossaries.

Published titles:

The Ethics of War and Peace: An Introduction
Second Edition
Helen Frowe
978-0-415-72481-4

The Ethics of Global Poverty: An Introduction
Scott Wisor
978-1-138-82706-6

The Ethics of Surveillance: An Introduction
Kevin Macnish
978-1-138-64379-6

You can find all available titles in this series at: https://www.routledge.com/The-Ethics-of-/book-series/ETHICSOF.

The Ethics of Climate Change

An Introduction

Byron Williston

Routledge
Taylor & Francis Group

LONDON AND NEW YORK

First published 2019
by Routledge
2 Park Square, Milton Park, Abingdon, Oxon OX14 4RN

and by Routledge
711 Third Avenue, New York, NY 10017

Routledge is an imprint of the Taylor & Francis Group, an informa business

British Library Cataloguing-in-Publication Data
A catalogue record for this book is available from the British Library

Library of Congress Cataloging-in-Publication Data
Names: Williston, Byron, 1965- author.
Title: The ethics of climate change : an introduction / Byron Williston.
Description: Abingdon, Oxon ; New York, NY : Routledge, [2019] |
Series: The ethics of | Includes bibliographical references and index.
Identifiers: LCCN 2018006048| ISBN 9781138559783 (hbk : alk. paper) |
ISBN 9781138559790 (pbk : alk. paper) | ISBN 9780429471148 (ebk)
Subjects: LCSH: Environmental ethics. | Climatic changes–Moral and ethical aspects. |
Global environmental change–Moral and ethical aspects.
Classification: LCC GE42 .W56 2019 | DDC 179.1–dc23
LC record available at https://lccn.loc.gov/2018006048

ISBN: 978-1-138-55978-3 (hbk)
ISBN: 978-1-138-55979-0 (pbk)
ISBN: 978-0-429-47114-8 (ebk)

Typeset in Times New Roman
by Taylor & Francis Books

Contents

Introduction

In 1992, the Union of Concerned Scientists issued a "Warning to Humanity." The letter was signed by some 1,500 scientists, and warned of an impending biospherical crisis if rampant industrialization were not curbed. In November, 2017, 25 years after that warning appeared, more than 15,000 scientists signed an updated version of it. Apart from the number of signatories, the biggest difference between the two warnings is that the second one identifies climate change as one of the principal threats we now face:

> Especially troubling is the current trajectory of potentially catastrophic climate change due to rising GHGs from burning fossil fuels ... deforestation ... and agricultural production – particularly from farming ruminants for meat production ... Moreover, we have unleashed a mass extinction event, the sixth in roughly 540 million years, wherein many current life forms could be annihilated or at least committed to extinction by the end of this century.[1]

And yet, according to the 2017 report on global energy use from the International Energy Agency (IEA), demand for energy is expected to rise by 30% by 2030, with the bulk of this demand being met by fossil fuels.[2] The IEA is a notoriously conservative organization, so these projections cannot easily be dismissed.

The picture these two recent documents leave us with is not pretty. Together, they testify to the seemingly growing gap between our understanding of the accelerating damage being done to the biosphere by human activity and the creeping pace of our institutional response to this reality. Clearly, we require a shift in our thinking about our place in the Earth system if we are to minimize the impact of, or even just survive, the crises we are bringing upon ourselves through our profligate carbon emissions. This book is an attempt to help us come to grips with this task. It shows that our chief failing so far is an ethical one, and that the solution to the problem – if there is one – must also be ethical.

What does this mean? Well, the book as a whole supplies a comprehensive answer to this question, but here's a thumbnail version of it. As I understand it, we have compelling reasons to act aggressively towards the goal of reducing our carbon footprint dramatically. We must have a carbon-neutral global economy within two or three decades, a requirement entirely contrary to the IEA's prediction about the shape of our near future global energy regime. The reason for the requirement is straightforward. The impact anthropogenic climate change is having on the planet's most vulnerable groups – the global poor, future generations, and non-human species – is both profound and ethically outrageous. When I say "we" or "our" here, and throughout the book, I am referring principally to currently existing citizens of the rich, developed countries of the global north. These people have strong duties to constrain themselves so as to protect the vital interests of the groups just mentioned. "Constraint," for its part, is a catch-all for the diverse things that must be done, from curbing carbon-intensive consumption to building just global and national institutions.

Before getting to a summary of each chapter, let me make two methodo-logical points. The first is that this book is written from the standpoint of what has come to be known as Anglo-American philosophy. The approach taken here does not consider at any length the manner in which the climate crisis has been explored by philosophers working in non-Western traditions. Climate change is a quintessentially global problem, and it is being subjected to rigorous analysis by, among others, Indian, African, Chinese and Japanese philosophers, not to mention all those scholars and thinkers representing the world's diverse indigenous peoples. I am not an expert in any of these traditions and it would be both disrespectful and disingenuous of me to pose as one. So I have not considered them. This is a genuine pity. But even if I were equipped to write intelligently about these philosophical traditions and positions, doing so here would have made this book impossibly long and unfit for its primary function: a textbook introducing the main contours of philosophical debate in this area. It is an attempt to summarize the large body of existing literature known as Climate Change Ethics in Anglo-American philosophy.

This brings me to the second point. The other broad philosophical approach *not* represented here is "continental" philosophy (hermeneutics, phenomenology, existentialism and their offshoots). The body of literature just mentioned is, by contrast, largely "analytic" in orientation. Again, there is excellent work being done on the phenomenon of climate change generally in continental philosophy, but including it here would have increased the size of the volume substantially. These two points do indicate the need for a larger climate change ethics project, one that brings together Western and non-Western work on the one hand and continental and analytic work on the other. But that would be a different kind of book than this one.

Neither of these points should be taken to imply that there is something objectionably parochial about the methodology adopted here. The book is meant to be both comprehensive in scope and accessible to anyone who gives it serious consideration. Were the book to open up a dialogue with non-Western or non-analytic sources about the ethical challenges of climate change that would be a happy by-product of its primary aim. The more people representing a diversity of philosophical traditions and perspectives we can get talking about these issues the better. With that apology out of the way, here's a brief summary of each chapter.

Chapter 1 lays out the basic science of climate change. The goal of the chapter as a whole is to provide the reader with an up-to-date account of where things stand regarding the physical science of anthropogenic climate change. We start with an explanation of the greenhouse effect, moving next to projections of the effects of climate change in four areas of concern: heat waves, droughts, wildfires, sea-level rise and extreme precipitation events. Following this, we will see what impacts these effects will have on human and non-human systems. We close with some brief reflections on the nature of ethical scientific communication.

Chapter 2 examines the philosophical discipline of climate change ethics. We begin with an analysis of the distinction between ideal and non-ideal ethical theory. As we will see, the distinction is especially illuminating in the effort to find rationally justifiable climate policy. We will ask how climate change ethics fits into the larger field of environmental ethics, how economics provides a challenge to it, whether it is required to make sense of the threats of climate change, and, finally, whether it is adequate to that task.

In Chapter 3, we take a look at international climate change policy. We examine the ethical foundations of international climate policy, as well as the history of climate diplomacy. We begin with an analysis of the precautionary principle, moving next to the main objectives of international climate policy (namely, to help get a grip on the challenges of adaptation and mitigation), three key drivers of climate change, and some of the most important developments in climate diplomacy over roughly the last 20 years.

In Chapter 4, we begin the work of climate change ethics proper by looking at international justice. We begin with an analysis of the connection between climate change and human rights, before moving to a consideration of the nature of climate justice and why so many in the developed world have resisted justice-talk in this area. Next, we examine climate change as an example of the tragedy of the commons. This brings us to a detailed analysis of some important principles of climate justice, with a focus on the polluter pays principle. We close with an examination of the right to development and its problematic connection to the imperative to curb global carbon emissions radically.

Chapter 5 extends the analysis of justice to the intergenerational sphere. How should we think about the interests of future people in our policy deliberations? Why should they count and how much? This chapter examines those questions. We begin with Stephen Gardiner's analysis of how bad things might get for future people under business as usual. Next, focusing on Derek Parfit's non-identity problem, we examine why it is so problematic to say we wrong them by continuing down this path. This brings us to a sustained engagement with a broadly contractarian approach to intergenerational obligations, rooted in the philosophy of John Rawls. We close with some skeptical reflections on this approach to the problem.

Everything so far has been about humans. What about the rest of the biosphere? Chapter 6 takes up this issue. The chapter begins by asking why species and ecosystems matter morally. Why are they valuable? The discussion brings us to an analysis of what our duties of species preservation look like in the age of climate change. This is a difficult task because we are now in the Anthropocene, a new geological epoch defined by pervasive human influence in the Earth system. Next, applying some traditional moral doctrines, we ask whether or not it is permissible for us to engage in the sort of "activist preservationist" projects the new epoch seems to demand of us. This is followed by critical analysis of the claims (a) that the Anthropocene is a welcome moment in human history; and (b) that nature is at an end.

The chapters on justice had to do mainly with the duties of collectives, or individuals just to the extent that they belong to collectives. Chapter 7 extends the analysis by looking directly at the question of individual duties. We begin by locating it in the inescapable context of collective action problems. In an effort to understand the psychological dynamics that make those situations go awry so often, we look at the idea any individual might have that his or her contributions to the problem are "negligible." We will attempt to find a way around this very compelling thought, first by showing how to moralize the small consumption choices we make all the time; and second, by turning to a virtue-ethical analysis of the problem. This will bring us to a direct consideration of what individuals should do in our non-ideal situation. We examine two options: (a) working for meaningful political change; and (b) carbon offsetting.

Why have we done virtually nothing about climate change? A large part of the answer to this question is that we have denied the existence or severity of the problem. Climate change denial is therefore the focus of Chapter 8. We begin with a sketch of virtue epistemology, moving next to a description of what the ideal epistemic agent believes about climate change. This brings us to climate change denial, which we examine in the subsequent three sections. The first two deal with a familiar form of denial – here, following Harry Frankfurt, analyzed as climate change 'bullshit' – the third with a less familiar form that can show up among otherwise progressive people.

Chapter 9, our final chapter, considers the ethics of geoengineering – the suite of technologies designed to cool the planet as a response to dangerous heating. As we will see, proposals to research and deploy geoengineering technologies raise profound ethical questions. Our focus is on the many challenges of responding to geoengineering proposals in accordance with the principles of justice examined in earlier chapters. We thus look at this phenomenon through the lenses of distributive, intergenerational, procedural and corrective justice. We conclude with some brief reflections on what the very idea of geoengineering tells us about our ethically precarious position.

Two final points. First, I want to reiterate that this is an *introduction* to climate change ethics. As I have said, it seeks to gather together the most important developments in the existing literature, not develop new positions. Much like IPCC reports, it is essentially a work of synthesis. Moreover, while we will assess the soundness of numerous arguments over the following nine chapters, these assessments should not be mistaken for final pronouncements on the topic at hand. They are better viewed as invitations to take philosophical reflection even further than I have done here. For readers wanting to track down the original work on which I have drawn here, the suggested reading lists at the end of each chapter are a good place to start.

Second, no reader will fail to notice that I think the climate predicament into which we have stumbled is quite dire, even tragic. As I see it, that view is an inescapable reaction to the facts staring us in the face. But this book is not a requiem for our species. Climate change ethics makes sense as a discipline only if the assumption that we can still change things is warranted. The book in your hands or on your screen is evidence of my opinion that it is.

This book would not have been possible without the hundreds of conversations about climate change I have had over the last decade or so with friends, colleagues, family members and students. I derive a lot of energy from the profound commitment so many people evidently still have to figuring this thing out rationally and humanely, and I thank all of them for this. I am also grateful to Dale Jamieson, William Throop, Philip Cafaro, Jennifer Welchman, Tyler DesRoches, Frank Jankunis, Jason Kawall and Henry Shue for general philosophical encouragement on this topic. Special thanks to Shohini Ghose, Joel daSilva, Shanna Braden, Simon Dalby and the anonymous reviewers at Routledge for their perceptive comments on earlier drafts. My editors Rebecca Shillabeer and Gabrielle Coakeley have been enthusiastic supporters of the project since its inception and have guided me expertly through the publication process. I thank them, as well as my excellent copyeditor, Fliss Watts, warmly. Finally, a special shout out to my two kids – George and Pippa – for listening to my periodic rants on this topic with such forbearance.

Notes

1 William J. Ripple, Christopher Wolf, et al., "World Scientists' Warning to Humanity: A Second Notice," *BioScience* 67 (12), 2017, 1026–1028. DOI: 10.1093/biosci/bix125.
2 Madeline Cuff, "10 Things You Need to Know About the World Energy Outlook 2017," *Greenbiz*, November 15, 2017. https://www.greenbiz.com/article/10-things-you-need-know-world-energy-out look-2017. Accessed: November 17, 2017.

1 The basic science

Introduction

At or around the time of writing, the American southwest has just emerged from an unprecedented heat wave (described by a resident of Phoenix, Arizona as more like a "heat attack"), huge tracts of forest in California, Portugal and British Columbia are on fire, much of Australia's Great Barrier coral reef is in its death throes, there is drought-induced famine looming in South Sudan, an iceberg three times the size of Madrid has calved from the West Antarctic Ice Sheet, a succession of monster hurricanes has laid waste to several Caribbean islands and the Florida Keys, and Arctic sea ice is melting faster than most scientists had predicted. Though the causal chains can sometimes be difficult to specify these are all likely effects of **anthropogenic** (human-caused) climate change. To understand them, and related phenomena, we begin this book with a look at the basic science of climate change. We start with an explanation of the greenhouse effect, moving next to projections of the effects of climate change in four areas of concern: heat waves, droughts, wildfires, sea-level rise and extreme precipitation events. Following this, we will see what impacts these effects will have on human and non-human systems. We close with some brief reflections on the nature of ethical scientific communication.

The greenhouse effect

Since the advent of the agricultural revolution some 12,000 years ago, and then much more intensively from the beginning of the Industrial Revolution (circa 1750), humans have been altering the global climate through such processes as deforestation, livestock cultivation and the burning of fossil fuels. At the time of industrialization the concentration of **greenhouse gases (GHGs)** in the atmosphere was about 280 parts per million (ppm). It is now over 400 ppm and climbing 2–3 ppm/year. In its most recent report, the **Intergovernmental Panel on Climate Change (IPCC)** makes a clear and confident statement about the reality of climate change that this increase has produced:

Warming of the climate system is unequivocal, and since the 1950s, many of the observed changes are unprecedented over decades to millennia. The atmosphere and ocean have warmed, the amounts of snow and ice have diminished, sea level has risen, and the concentrations of greenhouse gases have increased.[1]

Although climate change deniers sometimes speak as though scientists invented the concept of climate change or global warming out of the blue a few decades ago, in fact we have known about the phenomenon for well over a century. The first articulation of it as a "greenhouse effect" came in the early decades of the nineteenth-century from the French scientist Jean Baptiste Joseph Fourier. Fourier wondered how the earth could retain its heat and speculated that the atmosphere must have a role to play in this. He thought of the earth as something like a glass-covered box – a greenhouse – and thus became known as the inventor of this (somewhat misleading but nevertheless useful) analogy.[2]

Although GHGs can pack a big warming punch, they comprise only a tiny fraction of atmospheric gases. Nitrogen and oxygen together make up 99% of the gases in the atmosphere. The remaining 1% is taken up by relatively small concentrations of neon, helium, methane, carbon dioxide, water vapor, and other gases. Only a few of these gases – methane, water vapor, carbon dioxide, ozone and nitrous oxide – have heat-trapping properties. As the earth absorbs solar radiation and heats up, it radiates heat back out. GHGs absorb and reradiate infrared energy from incoming sunlight, but incoming sunlight is not just infrared radiation. It also includes visible light which is not blocked by the atmosphere. This incident light is also reradiated by the earth mostly as infrared radiation that can be absorbed by the atmosphere.

For purposes of understanding the human role in all of this, it makes sense to concentrate on the role of carbon dioxide (CO_2) in this process. Carbon moves through the Earth system in a cycle, passing in different forms though various "reservoirs" – oceans, rock strata, ice formations, the atmosphere, the bodies of living things, etc. – in the process. Consider a hyper-simplified illustration. Atmospheric carbon is drawn down by plants through the process of photosynthesis – which converts CO_2 to sugar, used by plants to build biomass – and passed along to other organisms through the food chain. Dead plants and animals transfer their carbon to the soil, where bacterial decomposers get to work on it, releasing the carbon back to the atmosphere as they do so. Barring major climatic upheavals, such as volcanic eruptions, this process can stay in rough equilibrium for millennia, meaning that the amount of heat-trapping CO_2 in the atmosphere remains relatively fixed over such periods. But the climate system can also be "forced" – thrown out of equilibrium – by natural or human causes.

Fossil fuels are stores of carbon built up over hundreds of millions of years. They are the remains of ancient plants and animals sequestered in oxygen-starved geological strata, so that they could not decompose. When we extract and burn them we introduce this carbon into the **carbon cycle**. This is an anthropogenic (human-caused) climate forcing. On a small scale it would make no appreciable difference to the Earth system, but since industrialization humans have been doing it at such a furious rate that we have upset the carbon cycle's balance. Because there is a correlation between the concentration of greenhouse gases in the atmosphere and the amount of thermal energy trapped in the lower atmosphere, introducing more GHGs into the Earth system will, other things being equal, lead to an increase in surface temperatures. And this is just what we have seen. But not quite at the rate we might have expected because the climate system includes the oceans and 90% of the solar energy absorbed by the earth between 1971 and 2010 has gone into heating these vast liquid bodies.[3]

There are two distinct time frames of relevance here, though each tells much the same story about the unprecedented warming humans have caused. The first is the change in global surface temperatures since about 1880. This is when the **instrumental temperature record** begins. Scientists are most confident about these results, simply because they have direct access to temperatures through thermometer records in this period. The instrumental record shows clearly that temperatures across the oceans and land have risen steadily since 1880. We have seen a global temperature rise of almost 1.0°C (1.8°F) since this time, from 13.5°C (56.3°F) to 14.5°C (58.1°F). Moreover, although the average increase over the 20[th]century as a whole is 0.10°C (0.18°F) per decade, the rate of warming has increased substantially since about 1980, to 0.15°C (0.27° F) per decade.[4] This is correlated with dramatically enhanced consumption of fossil fuel products, as well as deforestation, by humans in this period.

It is much more difficult to reconstruct temperatures before the instrumental record, but scientists have devised ingenious ways of doing so. These methods provide indirect or **proxy data** of past temperatures, meaning that temperatures are *inferred* from other data that bear a consistent relation to them. For example, over millions of years layers of snow build up and are compressed on the ice sheets of Greenland and Antarctica. Scientists extract long, tubular cores of this ice. These layers of ice trap bubbles of air, so they can be analyzed to determine the air's gaseous makeup at specific years.

Because each layer represents a year, the whole ice-mass can be considered a coded record of the past. Using similar methods on tree rings, corals and lake sediments, scientists have been able to reconstruct temperatures going back millions of years. Coming a little closer to our time, from proxy data we now know, for example, that atmospheric concentrations of CO_2 were not far off 280 ppm – the **pre-industrial baseline** – for at least 10,000 years before the 20th century.[5] On any time scale that is relevant to us what we are now witnessing is therefore unprecedented.

This is worrisome enough, but there is yet another feature of the climate system we need to mention. Earlier, we noticed that "other things being equal" increasing the atmospheric stock of GHGs will raise temperatures a corresponding amount. The assumption behind this statement is that there is a stable or linear relation between the two phenomena, that with, say, every extra 50 ppm of CO_2 we can expect a temperature rise of 1.0°C (these are arbitrarily chosen numbers). The problem with this assumption is that the climate system is full of feedbacks, which can make the assumption of a linear correlation between GHGs and temperatures difficult to sustain. It can be very difficult to understand the relation between these two phenomena accurately, because the complexity of feedbacks makes them difficult to model on computers. Feedbacks are effects of causal processes that turn back to affect those causal processes themselves. They come in two varieties, negative and positive. A **negative feedback** diminishes the force of the causal process, while a **positive feedback** enhances it.

Here's an example of a climatic phenomenon that exhibits both kinds of feedback. Because warmer air causes more evaporation of water, global warming increases the amount of water vapor in the atmosphere. One effect of this is a tendency to enhance the warming process, since water vapor is a greenhouse gas. This amplifies or enhances the force of the causal process and is thus a positive feedback. A second effect, however, is to create more cloud cover over the earth's surface. Because low clouds reflect incoming sunlight, this effect can slow or dampen the causal process. This is a negative feedback. So in this case we have two effects of a global warming-induced increase in evaporation, one of which enhances the warming while the other diminishes it. But before rushing to the conclusion that climate change is no problem, because these effects are likely to balance each other out in the climate system as a whole, it is crucial to note two points.

First, there is strong evidence that positive feedbacks outweigh negative feedbacks in the climate system.[6] In other words, processes that accelerate warming dominate those that accelerate cooling. Second, and more important, the climate system contains some positive feedbacks that have the potential to accelerate climate change *dramatically* if they are tripped. One example is the permafrost in the Siberian tundra. Permafrost is frozen organic material, lying just below the top layer of soil. It is now melting because of elevated temperatures. Permafrost is loaded with methane (CH_4), a powerful greenhouse gas. The problem is that when it melts, this gas is released into the atmosphere, where it can act as a super-accelerant of heat increase. Methane is 86 times more potent than CO_2 at trapping heat over a 20-year period, though this potency diminishes to 34 times the effect of CO_2 over 100 years.[7] So even though it does not remain in the atmosphere for as long as CO_2, it can enhance warming significantly while it is active in the climate system.

Depending on what measures we take to address climate change, between 37% and 81% of permafrost will be lost this century, which could release up to 250 billion metric tons of methane to the atmosphere.[8] Again, the key is that this will *accelerate the warming process*, not simply increase warming in a linear fashion. Scientists are also worried about positive feedbacks in Arctic sea ice melt, land ice melt, potential for wildfires, and more. Positive feedbacks like these are especially alarming because the paleoclimatic record reveals that the climate can switch "abruptly" from one regime to another once they kick in. **Abrupt climate change** can happen within centuries or even decades. It's as though a switch or tipping point is reached, after which nothing much can stop the momentum of the system.

In our case, even if we realized this was happening and ceased our GHG emissions immediately in a desperate attempt to reverse it, our efforts would be in vain. This is **runaway climate change** and we may be closer to it than we suppose. Here is what climate scientist Stefan Rahmstorf says about this prospect:

> What climate scientists have feared for decades is now beginning to come true: we are pushing the climate system across dangerous tipping points. Beyond such points, things like ice sheet collapse become self-sustaining and unstoppable, committing our children and children's children to massive problems. The new studies strongly suggest the first of these tipping points has already been crossed. More tipping points lie ahead of us. I think we should try hard to avoid crossing them.[9]

The "first" tipping point to which Rahmstorf alludes here are some ice sheets in Western Antarctica whose collapse, according to the latest research, *may* now be inevitable. All by itself, this will raise sea levels by 1.2 metres (4 feet).

But even if we accept the IPCC's claim that the late-20th-century warming trend is unequivocal, how can we be sure that we are the cause of it, that the current forcing of the climate system is truly anthropogenic? The planet has gone through wild climatic swings over its 4.5 billion year history. For the past 2 million years we have been in the Pleistocene glacial age, characterized by the pendulum swing of glacial and interglacial periods (we are currently in an interglacial known as the Holocene). But prior to the Pleistocene, the planet was generally much warmer than it is now, with correspondingly higher concentrations of atmospheric CO_2. Sixty-five million years ago, alligators were roaming above the Arctic circle.[10] Since we were not around yet, significant climate change can obviously happen without us.

There are a number of natural forces that can cause climate change. Minute shifts in the planet's orbital route, sunspots and explosive volcanic activity have all been identified as important natural causes of climate change. To find out whether or not 20th-century warming can be attributed to these kinds of phenomena, scientists use computer models to determine what effect known natural causes alone would have had on temperatures, then compare the results with what has actually been observed. The models consistently show a large discrepancy between the two data sets. Natural causes alone cannot explain what the instrumental temperature record reveals, but when the models add in anthropogenic sources, the two sets fit together nicely. This is observable at both global and regional levels, and for terrestrial as well as ocean temperatures.[11] What's more, since industrialization human sources begin to swamp natural ones. The data now show clearly that our activities are the dominant forcing mechanism in the global climate.

Could there be other natural variables of which we are simply ignorant? Why convict humanity before *all* the facts are in? There's a chance of this but only because it's impossible to prove a negative. This is as true of the claim that "there is no other natural cause that could explain the observed climate data" as it is of the claim that "there is no God." Surely, however, the argumentative burden lies with the skeptic at this point. This person should be able to show that the purely natural variables *we know about* are sufficient to explain the observed data. But, again, they are clearly *not* sufficient. In a telling analogy, the climate scientist David Archer argues that we know the identity of the real "culprit" here so the search for an alternative one seems bizarre:

> Shifting the blame to something else would require an explanation of why the CO_2 would not be trapping the heat as we expect it would be doing. Think of it like a murder mystery. The butler (CO_2) was caught with a smoking gun in his hand in the room with the dead guy … . Yes, the bullets came from the gun … . Yes, the gun was purchased by the butler. Everything checks out. But now your partner, Bob … argues that it was really the chauffeur [who] did it. Actually you find out that the chauffeur was at his sister's wedding on the other side of town for the whole time and lots of people saw him … . [I]f Bob is going to convict the chauffeur, he has to think of a way to unconvict the butler. He would have to come up with an innocent explanation for the butler's smoking gun and the bullets, and all that.[12]

We should therefore have no compunction about pointing to the anthropogenic sources of the current problem. But why should we worry about it? So far, we have been looking at the past and the present. What does the future have in store for us?

Climate projections

These questions bring us to the IPCC's construction of climate change scenarios. Obviously, the climate future we get will in part be a function of the policies we adopt in the coming years, especially with regard to our use of fossil fuels. To guide the modeling process, the IPCC considers four distinct possibilities, which they call **Representative Concentration Pathways (RCPs)**. The numbers in each case refer to the "total radiative forcing" each path would lead to, measured in watts per square meter, by 2100:

- a "stringent mitigation scenario" (RCP 2.6)
- two "intermediate scenarios" (RCP 4.5 and RCP 6.0)
- a "scenario with very high GHG emissions" (RCP 8.5).

The first and third of these scenarios are especially important. RCP 2.6 describes the policy measures that are required in order to make it "likely" that we stay below 2°C, relative to the pre-industrial baseline. RCP 8.5, by contrast, describes a world in which no significant policy measures are adopted to reduce emissions. It is the path we are currently on, often referred to as **business as usual** (a convention we will follow in this book). RCP 8.5 will bring 2.6°C to 4.8°C of warming this century.[13]

These numbers and acronyms can look pretty abstract, so it is important to point out that each scenario is meant to represent concrete aspects of the real world, as reflected in the policy choices we make. We can see this clearly by comparing the RCP scenarios with those laid out in previous IPCC reports. RCP 8.5 corresponds (roughly) to what AR4 labelled A1F1. It involves rapid economic growth, a population that peaks around 2050, and a fossil-fuel intensive energy mix. RCP 2.6 corresponds (again roughly) to what AR4 calls B1. Here, humanity has become committed to protecting the environment and to promoting social equity. This dual focus has, accordingly, moved us away from a fossil-fuel intensive energy mix. There is much more detail contained in these older projections, but this brief comparison between them and the RCP scenarios should help concretize the possibilities we are talking about.

Two more preliminary points about the RCP projections are worth emphasizing. First, since (as we have seen) feedbacks are notoriously difficult to model, even on our fastest computers, none of the scenarios takes them fully into account. And because positive or enhancing feedbacks dominate negative or diminishing ones this means that *all* of the scenarios probably underestimate the amount of warming we are likely to get. So, for example, we should be most worried about the upper end of the range specified in RCP 8.5 temperature projections (i.e., close to 5°C). Second, since it is the path we are currently on, it makes sense to focus on the implications of the world described by RCP 8.5. This is what we will do in the rest of this chapter.

What does a world with close to 5°C of extra warming look like? Before answering that question, it is crucial to emphasize the basic distinction between weather and climate. Confronted with the possibility of a 5°C increase in temperature, many people, especially those living in cold regions, are apt to shrug their shoulders. After all, the temperature can rise that much within a few hours on any spring day, and some might welcome the prospect of slightly less frigid winter temperatures. The mistake here is to take claims about climate, which measures long-term statistical averages, to be about weather, which relates to what is happening with temperature, precipitation, etc. in a relatively small time-frame. It is a very serious error to make because temperature changes of little significance from a weather standpoint can be very significant from a climate standpoint.

For example, it is often pointed out that in the midst of the last period of glaciation, when much of North America was covered by a thick sheet of ice, average global temperatures were just 5°C colder than they are now. The difference between that world and ours with respect to human habitability is obviously profound, so it makes sense to wonder what a similar temperature change in the opposite direction might portend for us. Indeed, there is some reason to think that 5°C of warming would be a much more significant challenge for us than 5°C of cooling would be. Of course, there is obviously a connection between weather and climate because weather events depend on local climate. Residents of Vancouver, Canada won't be surprised to wake up to cold rain some November morning precisely because they live in a temperate climate on the edge of a mid-latitude coastal rainforest.

Does this mean we can attribute specific weather *events*, like hurricanes, to climate change? An analogy originating with Dale Jamieson shows what is potentially misleading about this question. Suppose a baseball player has a .333 batting average, and that on his third and final time to the plate in a particular game he hits a homerun. It would not make much sense to ask whether or not his batting average caused that hit. Statistics do not intervene in the material world in this fashion. What we *can* say is that it is more likely that he was going to get the hit at that point in the game than he would have been had his average been lower. This leaves open the possibility that the homerun might *also* be attributable to factors other than the player's batting prowess: a bad pitch, a sudden up-swelling of wind, and so on. Even so, a less accomplished hitter might not have been able to exploit these factors to his advantage.

Like homeruns, weather events are the product of tangled causal chains, some of whose elements have nothing to do with us. The baseball analogy nevertheless makes it plausible to say that by loading the atmosphere with GHGs we are making extreme weather events more likely. This both (a) avoids the direct attribution of any particular event directly to climate change, while (b) making that event – a category 5 hurricane, say – less surprising than it would otherwise have been.

In thinking about impacts of climate change on the physical world we all inhabit, there are five key phenomena to watch: heat waves, drought, wildfires, sea-level rise and extreme precipitation events. This list is not meant to be exhaustive, but though incomplete it does convey the gravity of the threats we are creating.

Heat waves

A heat wave occurs when five consecutive days are at least 5°C (9°F) hotter than the historical average in a particular place.[14] In 2003, a heat wave killed about 35,000 people in Europe. In much of North America in 2012, temperatures soared throughout June and July, leading to massive crop failure, wildfires and death. These events were caused by an expansion of high-pressure subtropical weather patterns into higher latitudes, like North America and Europe. This is a predicted effect of global warming. In fact, heat waves are expected to become more intense and longer-lasting under business as usual (i.e., RCP 8.5).

For example, in St. Louis Missouri, which experienced massive heat-related problems in 2012, there are currently fewer than three days per year above 38°C (100°F), but this number is projected to rise as high as 40 per year by 2100.[15] A similar pattern is expected in the southwest U.S., western Europe and parts of Australia. And in the Middle East and North Africa the end of the century could see temperatures regularly reach 50°C (122°F), with ten times the number of heat waves currently seen. This would render this vast region literally uninhabitable for parts of the year.[16]

Drought

The hot, dry air of the subtropics that global warming is pushing to higher latitudes is having a drying effect in large parts of North America, the American tropics, Africa, Asia, Indonesia and Australia. This has led to often severe drought conditions in these areas.[17] Two other phenomena can enhance this effect. The first is that climate change appears to induce "blocking patterns" in weather systems, one effect of which is that high-pressure systems that cause drought can get stuck in place for relatively long periods of time. The second is that because warming causes increased evaporation, the sun bakes the desiccated earth. This raises air temperatures still further, another good example of a positive feedback.[18]

At this point, even if rain begins to fall again, the water tends to run off the surface of the soil rather than penetrating it. The problem is projected to be worst in Mexico and West Africa, which could lead to dramatic reductions in crop yields as well as mass migrations out of those regions. Indeed, the U.S. southwest, western and southern Africa, much of South America and the Mediterranean region must brace for "multidecadal megadroughts" on a scale that "in the past destroyed entire civilizations."[19] It is expected that with moderate warming (no more than 3°C (5.4°F)), some regions could see their agricultural productivity increase because there will be more frost-free days. But even in those places – parts of Canada, for example – anything above 3°C is likely to lead to declines in agricultural productivity.

Wildfires

In May-June 2017, wildfires swept through a region northwest of Lisbon, Portugal, killing more than 60 people (many of them trapped in their cars) and destroying 14,971 hectares of forest. In an area prone to wildfires, this decade has seen a 16% increase of them over the previous decade. In Australia, another fire-prone country, wildfires in February 2009 burned more than 3,500 km^2, killing 173 people, and causing about AU\$4 billion in damages.[20] Here again, we have a clear and powerful positive feedback. Global warming increases drying through enhanced evaporation, higher temperatures and earlier snowmelt, providing extra fuel for fires. Fire releases the CO_2 sequestered in that fuel (trees, etc.), which causes even more warming, leading to more drying out of forested regions, hence more potential for fires, and so on.[21] So it makes intuitive sense to say that wildfires will likely increase in frequency and intensity in years and decades to come. According to one report, 20 million acres a year in the U.S. (especially California and the Pacific Northwest) will burn by 2050.[22] Large increases in fire frequency will also hit southern Africa, southern Australia, New Zealand, Central Europe, northern India and central South America.[23]

Sea-level rise

Sea-level rise occurs as a result of global warming for two principal reasons: thermal expansion of the water (known as "thermosteric" expansion) and melting of land-based ice sheets. According to the IPCC, under business as usual these factors will cause mean global sea levels to rise 0.7 meters by 2100, and somewhere between 1.5 and 6.6 meters (4.9–21.8 feet) by 2500.[24] However, scientists are now beginning to think that the 2100 number may be unrealistically low. The reason for this is that the IPCC does not feel confident about including the effects of a collapse of the West Antarctic Ice Sheet (WAIS), which many scientists now consider likely.

Moreover, recent research has revealed that there is also a large glacier on the East Antarctic Ice Sheet that looks alarmingly unstable. Given these observations, climate scientist Joseph Romm concludes:

> we are likely headed toward what used to be the high end of projected global sea-level rise this century (i.e., 4 to 5 feet [1.2 to 1.5 meters]) and the worst-case scenarios where humanity fails to take aggressive action to cut greenhouse gas emissions are considerably higher than that.[25]

In other words, we are "likely" to hit the low end of the IPCC projections for 2500 fully 400 years before that date.

Extreme precipitation events

Finally, let's consider the effects of climate change on severe storms. Warmer temperatures can increase the intensity of storms by providing more fuel for them in the form of warmer ocean surface temperatures. While there is little confidence that global warming will increase the frequency of hurricanes and typhoons, there is general agreement that it will increase the number of severe storms, especially in the tropical Atlantic ocean basin (although less so for the Pacific and Indian ocean basins).[26]

For example, events like the extreme storm surge of Hurricane Katrina that struck New Orleans and the Gulf Coast in 2005 could become much more frequent. With a 1°C rise in temperatures, the frequency of high-magnitude storms like this would likely increase 3–4 times, while a 2°C increase would increase them 10 times (roughly one every other year). One recent study predicts that under business as usual, category 4 (wind speeds of 209–251 km/h (130–156 mph)) and 5 (wind speeds of 252 km/h (157 mph) or higher) storms will eventually represent up to half of all hurricanes.[27]

Four final points about all of these phenomena. First, they will not necessarily happen in isolation from one another in any particular region. This will make adapting to them even more difficult than it would otherwise be. For example, the U.S. is likely to experience severe flooding and salt-water intrusion along its eastern coastline from sea-level rise and storm surges, even as it battles prolonged drought conditions in the southwest and more frequent and intense wildfires in the northwest.

Second, although we have been talking quite a bit in terms of average increases in this or that event or phenomenon, the real danger might be "the variations around [the] average." That is, we should focus not just on the "constant effects" of climate change but also on its "episodic effects." For example, if average temperatures in some regions reach 45°C (113°F), 49°C (120°F) highs will likely become much more frequent.[28] The same point applies to storm surges.

Third, most of the conclusions we have been considering in this section are derived from climate models, which are by definition forward-looking. This method must however be supplemented with a comparative analysis between the projected futures and the deeper past (the field of **paleoclimatology**). This allows us to appreciate the extent to which the future we are creating is historically anomalous, unprecedented for our species. Paleoclimatologist Jeffrey Kiehl summarizes the issue this way:

> Earth's CO_2 concentration is rapidly rising to a level not seen in 30 to 100 million years, and Earth's climate was extremely warm at these levels of CO_2. If the world reaches such concentrations of atmospheric CO_2, positive feedback processes can amplify global warming beyond current modeling estimates. The human species and global ecosystems will be placed in a climate state never before experienced in their evolutionary history and at an unprecedented rate. Note that these conclusions arise from observations from earth's past and not specifically from climate models. Will we, as a species, listen to these messages from the past in order to avoid repeating history?[29]

Finally, it is crucial to emphasize that RCP 8.5 is not inevitable. It is a pathway we are on, one we can in principle get off. The futures we are contemplating here are not like the proverbial asteroid rushing towards the planet and destined to kill us all. It is important to say this because the asteroid scenario leaves no scope for an ethics (or does so only in some specialized or attenuated sense: depending on how much time we had left there might be genuine ethical questions about our procreative choices, for example), whereas climate change does. Ethics depends on the possibility of a *way out*, even when things look very bad.

These points bring us to an assessment of the key risks and vulnerabilities of a climate changed world.

Risks and vulnerabilities

We will consider climate change risks and vulnerabilities under two headings: those facing human systems, and those facing ecosystems and the living things that make them up. This distinction is not meant to indicate a fundamental split between humans and the rest of the biosphere. Human activities have profound effects on ecosystems, and humans are themselves fully embedded in such systems. The distinction is nevertheless analytically useful.

Human systems

The IPCC lists six main threats to humans systems from climate change. First, storm surges, coastal flooding and sea-level rise in small island states increase the risk of death, ill-health, displacement and injury to people living there. Second, many regions will see inland flooding on a massive scale, due to rising seas and storm surges, which threatens human health and livelihoods. Third, extreme weather events can threaten water supply and electricity services to vulnerable populations. Fourth, there is risk of morbidity during heat waves, and a general loss of labor productivity for those working outside (like construction workers and seasonally employed agricultural workers). Fifth, there is a risk of profound food shortages resulting from more frequent and intense droughts. And sixth, there is risk of an increase in global and regional insecurity.[30]

These risks are not evenly spread across the global population, of course, nor is the capacity to deal with disaster as it arises. Very generally, the biggest threats are faced by those nations of the global south – especially in east and south Asia and Africa – who (a) have historically contributed the least to the problem of carbon pollution and (b) are least equipped economically to adapt to the coming changes. These points are pivotal to grasping the nature of international justice, to be explored in a later chapter. For now, because of the potential they have to affect the lives of billions of people, we will focus more closely on four of the six key threats: direct health impacts, loss of agricultural productivity, coastal flooding and security.

Direct health impacts

What are the likely health impacts of climate change and which populations will experience them most dramatically? According to a 2009 study commissioned by the *Lancet*, "climate change will have devastating consequences for human health."[31] These will come from changing patterns of vector-borne diseases like malaria, a rise in malnutrition and diarrhoeal diseases resulting from food and water insecurity, direct injury from more intense storms, increased morbidity due to warming-enhanced urban smog (higher temperatures trap ground-level ozone), and direct death from wildfires and heat waves.[32]

These effects will be experienced globally, though countries in the developing world will have a much more difficult time than developed countries coping with them because of less well-funded and responsive health care systems in those parts of the world. For example, much of West Africa and the Sahel will see large changes in the incidence and geographic range of vector- and water-borne diseases. Avoiding large-scale disaster from this source will require resolute attention to development goals in this region, with a focus on improvements in sanitation and water access as well as public health infrastructure.[33]

Loss of agricultural productivity

The problem here is brutally simple: most of the places hit hardest hit by drought will also be experiencing population increase. By 2050, world population is expected to rise to approximately 10 billion. This rise will happen very disproportionally across the globe, being concentrated in developing countries. The reason for this is that most of these countries have not passed through the **demographic transition** already experienced in much of the developed world. Population is a function of two factors: death rates and birth rates. In the developed world, birth rates have generally fallen in concert with a fall in death rates. People live longer but also have fewer babies, the result of which is a rough balance in population or even – in countries like Russia and Italy – negative fertility rates.

Many developing countries are now experiencing a fall in death rates due to advances in the quality of medical care, but in some of them this has not been matched by a decline in birth rates. The result is a net increase in population in these countries. In fact, it is predicted that half of the population growth this century will occur in just eight countries, all of which fit this broad pattern: Nigeria, India, the United Republic of Tanzania, The Democratic Republic of the Congo, Niger, Uganda, Ethiopia and the United States.[34] With the exception of the United States, these are all countries whose agricultural systems are going to be stressed to the breaking point by climate change induced drought in the near term.

Coastal flooding

Coastal flooding poses two broad threats. The first is intrusion of salt-water into inland freshwater systems that are essential for irrigation and human consumption. The second is displacement due to inundation. The most dramatic effects of inundation will occur in small island states like Tuvalu and the Solomon Islands, which are literally disappearing under the waves. But the problem goes well beyond the fate of island nations. Recent research suggests that by 2060 there could be 1.4 billion climate refugees because of sea-level rise, a number that increases to 2 billion by 2100. That is approximately 20% of the total human population that will be affected by this phenomenon in a significant way at some point this century.[35] The study points to an important factor: the difficulty many people who are fleeing inundated coasts will have in resettling inland. They will not likely be moving into empty spaces, and the people already living there may be facing resource scarcity of their own or be members of a hostile ethnic or religious group. This point brings us to our final area of concern.

Security

Because climate change places enormous stresses on a country's or region's environment it can lead to scarcity of essential resources which, in turn, is an important potential driver of conflict among groups of humans. The IPCC is careful to avoid making direct links between climate change and violent conflict, noting that it is an important causal factor among many others.[36] The American military establishment is far less circumspect about the connection, however. They have identified climate change a key "threat multiplier" in many regions of the world, a threat that could topple governments, lead to large-scale crimes of atrocity and perhaps even to nuclear war.

John Beddington, a scientific advisor to the UK government, argues that we could begin to see significant global security challenges by 2030: "A 'perfect storm' of food shortages, scarce water and insufficient energy resources threaten to unleash public unrest, cross-border conflicts and mass migration as people flee from the worst-affected regions."[37] Although we should be wary of such pronouncements from the military establishment, since it clearly has an interest in characterizing security threats in a way that will enhance its own power, it would be foolish to ignore these warnings altogether.

Finally, as was the case with the physical impacts of climate change on the Earth system, it is important to emphasize that the four main areas of concern just considered will not appear in isolation from one another. For example, in Bangladesh, most of which is perilously close to sea-level, rising waters in the south will force millions of people north. There, they will likely confront a security nightmare because India lies directly in their path and the Indian government has already made it clear that it does not want them entering the country en masse. If the Bangladeshi government cannot cope with the displacement, what will happen to these people?

Similar problems will confront southern Europe, facing a refugee influx from North Africa as well as the United States facing the same phenomenon from Mexico and Central America. This massive global movement of people all looking to escape drought, rising seas, hostile neighbors and so on will place enormous pressure on our capacity to coexist peaceably in the coming decades.

Ecosystems

Although it is much less talked about in the larger culture, climate change is going to have a profound effect on ecosystems. We cannot hope to do justice to the full scope of this threat here, but let's take a brief look at it under two headings: terrestrial and freshwater ecosystems on the one hand, and ocean ecosystems on the other.

Terrestrial and freshwater ecosystems

The IPCC predicts that "climate change will be a powerful stressor on freshwater and terrestrial ecosystems." This will have negative repercussions for the species that make up these ecosystems:

> A large fraction of both terrestrial and freshwater species faces increased extinction risk under projected climate change during and beyond the 21st century, especially as climate change interacts with other stressors, such as habitat modification, overexploitation, pollution, and invasive species.[38]

As temperatures rise, both plant and animal species will migrate in search of a climate like the one they are used to. In general, this means two broad patterns of movement: to higher latitudes (horizontal migration) and into alpine regions (vertical migration).

The problem here is much like it is for humans on the move because of climate change. First, there may simply not be any space into which species can move. If, for example, there are no mountains or hills around, they cannot migrate vertically. As for horizontal migration, species like the polar bear might simply run out of planetary real estate. Second, many species may simply not be able to move *quickly* enough to escape the heat. Freshwater mollusks, plant-feeding insects, carnivorous and split-hoofed mammals can generally move across landscapes quite quickly (measured in kilometers per decade); but trees, herbaceous plants, rodents and primates move much more slowly.[39] Finally, even if they can migrate – vertically or horizontally – species may not be able to compete with indigenous species for scarce resources, or, if they are especially aggressive, they may drive indigenous species out. Either way extinctions will rise.

Ocean ecosystems

One of the major dangers for ocean ecosystems is **acidification** of the seas. Burning fossil fuels releases carbon into the atmosphere, as we know. Eventually some of this is transferred to the oceans, where it reacts with the chemicals in the water to increase the concentration of hydrogen ions and reduce the concentration of carbonate ions. This is acidification. The problem with it is that many ocean organisms require carbonate ions to build their shells and skeletons. Some of these organisms are important links in marine food chains, so if they cannot reproduce at sufficient levels, entire food webs may be undermined. This could cause a crash in ocean biodiversity.

The most vulnerable marine ecosystems are coral reefs, richly biodiverse low-lying ecosystems. Although they occupy less than 0.1% of the ocean floor they support a disproportionate quantity of marine biodiversity. There are multiple threats here. Acidification and overfishing are prominent. But the main threat is that corals are very sensitive to temperature. As oceans warm, the corals expel the colorful algae that live symbiotically on them. This leads to bleaching, the death of coral reef ecosystems. It is already happening on an alarming scale and is projected to become much worse throughout this century.

Although our ignorance of the total number of species in existence makes it hard to say what percentage of that total is under threat of extinction, scientists have noticed that current rates of extinction are almost 1000 times the background or natural rate. Climate change is not the only cause of this, but it is a major one. Five times in its roughly 3 billion-year history of life this planet has come close to losing all its species. Some of these extinction events have been associated with a CO_2 spike. We are now in the midst of the **Sixth Mass Extinction**, also associated with a sharp rise in atmospheric CO_2. The potential consequences of this are momentous, as Elizabeth Kolbert notes:

> Right now, in the amazing moment that to us counts as the present, we are deciding, without quite meaning to, which evolutionary pathways will remain open and which will forever be closed. No other creature has ever managed this, and it will, unfortunately, be our most enduring legacy. The Sixth Extinction will continue to determine the course of life long after everything people have written and painted has been ground into dust and giant rats have – or have not – inherited the earth.[40]

Chapter 6 explores the ethical dimensions of this massive loss of non-human lives. For now it is sufficient simply to note that the destruction being wrought by anthropogenic climate change is not confined to human systems.

Let's switch gears at this point and begin the task of climate change ethics proper. There's much groundwork to be done in the next two chapters before we can get at the key issues in a comprehensive fashion. But we can begin, more modestly, by exploring an issue of relevance to this chapter: how climate science should be communicated from experts to non-experts. Specifically, we will explore the idea that such communication might be more *effective* if it is informed and constrained by ethical considerations.

Ethical communication of science

Most people accept that in a democratic polity it is not acceptable to get people to do the right thing through manipulation and deceit. A large literature in social psychology has emerged to address the issue of proper "climate change communication," but philosophical ethicists have not accorded the issue the attention it clearly deserves. This is unfortunate because, although the social psychological research is important it cannot by itself address the normative dimensions of the problem. Social psychologists have shown that scientific communication must go beyond the delivery of dry facts to audiences. It must, in addition, engage the affects of the audience because facts alone are insufficiently motivational. But does this characterization of the issue exhaust what we mean by appropriate communication? Is communicating the facts and engaging the affects all there is to it? This seems like an oversimplification.

We might also wonder about what Michael Lamb and Melissa Lane refer to as the "moral values that define legitimate communication."[41] These philosophers show that Aristotle's concept of rhetoric can do illuminating work here. For Aristotle, rhetorical communication has an intrinsically ethical component to it. It seeks to engage not only the reason and the affects of the audience members but also their conception of themselves as *citizens*. So expert speakers are enjoined by Aristotle to communicate in a way that recognizes the "civic equality between speaker and auditor."[42] From this standpoint, expert communication lacking this element is inadequate even if it is otherwise effective in rousing people to action. But there is good reason to believe that it would in this case simply *not* be effective at moving people to appropriate action. Facts alone tend not to motivate people sufficiently or reliably, and purely emotional arousal is often seen by its target audience as a form of manipulation.

No-nonsense delivery of the facts and affect-arousal are still important, but audiences are much more likely to be mobilized by these forces if they perceive that they are being treated as genuine *deliberators* in the social and political articulation and dissemination of information. Lamb and Lane summarize the specifically ethical focus on the relationship between speaker and audience this way:

> Such relationships can facilitate ongoing acts of successful communication, even when factual uncertainty and expert disagreement threaten to incite division. Ultimately, by alerting climate change communicators to the importance of these ethical and political relationships, an Aristotelian

approach highlights how rhetoric can be an art of earning trust. Contemporary climate change communicators can learn much from Aristotle's ancient advice.[43]

Otherwise put, it is crucial to convey to a broad swath of the public that *climate change is a choice* for which we are all responsible (albeit in different ways and to differing degrees). Fundamentally, we are, as Dale Moellendorf puts it, "coauthors of the rules of our common life," and the way the science of climate change is disseminated from experts to non-experts must reflect this fact.[44]

Fortunately, we have science communicators who seem to understand this, however implicitly. For example in the quote just above from Kolbert we find a reference to "what we are deciding" with respect to the Sixth Extinction Event. This implies a refusal to shift blame to someone else. It brings the reader into a conversation about this tragic event, asking her – again implicitly – to reflect on the ways in which she might be able to address the crisis as a morally engaged citizen.

The same goes for the accounts of climate change in the books by Romm and Mann on which this chapter has relied extensively. Both are scientists, and both understand that the facts about climate change must be communicated in a way that also engages the affects. But these books are also addressed to their readers as co-deliberators in a democratic polity. In his preface, Romm, for instance, notes that his book is aimed at "those interested in joining the growing public debate and discussion" about climate change.[45] It's a simple message but it has the power to make all the difference.

Chapter summary

In this chapter we have examined the basic, and latest, science of climate change. This is obviously not philosophy, but since our approach to the ethical challenges of climate change depends so heavily on the precise nature and scope of the physical phenomenon of climate change it is necessary to ground our analysis this way. We began with a look at the greenhouse effect, noting in particular the extent to which the climate system is prone to surprises because of positive feedbacks. Next, we examined the IPCC's projections of future climate change, focusing on heat waves, droughts, wildfires, sea-level rise and extreme precipitation events. The path we are on – RCP 8.5 or "business as usual" – could result in GHG concentrations the planet has not seen on any timescale that is relevant to human concerns. Following this analysis, we looked at the potential for these disturbances to affect both human and non-human systems (ecosystems). We concluded with some thoughts about the ethical communication of scientific results from experts to non-experts.

Questions for discussion

1   In this chapter, we separated human and non-human systems (ecosystems) for analytic purposes. This, as noted, is highly artificial. What are the ways in which these systems interact in the real world?
2   What is the greenhouse effect and how does it affect the regulation of the climate system?
3   What are the likely effects of climate change in the area or region in which you live? Have the risks been adequately laid out and addressed by your governmental officials or prominent civil society groups?
4   What is your reaction – intellectually and emotionally – to Kolbert's description, quoted in this chapter, of the Sixth Extinction?
5   How do you think the international community should respond to the security threats of climate change? Is the military to be trusted here? Do we have global institutions that are capable of responding to these threats in a way that does not exacerbate them?

Suggested reading

IPCC 2014. *Synthesis Report. Summary for Policymakers.* An accessible summary of the latest report from the most authoritative source. Available at: https://www.ipcc.ch/pdf/assessment-report/ar5/syr/AR5_SYR_FINAL_ SPM.pdf

Elizabeth Kolbert. 2014. *The Sixth Extinction: An Unnatural History.* New York: Henry Holt. A masterful and stirring description of the effects of anthropogenic climate change on biodiversity loss. It is journalism of the highest caliber.

Michael E. Mann and Lee R. Kump. 2015. *Dire Predictions: Understanding Climate Change: The Visual Guide to the Findings of the IPCC,* second edition. New York: DK Publishing. Mann is one of the world's leading climate scientists (as is Kump) and communicators. He has been at the forefront of the battle against industry-funded climate change denial. This is a vivid, pictorial guide to the latest IPCC report.

Joseph Romm. 2016. *Climate Change: What Everyone Needs to Know.* Oxford: Oxford University Press. Romm, like Mann and Kump, is a brilliant science communicator. This book not only summarizes IPCC findings, but goes beyond them to include more updated information.

Notes

1   IPCC 2013: Summary for Policymakers. In Stocker, T.F., D. Qin, G.-K. Plattner, M. Tignor, S.K. Allen, J. Boschung, A. Nauels, Y. Xia, V. Bex and P.M. Midgley (eds.), *Climate Change 2013: The Physical Science Basis. Contribution of Working Group I to the Fifth Assessment Report of the Inter-governmental Panel on Climate Change* (Cambridge, United Kingdom and New York, NY, USA: Cambridge University Press, 2013), 4.

2 Dale Jamieson, *Reason in a Dark Time: Why the Struggle against Climate Change Failed and What it Means for our Future* (Oxford: Oxford University Press, 2014), 13.

3 IPCC 2013, 4.

4 Michael E. Mann and Lee R. Kump, *Dire Predictions: Understanding Climate Change: The Visual Guide to the Findings of the IPCC*, second edition (New York: DK Publishing, 2015), 34.

5 Mann and Kump, *Dire Predictions...*, 31.

6 Mann and Kump, *Dire Predictions...*, 25.

7 Joseph Romm, *Climate Change: What Everyone Needs to Know* (Oxford: Oxford University Press, 2016), 81.

8 Mann and Kump, *Dire Predictions...*, 148.

9 Quoted in Romm, *Climate Change...*, 30.

10 Mann and Kump, *Dire Predictions...*, 41.

11 Mann and Kump, *Dire Predictions...*, 72–74.

12 David Archer, *The Long Thaw: How Humans are Changing the Next 100,000 Years of Earth's Climate* (Princeton, NJ: Princeton University Press, 2009), 3–4.

13 IPCC 2013, *Summary for Policymakers...*, 10.

14 Mann and Kump, *Dire Predictions...*, 113.

15 Mann and Kump, *Dire Predictions...*, 57.

16 J. Lelieveld, Y. Proestos, P. Hadjinicolaou, M. Tanarhte, E. Tyrlis and G. Zittis, "Strongly Increasing Heat Extremes in Middle East and North Africa (MENA) in the 21st Century," *Climatic Change*, 137 (July), 2016, 245–260.

17 Mann and Kump, *Dire Predictions...*, 55.

18 Romm, *Climate Change...*, 43.

19 Romm, *Climate Change...*, 98–99.

20 IPCC 2014 (a): Summary for policymakers. In Field, C.B., V.R. Barros, D.J. Dokken, K.J. Mach, M.D. Mastrandrea, T.E. Bilir, M. Chatterjee, K.L. Ebi, Y.O. Estrada, R.C. Genova, B. Girma, E. S. Kissel, A.N. Levy, S. MacCracken, P.R. Mastrandrea, and L.L. White (eds.), *Climate Change 2014: Impacts, Adaptation, and Vulnerability. Part A: Global and Sectoral Aspects. Contribution of Working Group II to the Fifth Assessment Report of the Intergovernmental Panel on Climate Change* (Cambridge, United Kingdom and New York, NY, USA: Cambridge University Press, 2014), 304.

21 Romm, *Climate Change...*, 45

22 Romm, *Climate Change...*, 46.

23 IPCC 2014(a), 1400.

24 IPCC 2014(a), 369.

25 Romm, *Climate Change...*, 94.

26 Mann and Kump, *Dire Predictions...*, 62–63.

27 Romm, *Climate Change...*, 97.

28 Philip Kitcher and Evelyn Fox Keller, *The Seasons Alter: How to Save our Planet in Six Acts* (New York: WW Norton, 2017), 47–48.

29 Quoted in Romm, *Climate Change...*, 139–140.

30 IPCC 2014(a), 13.

31 Cited in Romm, *Climate Change...*, 104.

32 Romm, *Climate Change...*, 103–105.

33 IPCC 2014(a), 21.

34 Anthony D. Barnosky and Elizabeth A. Hadley, *Tipping Point for Planet Earth* (New York: St. Martin's Press, 2015), 40–41.

35 Charles Geishert and Ben Currens, "Impediments to Inland Resettlement under Conditions of Accelerated Sea-level Rise," *Land Use Policy* 66 (July), 2017, 233–330.

36 IPCC 2014(a), 772.

37 Quoted in Romm, *Climate Change...*, 131.

38 IPCC 2014(a), 67.

39 IPCC 2014(a), 67.

40 Elizabeth Kolbert, *The Sixth Extinction: An Unnatural History* (New York: Henry Holt, 2014), 268–269.

41 Michael Lamb and Melissa Lane, "Aristotle on the Ethics of Communicating Climate Change," in Clare Heyward and Dominic Roser (eds.), *Climate Justice in a Non-ideal World* (Oxford: Oxford University Press, 2016), 229–254 (233).

42 Lamb and Lane, "Aristotle…," 237.

43 Lamb and Lane, "Aristotle…," 250.

44 Dale Moellendorf, *The Moral Challenge of Dangerous Climate Change* (Cambridge: Cambridge University Press, 2014), 30.

45 Romm, *Climate Change…*, xix-xx.

2   What is climate change ethics?

Introduction

So far we have examined the basic science of climate change. This sets us up nicely to begin the work of climate ethics proper, though there's still some preparatory work to be done before we get fully into that. Although it had more or less ignored the ethical dimensions of climate change since its inception, in its latest report the IPCC claims that climate change "raises difficult issues of justice, fairness, and rights, all of which lie within the sphere of ethics."[1] That is a salutary insight and also a challenge to us to come to grips with this aspect of the problem. In this chapter we will therefore look closely at the *discipline* of climate ethics. We begin with an examination of the distinction between ideal and non-ideal ethical theory. As we will see, the distinction is especially illuminating in the effort to find rationally justifiable climate policy. We will ask how climate change ethics fits into the larger field of environmental ethics, how economics provides a challenge to it, whether it is required to make sense of the threats of climate change and, finally, whether it is adequate to that task.

Ideal and non-ideal theory

Climate change ethics is usually considered a branch of environmental ethics. The larger field came into its own beginning in the 1960s and began to flourish as a discipline in the 1970s. At that time, climate change was not a significant worry for the culture at large nor, therefore, for philosophical ethicists. The big environmental issues of the day had to do, among other things, with nuclear waste disposal (this in an age of profound angst about nuclear weapons proliferation), clear-cut logging and relatively localized, though often still severe, problems of pollution. And there was an abiding attempt to think through the larger questions about the human place in the natural order.

By 2004, this situation had not changed dramatically. There were now a handful of philosophers – many of whose views will be explored in upcoming chapters of this book – writing about climate change, but the paucity of attention devoted by philosophers to this issue was seriously out of step with what the scientific community was saying about the threat posed by climate change. Things have now altered significantly in the philosophical community. There is a large and growing literature on the ethics of climate change, with many philosophers now recognizing that the climate crisis has effectively eclipsed all other environmental problems in scope and severity.

It's easy to understand this assessment of the situation. In one of the earliest treatments by a philosopher of the ethics of climate change, James Garvey said this:

> We can expect a future with hundreds of millions, even billions of displaced, hungry, thirsty people in it, escaping not just sea-level rises but on the move away from scorched croplands and empty wells ... There is going to be a lot of death in the future, a lot of death which wouldn't have happened had we and those before us acted otherwise.[2]

This is exactly the kind of blunt talk the climate crisis requires, and not just from philosophers. It also seems to invite specifically ethical analysis of the problem, but with what principles should such analysis begin?

The most natural place to start is with the **harm principle**. First espoused in the 19th century by John Stuart Mill, the principle states that "the only purpose for which power can be rightfully exercised over any member of a civilized community, against his will, is to prevent harm to others."[3] This is a doctrine about the moral limits of state power in a liberal democracy, but it applies more generally as well. The broader claim is that, other things being equal, we have moral reasons to refrain from performing actions which bring harm to others. This means that we have duties of constraint with respect to those actions. Ethical analysis can show us both what these duties are and why we have reason to constrain ourselves in the appropriate way whether or not this is optimal from the standpoint of self-interest.

Avoiding or reducing prospective harms as well as compensating for past ones is not all there is to ethics but focusing on it takes us very far, especially in our understanding of climate change. Still, the harm principle is too general to provide policy guidance all by itself. Deciding in particular cases what constitutes harm requires more fine-tuned theoretical and empirical work. To take a simple example, we can argue about whether it is more important to protect people's rights or their welfare. And in any particular case, it may not be easy to determine which actions will give us the results we are looking for. Violation of either of these values can be construed as a harm, but sometimes a policy-maker might have to choose between them in a situation of conflicting interpretations of where the potential harms lie. A policy designed to maximize net welfare in a group of people might conflict with the rights of some members of that group or a different group.

For instance, a majority in some collective might have a preference for the military security provided by low-level jet fighter test-flights over their territory, even though the flights arguably violate the rights of a minority group within the territory because they disrupt the migratory path of a species this group hunts for subsistence. Members of the majority group might deny that members of the minority group are being genuinely harmed by the test flights, while members of the minority group might deny that members of the majority group would be harmed by the flights' cessation. But even if neither group engages in this sort of denial the disagreement can be protracted. They might in this case simply say that the harms to their group outweigh the harms to the other. In cases like this we can't have it both ways, so how do we decide? Whatever we decide, we must *justify* our decisions by appeal to reasons that are accessible to others. Here are four standard ways of doing this.

The first is **consequentialism**, the notion that we ought to evaluate actions on the basis of their outcomes. **Utilitarianism** – the most widely employed form of consequentialism among philosophers – holds that what counts in terms of outcomes is welfare, broadly construed. So, if I have a choice between two courses of action I should assess whose welfare will be affected by each course, then choose that course which maximizes total welfare for this group. The second theory is **deontology**, which assesses actions on the basis of whether or not they treat other moral agents respectfully. Deontology has become the theoretical basis of moral and political "rights" in our culture. The third theory is **contractarianism**. Here, actions are morally permissible just insofar as they are the product of an agreement among properly- informed moral agents. The final theory is **virtue ethics**. On this theory actions are permissible to the extent that they are the product of ideal character traits in agents. For example, we can praise an agent for an action she performed if we judge that she acted bravely, where bravery is, let's suppose, a character trait admired in our group.

Each of these theories is designed to provide a general description of our duties. They help us organize the latter at a relatively abstract conceptual level. They provide "rules" that we can apply to the assessment of particular actions, defining the boundary between the permissible and the impermissible. They are all examples of "ideal theory." That is, they specify ideals towards which society and individuals should be moving and on the basis of which they can be criticized for failing to do so. Ideal theory is to be contrasted with "non-ideal theory." The ideal/non-ideal distinction originates in John Rawls' political philosophy and is important for two reasons. The first is that more and more moral and political philosophers are being drawn to non-ideal theory in light of the evident failures of ideal theory; the second is that this trend has spread to climate ethicists..

Rawls' philosophy deals for the most part with "the principles of justice that would regulate a well-ordered society." This is a society in which people are "presumed to act justly and to do [their] part in upholding just institutions." In sum, for Rawls "the nature and aims of a perfectly just society is the fundamental part of the theory of justice."[4] In constructing the theory of justice, Rawls is operating with two assumptions. The first is that of "strict compliance," i.e., a situation in which everyone does her part in maintaining the institutions of justice; the second is "favorable circumstances", e.g. merely moderate material scarcity as well as a generally well educated and suitably skilled citizenry. Non-ideal theory, then, concerns situations in which these assumptions do not hold. Rawls recognizes that a full understanding of such philosophical topics as punishment, just and unjust wars and how to oppose tyrannical regimes may be best approached by means of non-ideal theory.[5]

It is tempting to add climate change to this list of topics, as some philosophers are now realizing:

> In its broadest sense, non-ideal theory asks how to respond to an imperfect world. Some advocates of non-ideal theory emphasize a different approach to theorizing, others call for more practical action-guidance. The challenges of responding to climate change are further evidence, if any were needed, that we do not live in an ideal world.[6]

Given the repeated failures of international climate policy over the years (we'll look into this in Chapter 3), this is certainly an understandable position to adopt. Non-compliance with the terms of the various treaties that have been adopted has, if anything, been the international norm. Global carbon emissions have accelerated alarmingly in the past two decades or so. "Favorable circumstances," on the other hand, exist in some places but not everywhere. Absolute poverty, economic inequality, global institutional failure, a generalized distrust of democratic politicians and technocrats and organized climate change denial are just a few of the forces which challenge the notion that we can reason as though the circumstances of climate justice were unproblematically ideal.

Bearing these points in mind will pay dividends as we examine the nature of climate justice in Chapters 4 and 5. But we need to be more specific about what non-ideal theory is aimed at elucidating. Laura Valentini mentions three areas. Non-ideal theory must (a) pay attention to the fact of only *partial compliance* among relevant parties; (b) be *realistic*, rather than utopian, especially about global politics; and (c) be concerned not just with the end-state we want to achieve but also the *transition* to that state from where we are now.[7]

Many climate ethicists have now embraced these recommendations. As we have just seen, one cannot, for example, construct ideal theories of justice as though full compliance were either an achieved reality or in the offing. The Trump administration's decision to exit the Paris Agreement changes the game for *everyone* else, for example. The best we can do right now therefore, is to provide a transitional ethics, a way to understand how to get through the climate crisis with our moral integrity not too badly damaged. That is one way to understand what we are up to in this book.

Another general reason for endorsing non-ideal theory in climate ethics is that it embraces a broader pragmatic turn in ethical theory. Some critics of ideal ethics have argued that theories like utilitarianism, rights-theory, con-tractarianism and virtue ethics can actually make our policy disagreements more protracted. How? Well, think of the metaphors typically employed in this area. For example, justification by way of theory-construction is meant to "fortify" one's stance, provide it with more secure "foundations" and so on. The point of fortification and foundation-building, of course, is to make it more difficult to dislodge you from your position. It fixes you in place, impervious to onslaughts from would-be theoretical raiders. So the effort to provide theoretical justifications for our policy choices can make us less open-minded to the views of others. This is, we might think, contrary to the broadly pragmatic goal of getting things done.

But there are dangers lurking here. Ideals remain important because they both tell us what our deepest aspirations are and provide an ultimate goal towards which we can work. In spite of the potential pitfalls of the search for foundations, justification is probably indispensable if we are to avoid brute force as the final court of appeal in our deliberations. The danger with the insistence on purely non-ideal theory in climate ethics, then, is that it might degenerate into an apology for the status quo. The call to pay attention to non-compliance, to be realistic and worry less about the end-state than the transition to it can be summarized in the advice to make climate policy feasible. But as Gardiner has noted, the focus on the "feasible" excludes:

> *whole categories of concern* from climate policy (e.g., distributive and corrective justice), even despite their importance to the large emitting economies whose cooperation is essential (e.g., I doubt the political wisdom of saying to India "feasibility" means accepting our world view – where you are the problem and your concerns about justice are irrelevant). Notably, it underestimates the extent to which the feasible is political.[8]

That last line is key: "the feasible is political." Talk of sticking to what is "feasible" can be music to the ears of those who benefit the most from dra-matically skewed social and economic relations. We need to take care that we are not using considerations of pragmatism, realism, feasibility, etc. to prop up unjust power relations. Keeping an eye on ideals can aid us in this task.

The trick for a sound climate ethics, then, appears to be to cleave to the middle ground between two extremes. We want to avoid both (a) the sort of moral idealism that takes no account of the constraints imposed by current social, political and economic reality; and (b) a hard-nosed realism that is likely to leave entrenched inequities untouched. One thing to say about both (a) and (b) is that neither is likely to work. To embrace either dogmatically is to alienate too many people to expect one's proposals to gain real political traction. Politics unfolds in the space between the ideal and the real.

Let's bring this back to the harm principle. The actions leading to climate change – for example, profligate use of fossil fuels – look to be paradigm examples of harm causation. Other things being equal, it should therefore be easy to justify constraining people from doing these things. Things are, alas, not so straightforward. Much of the rest of this book is aimed at laying bare just how complex all of this can get. For instance, if there are duties of constraint in this case, who has them? Towards whom? What specific actions do they prescribe or proscribe? And finally, what is the force of that sneaky clause just above that we have reason to refrain from acting in harm-causing ways, "other things being equal"? It seems to imply that the moral reasons which apply for the most part might not apply in the real world of messy politics, clashing interests, competing rights claims, and so on.

We'll get to all of these questions, but there's a more pressing task right now, for there are two broad challenges to the enterprise of climate change ethics. The first comes from those who deny that ethical analysis is relevant to climate change; the second from those who claim that ethics is relevant but that it is conceptually inadequate to help us address the issue. The first claim has been made by economists who embrace **cost-benefit analysis (CBA)**, the second by some prominent climate ethicists. We'll address these in order in the next two sections.

Climate economics

Making decisions about climate policy in one way rather than some alternative expresses a commitment to a specific conception of value. Most economists think that value is determined by individual preferences, that these can be "revealed" in markets and that the job of policy makers is to tailor public policy so as to allow for the smooth expression of such preferences. This can be done through the application of CBA to competing policy options. CBA attempts to monetize a more general pros and cons approach to problems. For any proposal it translates preferences into monetary terms, then simply compares the costs against the benefits. The most "rational" course of action is the one that is least costly. Although the approach has the virtue of clarity, it has been subjected to withering critique as an instrument of public policy. Let's focus on three criticisms of it, chosen for their importance to climate ethics.

CBA is monistic about value

Value-monism is the idea that there is just one kind of value, or that if there are different kinds they can all be translated into the one master-value. Of course, for the economist that master-value is economic value. But this leaves out of account spiritual, aesthetic and political values, among others. It cannot account for environmental values, for example the value a person might place on the mere existence of an economically useless species.

Economists have responded to this worry by invoking the idea of "willingness to pay." Briefly, the claim is that the value of these things can be fully accounted for by our willingness to pay to have them protected. If we care about a tree species threatened by the development plans of the logging industry, for example, then we can express this concern through financial support of environmental groups devoted to preserving the forests containing this tree species. If such support outweighs the financial benefits of cutting down the trees, then governments have a duty to prevent or restrict the logging. As this example makes clear, the approach assumes a rough equality of economic power in society that may not exist. The logging company's financial power, and that of its supporters, might vastly outstrip the financial power of concerned environmentalists.

The alternative to value monism is value pluralism. Value pluralists take it for granted that there are sources or kinds of value not reducible to money. If you are a pluralist in this sense, and also a policy-maker, you will emphasize dialogue with and consultation among the various groups affected by a proposed policy. It is important to say this, because CBA is often characterized by its supporters as *the* democratic approach to policy making. After all, it takes everyone's preferences seriously, throwing them all into the great melting pot of monetization to see which ones come out victorious. But if the approach favors the economically powerful, it is not democratic at all.

Moreover, we might question the assumption behind CBA that democracy is essentially about finding a way to satisfy people's preferences. This may in fact be a category mistake. That is, values might be more like mathematical truths than tastes. When it comes to preferences for ice-cream flavors, there's no problem reducing "value" to the intensity with which the preference is held. But we would not judge mathematical claims this way: their truth has nothing to do with what we want to be the case.[9] Again, imagine someone wanting to preserve a beautiful tree species because she thinks it is important that future generations have access to it in its relatively untouched forest ecosystem. She might be outraged if it were suggested to her that her preference for preservation over destruction is not qualitatively different than her preference for maple walnut over chocolate ice-cream. CBA is constitutionally incapable of comprehending this outrage, but value pluralism is not.

At the end of the day, there are two dangers to avoid here. Pluralism can lead to policy paralysis, whereas monism can lead to misguided policy. It's likely best to insist on pluralism, so long as all parties to policy disputes agree on the necessity of compromise. That way, we can get things done while not running roughshod over the concerns of minority groups or the economically disadvantaged. This is essential to bear in mind in climate policy. Climate change is such a wide-ranging phenomenon, creating potential harms for such a diversity of entities – the poor, nature, future people, indigenous groups – that to think we can capture its challenges solely in the language of money is unhelpfully dogmatic. CBA is admirably clear but it badly misrepresents how we think, and ought to think, about value. It is the perfect example of the person looking for his keys at night under a bright lamp, not because that's where he lost them but simply because the light is better there.

CBA cannot support aggressive climate measures

Some economists believe that (a) we require aggressive action to combat climate change, but (b) we can ground this policy in economics. Ethics has no bearing on this issue.[10] The reason for this is that ethics is about transcending individual self-interest whereas climate change is a problem, if it is at all, only because individuals – and therefore also the societies they make up – have misunderstood their genuine self-interest. For instance, most people love their children and grandchildren, but because climate change is going to harm these people, it is in the interest of loving parents and grandparents to do something about the problem now. To fail in this task is to neglect one's genuine self-interest. David Weisbach, an economist, claims that we need to make aggressive emissions cuts but only because doing so is a way of "saving our own necks."[11] In other words, there's simply no significant work for ethics in this domain.

Here's the challenge laid out more formally:

1   Ethics demands that we sometimes look beyond self-interest for solutions to our problems.
2   Climate change is happening because we have misunderstood our genuine self-interest.
3   Determining our genuine self-interest is the task of CBA.
4   Therefore climate change is an economic problem, not an ethical one.

What can we say about this argument? It looks valid, but is it sound? There's little reason to dispute premise (1). Though it requires some elaboration, it expresses a commonsense understanding of morality that is good enough for our purposes here. We can let premise (3) stand as well, since it expresses the self-understanding of the discipline of economics. The real problem is premise (2). As we have noted, the argument for it depends on what we might call the three-generation gaze: parents and grandparents living now have entirely self-interested reasons to get serious about fighting climate change because the interests of those they love – hence their *own* interests too – will be adversely affected if they fail to do so.

Weisbach himself thinks this argument justifies very strong emissions reduction measures. He thinks we must move the global economy to zero or near-zero carbon emissions within a few decades. He *needs* premise (2) to ground this policy prescription. Unfortunately, premise (2) appears dubious, for two reasons. First, there are plenty of people who are not parents or grandparents. On Weisbach's analysis, such people have no duties of constraint in this area. If it suits them, they may as well live in the most carbon-intensive way they can, and they should actively oppose governmental efforts to regulate industry. This is counter-intuitive, especially if everyone else – those parents and grandparents – ends up having fairly stringent duties of constraint.

Second, the claim that it is in the interest of the procreators to act with constraint looks to be empirically false for parents and grandparents in relatively wealthy countries. For example, in the short to medium term the U.S. is, as Robert Paarlberg has shown, among the world's *least vulnerable* countries with respect to severe climate disruption. This is because it is rich enough to cope with most of the damages it will see. For instance, Hurricanes Harvey and Irma caused massive damage in Texas and Florida in 2017, but the cleanup in both places was relatively swift for storms of that size. More generally, William Nordhaus has argued that even if we cannot keep temperatures below 2°C by 2070 about 90% of the economy of the U.S. will be "only lightly or negligibly impacted" by the effects of climate change.[12] That means that with little or no aggressive action on climate change, the children and grandchildren of present citizens of the U.S. will be just fine, relative to the not-so-lucky elsewhere on the planet.

So while (2) might be true of some people, in some places in the world, it does not generalize and cannot therefore support the conclusion (4). Given this analysis, we can see that there is something perverse about the economist's claims here. What the three-generation gaze implies, in effect, is that those who are most wealthy, and who have therefore benefited the most from carbon-intensive economic activity, have the least stringent duties to change their lifestyles. This is because wealth brings with it the ability to protect one's progeny from environmental harms, and this, we have seen, is all economists like Weisbach think we are required to care about. The poor, on the other hand, are required to forgo economic development to the extent that this requires burning fossil fuels because *their* children and grand-children really will be adversely affected by climate change. Some might suspect that this conclusion turns our moral intuitions on their heads.

In short, even if the economist agrees that strong measures are required in order to meet the climate challenge, the claim cannot be grounded in the economic assumption that self-interest is the ultimate justification for policy. This brings us to the final criticism of CBA.

CBA misunderstands our duties to future generations

A major component of environmental policy generally and climate policy in particular has to do with the value we place on the future. One question that arises is how much money we should set aside in the present so that people of the future can cope adequately with the environmental challenges we have left for them. One possible answer is: nothing at all, but that notion has few adherents. Almost everyone agrees that we are morally required to set aside something for the future. But how much? There is a major dispute between (most) economists and just about everyone else, regardless of disciplinary background, on this issue. Of course, economists are the experts in rational approaches to saving, so we should at least give them our ear on this question.

The approach taken by economists is an application of CBA to the future, known as **discounting**. The idea is simple. If you desire a certain consumer good sometime in the future, then in order to calculate how much money you should set aside for it now you should (a) determine how much money your investment can make in interest if you tuck it away someplace; and (b) calculate how long you are willing to wait to receive the good. For example, if I want to buy a $15,000 pony for my daughter in 10 years and I can get 5% interest every year between now and then, I should invest $10,000 right now. If I do, then I can say that the *present value* of that pony is $10,000 given a 5% *discount rate*.

Three features of this simple example jump out. First, the discount rate is key. The higher it is, the less is the present value of the good. Second, how far in the future we are investing affects the present value of the good in the same way. The farther out we are looking, the less we must invest now. Third, this way of reasoning makes perfect sense applied to the purchase of consumer goods like ponies and computers. The question is how applicable is it to climate policy?

Remember that we are talking about the state of the world in, say, 2100 (this is how far out the IPCC's projection scenarios go, for example). The question then becomes, what is the present value of a world that is not ravaged by climate change in 2100? The British economist Sir Nicholas Stern uses a very low discount rate, thus generating the claim that our current investment in avoiding climate disaster ought to be correspondingly high. Most mainstream economists disagree with Stern about this. There are usually two reasons given for this disagreement, and thus for adopting a relatively high discount rate.

The first reason is that future generations will likely be wealthier than us. If this is true, then it may be that we owe them relatively little. But as Stern notes, it cannot simply be assumed that they will be wealthier than us, since this will depend on our policy choices:

> What we do now on climate change will transform the circumstances and income of future generations and this will determine discount rates. It is therefore a serious mistake to see decisions in this context as being determined by a discount rate.[13]

For example, if we continue with business as usual – RCP 8.5 – we invite catastrophic climate change. World GDP may drop substantially in these circumstances. It is a measure of the blinders we wear that this type of consideration is so easily dismissed in our culture. Those of us in the developed world are culturally and psychologically wedded to the notion that things must always get better, that short of causing a nuclear war we in the present are literally incapable of making people of the future worse off than we are.

This is an unfounded article of faith, one born of the material progress of the developed world over the last half-century or so. It does not generalize to human history as a whole and should not therefore obscure the possibility that there are choices we might make in the present that can cause the prosperity of future people to decline sharply. A refusal to act meaningfully to curb our carbon emissions could be one of those fateful decisions. However, even if climate change does not diminish global GDP in the future, it may exacerbate global inequities in a manner that will be abetted by our choice of a high discount rate. This might happen, for instance, because in a climate ravaged world resources for adaptation will be hoarded by the rich. A high discount rate makes fewer of these vital resources available, making hoarding both more likely and more devastating in its impacts on the poor.

The second reason for adopting a high discount rate is known as the "pure time preference" approach to the issue. The idea is that people of the future matter less to us, and ought to do so, simply because they are people of the future and not the present. This difference in concern can be translated into investment decisions. To non-economists, this "justification" for discounting can look bizarre. Stern, however, notes that indirect support for it can be drawn from a philosopher, David Hume. Hume argues that the interests of members of one's family or other in-group have, quite rightly, more weight than the interests of outsiders. Our allegiances move outward in concentric circles: we should "invest" in those closest to us to a greater extent than those further away.[14]

Of course, if we go far out enough along these circles the people we encounter might not count at all to us. This made *some* sense in Hume's day – the 18th century – because the decisions taken in one part of the world had a relatively small impact, or no impact at all, in most other places. However, in a highly economically interconnected world it makes less sense. If the products I buy in one place affect social relations and environmental conditions halfway across the globe, then there's an ethically meaningful sense in which those people ought to matter to me. More to the point, if my consumption choices can affect the life prospects of future people, then, ethically speaking, they have become a part of my time. Their interests cannot be discounted simply because they are relatively temporally far-flung.

There is a more general point to make about both attempts to justify high discount rates. It is that while discounting is a rational approach to organizing financial affairs at the level of individual decision-making, it is much more difficult to justify when present decisions will affect other people. As Gardiner puts the point:

[I]t is one thing to prefer larger damages in the future over smaller costs now when these are both costs to oneself, but quite another to prefer larger damages in the future over present costs when this means that the damages will come to someone else ... Furthermore, it would be one thing for individuals to value deferring damages to the future, and quite another for governments to make it a central driver of national policy.[15]

Discounting the future, in other words, looks like unjustified bias towards our own interests to the clear detriment of the interests of others.

From the three problems considered in this section – value monism, the foundational appeal to self-interest, and the choice of high discount rates – we can conclude that economics, especially the tool of CBA, is a theoretically impoverished approach to the challenges of climate change. But two final points are worth emphasizing.

First, from this analysis it does not follow that economics is useless. On the one hand, it is probably the best – i.e., fairest – approach we have to making decisions in a situation of deadlock among policy options. On the other hand, even where there is no such deadlock, economics can specify the best way to implement a chosen policy option (though even here ethical considerations are also relevant). But options themselves must be selected in other ways. In other words, economics is instrumentally useful but it is not a fit tool for setting our ends. The second point is that from our analysis it also does not follow that ethics should set our ends for us. The failure of economics here does not entail a victory for ethics. To see why and how ethics *is* essential requires more argument, a task to which we turn next.

Why ethics is necessary

Gardiner has argued that there are at least two reasons for believing that ethics *is* essential in this area. First, it is difficult to say why climate change is a *problem* without invoking value judgments. For as soon as we begin to analyze what is problematic about climate change we will necessarily be drawn to the language of what matters to people, whose interests count, or ought to count, and so on.[16] Second, we cannot make sense of climate change policy decisions without invoking ethical considerations. Let's focus on this second point. The example Gardiner considers in support of it is one that has been at the front of public discussion on this issue for the last 20 years or so, namely CO_2 emissions reduction targets. This is sometimes referred to as the "trajectory issue." As we will see in greater detail in later chapters, the issue is ethically loaded on two distinct dimensions.

The first dimension is international. If we decide that cuts to greenhouse gases must be made, there is bound to be, and has been, heated debate about which countries should make the biggest cuts and whether the very poorest countries should make any cuts at all, at least in the short term. It should be obvious that we can't begin to answer these questions without invoking ethical considerations, in particular those surrounding the issue of who is most to blame for the climate crisis.

The second dimension is intergenerational. On the plausible assumption that the more aggressive our cuts are the less threatened by climate disaster people of the future will be, whatever level we decide on tells us something about how much we value the lives of future people. More to the point, since emissions are tied to the economic prosperity of the present generation, it tells us how much we believe their interests matter compared to our own.[17] We can think of this in terms of allocating costs. If we adopt very low reduction targets we are implicitly claiming that people of the future ought to be allocated a greater share of the costs of climate change than we are allocated. For them, these costs will be almost entirely in the form of adaptation to the effects of climate change whereas in our own case we are talking mainly of mitigation costs.

In spite of this difference the moral asymmetry of the allocation is clear: the low target implies the belief that it is *more important* for people of the present to avoid modest costs than it is for people of the future to avoid heavy costs. Of course, the point here is that it is always possible to question any such allocation. But we cannot do so effectively without using moral language, as Gardiner points out:

> Any allocation must (explicitly or implicitly) take a position on the importance of factors such as the historical responsibility for the problem, the current needs and future aspirations of particular societies, and the appropriate role of energy consumption in people's lives.[18]

This passage is loaded with normative language (which can be present even when words like "ought" or "should" are not explicitly invoked). Unpacking terms like "importance," "responsibility," "needs," "aspirations" and the "appropriate role" of energy in our lives puts us squarely in the territory of ethical deliberation.

For example, the concept of "needs" can sound merely descriptive, as when we assert that a healthy adult human male needs to consume about 2500 calories/day. But what do we say about the person who asserts that he *needs* to drive a Hummer because he finds smaller vehicles much less comfortable? Unfortunately, many of the "needs" that are defended as part of the refusal to cut CO_2 emissions on the part of people in the developed world are more like the Hummer case rather than the healthy calorie intake case. Again, to say why this is so, and what is wrong with it, would appear to require specifically ethical analysis. The Hummer owner must justify his actions to the rest of us in the context of a global situation that clearly demands constraint from individual consumers with respect to fossil-fuel use.

So climate change looks like an ethical issue if anything is. More specifically, it looks to be a question of justice in a fairly straightforward way. John

Broome argues that harms related to emitting GHGs are injustices in virtue of seven features:

- The harms are something the emitters *do*
- The harms are serious
- The harms are not accidental
- We do not compensate the victims of the harms
- Emissions are made for our own benefit
- The harms are not reciprocated (the victims do not harm us in an equivalent way)
- Our emissions could easily be reduced[19]

We will have a chance to expand on most of these claims in coming chapters. The point here is just to show that there is a strong *prima facie* case for climate change being a quintessentially moral problem, with a concern about justice at its core. However, some prominent climate ethicists themselves have argued that climate change defeats our efforts to understand it in terms of the standard categories and concepts of moral philosophy, at least as this is currently practiced in the analytic tradition.

Is ethics adequate?

For instance, Dale Jamieson has provided powerful reasons for thinking that climate change is not like a "paradigm moral problem," and that understanding it therefore defeats commonsense approaches to morality. Let's begin by clarifying the structure of a paradigm moral problem. It consists in one person intentionally causing harm to another, for example Jack intentionally stealing Jill's bicycle.[20] But climate change is not like this, for a number of reasons. First, the example is concerned solely with the present (and immediate past) whereas with climate change we are also concerned with future harms. Second, no individual intends to cause these harms. Our Hummer driver intends to have a comfortable ride, not to deprive future people of access to fresh water. Finally, the example is too individualistic. Jack causes the relevant harm all alone whereas our Hummer driver will be a harm-causer only if a significant enough number of other people engage in similarly carbon-intensive behaviors.

Jamieson concludes that the paradigm example would have to be amended to fit the case of climate change. Here's the amended version: "Acting independently, Jack and a large number of unacquainted people set in motion a chain of events that prevents a large number of future people who will live in another part of the world from ever having bikes."[21]

Let's isolate three features of *this* kind of case. First, the action is causally dispersed, in the sense that a large number of people whose actions are not formally coordinated are required to bring it about. Second, the harm caused by the action is dispersed among a number of people, both spatially (in the present) and temporally (in the future). Finally, unlike the paradigm moral case we have here no institutional framework allowing us to understand who owes what to whom by way of rectification for the harm caused. Put this way, we might find it very difficult to find Jack (or our Hummer driver) responsible for what transpires, in which case we can wonder whether or not there is a specifically moral problem here at all.

There's likely more we could add to distinguish this sort of case from the paradigm model, but this should be enough to get us worrying about the ability of commonsense morality to capture the problem of climate change. What about our moral theories? Gardiner, for one, doubts that they are adequate in their current form. He characterizes moral theories – including the big four we have noted above: utilitarian consequentialism, deontology, contractarianism and virtue ethics – as "research programs." They evolve historically and must evolve a good deal more to meet the challenge of climate change:

> Whatever their other merits, in their current forms these research programs appear to lack the resources needed to deal with problems like climate change. Moreover, it seems likely that in evolving to meet them they will be substantially, and perhaps radically, transformed.[22]

Jamieson makes much the same point, but appears to take it a step further. As he puts it, climate change is "world-constituting" because what we do, or fail to do, about our GHG emissions will alter radically the material conditions of the planet inherited by our descendants. It will also alter the *identities* of those people, an issue we look at in detail in Chapter 5. Commonsense morality, Jamieson's persistent focus in these remarks, is not equipped to grasp problems on this scale.[23]

To help assess this claim, notice that most of our morally important decisions are not world-making in this sense. We make decisions about whether or not to lie to someone on a particular occasion, whether we should become vegetarians, send our kids to public or private school, how much of our salary to give to charity, what portion of our time to devote to the abolition of the local puppy mill or to the promotion of our favorite political candidate, and so on. None of this appears to have anything to do with remaking a world, only tidying up our little corner of it, morally speaking. What we generally say as we go about making these decisions is that we are trying to improve things in some small way, and that if we fail to act as we think we should the world will be a bit worse for it.

But Jamieson is suggesting that with respect to our decisions about climate change it may not even make sense to ask whether or not the world we are making is "better" or "worse" than some alternative. Two analogies are mobilized to support his case. First, does it make sense to ask whether or not it is "better" that Christianity arose when it did and transformed the world in its image? We live in a world in which this transformation happened, so how we think about evaluative terms like "better" or "worse" takes place within this social and moral horizon. Climate change, we are told, is like this, making it impossible to even ask the question about the value or disvalue of a climate-changed world. Here's the second analogy: "Asking these questions can seem like asking whether it is a good thing that there is an oscillation between glacial and inter-glacial periods."

Jamieson summarizes the point of the two analogies this way:

> These are questions about the value of features that form the very structure of the world within which we make evaluations. Moral evaluations, at least those of the sort we are generally prepared to make, arise within these structures rather than being about these structures. Commonsense morality operates within a horizon of possibility. It is not well-equipped to make judgments about the conditions that fix these possibilities.[24]

Has Jamieson overstated the challenge morality faces? To see why we should probably be skeptical here, let's look at these two analogies in order.

First, it seems as though it is, and always was, possible to ask meaningful questions about the Christian horizon of moral meaning. With respect to questions about right and wrong, salvation and the nature of divine creation, for example, Christianity always had competitors (including atheism). It therefore does not, and never did, define the horizon of possible meaning in the *totalizing* way Jamieson's analogy apparently requires. Of course, living within Christendom in, say, the 14th century made it difficult, indeed perilous, for anyone to seek out alternative sources of moral meaning. But, again, there have always been atheists, apostates and heretics, people who challenged the evaluative terms of the system they inhabited from within it. In any case, in invoking Christianity in this context, Jamieson is talking not about people like this but about *us*. The claim is that *we* cannot evaluate the Christian worldview from our position inside of it. Since many of us do this all the time the claim seems false.

This brings us to the second analogy. Jamieson is surely correct to assert that the question about whether the oscillation between glacial and inter-glacial periods is a good or a bad thing is nonsensical. It is simply a fact. But this is surely *not* a good analogy to climate change, precisely because we are in this case choosing to bring about a specific future world, a world that will contain much avoidable suffering and harm. If we are able to refrain from bringing this world into being, it surely makes sense to ask whether it is a good thing, morally speaking, for us to try and do so. Indeed, if they believed their decision mattered morally, these considerations would also have applied to a hypothetical group of past people who *were* capable of doing something about the oscillation between glacial and interglacial periods, before the whole thing got started.

In trying to assess these complex issues, it might be helpful to distinguish commonsense morality and moral theory more carefully than we have been doing. To this end, the first question to ask is whether the person equipped with only the tools of commonsense morality can be critical of his horizon of moral meaning. The problem with this question is that commonsense morality is a vague notion. In their moral decisions most people likely operate with some shifting mixture of intuitions derived from various religious, political and scientific authorities, introspection, their peers, family traditions, the Internet and maybe even a smattering of moral theory picked up in college. It's an open question whether a bag of moral sources as motley as this can furnish material for criticizing the foundations or horizon of a moral culture. Maybe it can't, which is all the more reason to look beyond commonsense morality.

In any case, like Gardiner, Jamieson does not conclude from these reflections that moral *theory* is entirely inept when it comes to climate change, only that it needs to be radically revised or even revolutionized to meet this challenge. This sounds right. For one thing, it would probably not be possible even to recognize climate change as the profound moral problem it is if both our theories and commonsense morality could not make any sense of it. It shows up as a problem *from within* our moral horizon. It does not follow that it can be solved entirely from this perspective but it is worth pointing out that many climate ethicists – John Broome and Peter Singer, for instance – seem relatively unfazed by the sort of worries about moral theory's deep structure expressed by Gardiner and Jamieson.

A final point to make in this context is that nearly all the big moral issues we face can look as though they stretch our moral theories to the breaking point. This applies to abortion, euthanasia, the ethics of war and peace, the ethics of surveillance, the problem of global poverty and much more. It is easy to become frustrated with the capacity of any single moral theory to make full sense of these issues. Trying to grasp the ethics of terrorism from a utilitarian perspective or the ethics of abortion from the perspective of virtue theory can be illuminating but these approaches almost always leave gaps – sometimes significant ones – in our understanding of the issues. If we try to fill these gaps with some other theory, the results can look displeasingly *ad hoc*. We nevertheless rightly think it worthwhile to continue "applying" our moral theories to these kinds of problems.

Perhaps it's best to be agnostic here, at least provisionally. Keeping in mind the points made in this chapter both about the need to theorize (sometimes) in a non-ideal manner about climate change and about the unique challenges of this phenomenon as a moral problem, let's just *do* climate change ethics and let the philosophical chips fall where they may.

Chapter summary

This chapter has considered the nature, scope and limitations of climate ethics as a discipline. Such work is preparatory to doing climate ethics proper. We began by looking at the distinction between ideal and non-ideal ethical theory, noting that we should be skeptical of overly idealistic theory but that non-ideal theory threatens to be a simple apology for the status quo. Some middle ground between the two approaches was therefore recommended. Next, we examined cost-benefit analysis, the favorite policy making tool of the economist. It was necessary to do this because economics enjoys a good deal of power and prestige in our cultures. However, we found that it is not sufficient for making ethically sound policy choices. One of the chief areas of concern has to do with the theory of discounting the future employed by many economists. We saw that this is an inadequate way to make policy in the age of climate change. The failure of economics in this area seems to point to the need for ethics, but it is not clear that philosophical ethics is itself up to the job. Although we looked at some reasons for thinking this, and responded to the worries, the question remains open.

Questions for discussion

1 Explain the distinction between value monism and value pluralism. Is there a way to be a pluralist and a pragmatist? That is, can we be open to multiple value-perspectives without inviting policy paralysis?
2 Explain the theory of discounting. What are the justifications for adopting a high discount rate? Are they acceptable? Why or why not?
3 Do you agree with Weisbach that climate change is not an ethical problem at all?
4 Does climate change stretch the boundaries of our traditional moral categories to the breaking point (as the bike example illustrates) or is this claim an overstatement?
5 Explain the relation between ideal and non-ideal theory as applied to climate ethics. Can we retain our focus on an ideal while being attentive to messy realities?

Suggested reading

Nicholas Stern, *The Global Deal: Climate Change and a New Era of Progress and Prosperity* (New York: Public Affairs, 2009). A clear and accessible account of the economics of climate change, from an economics maverick. Builds on and summarizes The Stern Review.
Clare Heyward and Dominic Roser (eds.), *Climate Justice in a Non-ideal World* (Oxford: Oxford University Press, 2016). Great collection of essays examining the link between non-ideal theory and climate justice. Cutting-edge philosophy.
Dale Jamieson, *Reason in a Dark Time: Why the Struggle against Climate Change Failed and What it Means For Our Future* (Oxford: Oxford University Press, 2014), chapter 5. A thorough analysis of the enterprise of climate ethics. Jamieson was the first philosopher to think seriously about this problem, and this chapter represents the culmination of his work on it.

Notes

1 IPCC 2014 (b): Kolstad C., K. Urama, J. Broome, A. Bruvoll, M. Cariño Olvera, D. Fullerton, C. Gollier, W. M. Hanemann, R. Hassan, F. Jotzo, M.R. Khan, L. Meyer, and L. Mundaca, 2014: Social, Economic and Ethical Concepts and Methods. In Edenhofer, O., R. Pichs-Madruga, Y. Sokona, E. Farahani, S. Kadner, K. Seyboth, A. Adler, I. Baum, S. Brunner, P. Eickemeier, B. Kriemann, J. Savolainen, S. Schlömer, C. von Stechow, T. Zwickel and J.C. Minx (eds.), *Climate Change 2014: Mitigation of Climate Change. Contribution of Working Group III to the Fifth Assessment Report of the Intergovern mental Panel on Climate Change* (Cambridge, United Kingdom and New York, NY, USA: Cambridge University Press, 2014), 214.
2 James Garvey, *The Ethics of Climate Change: Right and Wrong in a Warming World* (New York· Continuum, 2008), 28.
3 John Stuart Mill, *On Liberty*, in Andrew Bailey (ed.), *First Philosophy* (Peterborough: Broadview Press, 2011), 200–240 (200).
4 John Rawls, *A Theory of Justice* (Cambridge, MA: Harvard University Press, 1971), 7–8.
5 Rawls, *A Theory of Justice*, 8.
6 Clare Heyward and Dominic Roser, "Introduction," in Clare Heyward and Dominic Roser (eds.), *Climate Justice in a Non-ideal World* (Oxford: Oxford University Press, 2016), 1–18 (9).
7 Laura Valentini, "Ideal vs. Non-Ideal Theory: A Conceptual Map," *Philosophy Compass* 7(9), 2012, 654–664.
8 Stephen Gardiner and David Weisbach, *Debating Climate Ethics* (Oxford: Oxford University Press, 2016), 252–253 (emphasis in original).
9 Gardiner and Weisbach, *Debating Climate Ethics…*, 78.
10 For example, David Weisbach. See Stephen Gardiner and David Weisbach, *Debating Climate Ethics*.
11 Gardiner and Weisbach, *Debating Climate Ethics…*, 156.
12 Quoted in Robert Paarlberg, *The United States of Excess: Gluttony and the Dark Side of American Exceptionalism* (Oxford: Oxford University Press, 2015), 152–154. This paragraph draws on Byron Williston, review of Gardiner and Weisbach, *Debating Climate Ethics*, Notre Dame Philosophical Reviews. At: http://ndpr.nd.edu/news/debating-climate-ethics/.
13 Nicholas Stern, *The Global Deal: Climate Change and a New Era of Progress and Prosperity* (New York: Public Affairs, 2009), 81.
14 Stern, *The Global Deal…*, 83.
15 Stephen Gardiner, *A Perfect Moral Storm: The Ethical Tragedy of Climate Change* (Oxford: Oxford University Press, 2011), 276–277.
16 Gardiner, *A Perfect Moral Storm…*, 20.
17 Gardiner, *A Perfect Moral Storm…*, 21.
18 Gardiner, *A Perfect Moral Storm…*, 21–22.
19 John Broome, *Climate Matters* (New York: W.W. Norton, 2012), 55–58.
20 Dale Jamieson, "Climate Change, Responsibility, and Justice," *Science and Engineering Ethics* 16, 2010, 431–445 (436).
21 Jamieson, "Climate Change, Responsibility…," 436.
22 Gardiner and Weisbach, *Debating Climate Ethics*, 38.
23 Dale Jamieson, *Reason in a Dark Time: Why the Struggle against Climate Change Failed and What it Means for our Future* (Oxford: Oxford University Press, 2014), 166.
24 Jamieson, *Reason in a Dark Time…*, 167.

3   Precautionary policy

Introduction

So far we have seen why climate change poses a grave threat to human and non-human systems and why it is, for this reason, an ethical issue at its core. Before we can appreciate the details and substance of the problem's ethical dimension, however, we need to describe what has been going on in the climate policy sphere in the recent past. What precise problems have we been trying to solve in our "official" deliberations about climate change? This is a large question since the tasks and challenges alter depending on the size and character of the political collective under analysis, and there is a vast range of these. To get a handle on the complexity, this chapter focuses on the ethical foundations of international climate policy, as well as the history of climate diplomacy. We will examine the precautionary principle, the main objectives of international climate policy (namely, to address the challenges of adaptation and mitigation), three key policy-relevant drivers of climate change and some of the more ethically salient developments in climate diplomacy over roughly the last 20 years.

The precautionary principle

Given the threats that await us under climate business as usual it seems wise for us to change course quickly. This, at least, is the conclusion that the international community has "officially" embraced. The founding document for understanding the normative dimensions of climate change is the **United Nations Framework Convention on Climate Change (FCCC)**. It was negotiated in the late 1980s and early 1990s, made available for signatures at the Rio Earth Summit in 1992 and entered into force in 1994. It currently has 197 Parties. The FCCC is steeped in ethical language and concepts. Perhaps the most important ethical concept it draws on is the **precautionary principle (PP)**, described this way:

> The Parties should take precautionary measures to anticipate, prevent or minimize the causes of climate change and mitigate its adverse effects. Where there are threats of serious or irreversible damage, lack of full scientific

certainty should not be used as a reason for postponing such measures, taking into account that policies and measures to deal with climate change should be cost-effective so as to ensure global benefits at the lowest possible cost.[1]

The FCCC sets the terms for the official international response to the problem of climate change. It therefore guides – provides the framework for – climate diplomacy. So if the PP is the ethical heart of the FCCC, which it is, then examining the principle with some care can help us understand what is going on at all those UN-sponsored climate change gatherings, the so-called Conference of Parties (COP) meetings. At the risk of oversimplification, we might say that these meetings are centrally *about* the meaning of the PP and the implications of taking it seriously in policy decisions about climate change.

The PP seems like an eminently reasonable principle to adopt with respect to serious environmental issues like this, but it has come in for a good deal of criticism over the years. Cass Sunstein thinks the principle fails because any attempt to understand its scope of application lands us in a dilemma. It is either so weak that it is simply banal or it is so strong that it is self-defeating. Either way it fails to be genuinely action-guiding in tough cases.

Consider the first horn of the dilemma. The PP is too weak if it tells us only that we should be careful in an environment of risk and uncertainty. Risk is generally understood as the product of the probability of a threat coming to pass and the magnitude of the damages that would be caused if it did. Other things being equal, the higher a threat scores on these two metrics, the riskier the situation is. Understood this way, we are almost always in an environment where there is some risk. After all, "full scientific certainty" on any issue is rarely if ever achieved. And yet we must often act, so the best option is to proceed with care.

That is indeed pretty banal advice. Imagine a pedestrian crossing a busy intersection. Her view is good and it looks like there is no traffic around, so she thinks it is probably safe to cross without waiting for the light to change. Applying the PP here would have the pedestrian nevertheless wait for the light to change since she can't be sure the intersection is clear. Cars drive very fast around here, so perhaps there is one just out of sight approaching at great speed. Better to wait. There's nothing objectionable about our pedestrian's reasoning here, and it does look like an accurate application of the PP, but it is difficult to see in what sense it provides an example to the policymaker, which is what we are really interested in.

But the real thrust of the principle is that it enjoins us to act decisively, and perhaps even aggressively, to combat threats we may understand only dimly, provided they are serious enough. So the best response to the first part of the criticism is that, while it is true that the PP can look banal, it also *permits* action that is anything but. For example, scientists might believe that, even though we lack certainty about the larger ecosystemic effects of using genetically modified organisms (GMOs) in agriculture, we should refrain from widespread development of these technologies, since these wider effects *could* be catastrophic. So the scientists advise policymakers and legislators to make them illegal. That's a bold policy option, arrived at by application of the PP on the basis of expert scientific advice.

However, this example throws us onto the other horn of the dilemma. Making illegal the widespread agricultural use of GMOs is itself not without risks. One of the main reasons for developing these organisms is to make crops more resistant to pests or extreme weather conditions like drought. Some believe that the only way we have a chance of feeding the roughly 10 billion of us who will inhabit the planet by mid-century – especially given the likely ravages of climate change on agricultural systems – is through the widespread adoption of GMOs. If this is correct, then making GMOs illegal is itself a deeply risky policy choice because it will lead to a lot of premature death, especially in the developing world.

Shouldn't a consistent application of the PP forbid this option? According to Sunstein, this would be incoherent because it would induce policy paralysis:

> The real problem with the PP in its strongest form is that it is incoherent; it purports to give guidance, but it fails to do so, because it condemns the very steps that it requires. The regulation that the principle requires always gives rise to risks of its own – and hence the principle bans what it simultaneously mandates.[2]

How should we respond to this challenge? It's worth noting that Sunstein eventually seems to back away from this dismissal of the PP. He argues that in the messy world of public policy, risk is ubiquitous and so we inevitably respond to those risks that are "especially salient or insistent." This will be different from one country (or city, state, region, etc.) to another. The real problem with the PP is that, in situations like this, it "wrongly suggests that nations can and should adopt a general form of risk aversion."[3]

We can agree that it makes little sense to adopt a general form of risk aversion, for we live in a sea of risks and if we did so we would indeed get next to nothing done. But there is nothing about the PP *per se* that forbids us from *comparing* the threats we face, recognizing that one of them, say, is an especially salient or insistent threat, and that our first task as policy-makers is therefore to address *it*. Our analysis of the science of climate change in Chapter 1 shows clearly that it is just such a threat, if anything is. It is especially "salient and insistent," even if addressing it robustly is itself risky. In a world that is still heavily dependent on fossil fuels for the provision of basic energy security, cutting carbon emissions aggressively risks lives and livelihoods.

The same point applies to diverting scarce resources to adaptation, which comes with opportunity costs (funding health care, for example), or responding to an alarming upswing in global temperatures by implementing a geoengineering scheme (examined in Chapter 9), which risks interfering with the climate system in potentially dangerous ways. And so on. The point is that deciding to act in one, or all, of these ways can be an expression of our commitment to the PP. In other words, we can interpret the PP so that it allows for risk-comparison among policy options. We might say that it bids us to choose the *least* risky option precisely because this is, in the circumstances, the safest thing to do. This interpretation of the principle allows us to side-step Sunstein's claim that the PP is undermined by incoherence.

Here is another way to make the point. Though he is only tangentially concerned with the PP, Henry Shue has argued that the climate change case fulfills three jointly necessary and sufficient conditions for strong policy action in this area. First, we are talking about potentially massive losses from climatic disruption. Second, we understand the physical mechanisms that will bring about these losses and we can see their conditions emerging.

Finally, the costs of action are not prohibitively high. Chapter 1 has provided reasons for taking the first two conditions to have been met. As for costs, Shue draws on the work of Sir Nicholas Stern, who has calculated that we could meet the challenge of climate change with an expenditure of 2–4% of global GDP per annum.[4] This is not pocket change, but for a global GDP projected to be around USD $90 trillion by 2020 it is surely manageable. In short, in the case of climate change we have (a) a robust grasp of potential damages; (b) a knowledge of relevant causal mechanisms; and (c) a feasible remedy.[5]

The PP recommends strong action to meet this threat, so it is a helpful and probably indispensable moral principle in this context. But we must note that it is not *foundational*. This is an especially pertinent observation in the context of multiple risks and the policy trade-offs they sometimes demand. For even if everyone agrees that it would be a good thing for us to act cautiously, there might be a good deal of disagreement about what to do because competing voices might weigh the various threats and risks we face differently. One set of stakeholders might view geoengineering as an especially dire threat to eco-systems, and therefore something to be avoided at all costs, while another sees it as the only viable response to the humanitarian crises that are likely in the event of runaway climate change. Because each group can invoke the PP in defence of its position, we need a deeper appeal to principles.

Here, it is possible to draw on any of the four normative theories we looked at in the previous chapter. We could say, for instance, that we should act with precaution with respect to climate change because if we do not our actions or omissions will (a) lead to the widespread violation of rights (deontology); or (b) violate the terms of an implicit contract between us and other members of the human community (contractarianism); or (c) display objectionable character traits like greed or selfishness (virtue ethics); or (d) fail to maximize utility or welfare (utilitarianism) among all those sentient beings likely to be affected by the choice. This is not the place to investigate these options in detail, only to underline the point that no appeal to the PP is theoretically complete in the absence of this kind of grounding.

In this respect the PP is much like the harm principle. In fact, though it is something of an oversimplification we might say that the PP simply *is* the harm principle expressed as a normative constraint on public policy deliberation and choice. It's helpful to put the point this way because the harm principle, recall, has mainly to do with what restrictions governments are permitted to impose on individual liberties. Mill's point is that the only time this is justified is when an individual's exercise of liberty threatens to harm other members of the community. Now, since citizens will never agree unanimously about every policy choice, the liberty of some will always be restricted in the implementation and enforcement of any policy. It follows that employing the PP in public policy choice is a way of justifying the restriction of individual liberty to some degree.

We want to avoid ungainly conceptual structures here, so let's put the point about how all these theories and principles relate to one another as follows. The PP is the harm principle pressed into the service of making sound public policy, in our case climate policy. But whether we talk about the policies we ultimately choose as expressing the harm principle or the PP we must always be prepared to provide foundations for them in the manner suggested just above. The result, hopefully, is an internally consistent set of principles and theories that can provide publicly defensible reasons for action to the policy-maker.

One final point. The PP is sometimes taken as a principle of prudence – we should act cautiously because it is basically in our interest to do so – but this is potentially misleading. These deeper theoretical positions just canvassed are all, in one way or another, impersonalist. They all ask us to consider what *any* rational agent would do in the circumstances that obtain. Because of this, they all take a stance on what is of ultimate value. The PP, in other words, is applicable in situations in which something of value – some *good* – is at stake and these theories attempt to specify what that thing most fundamentally is. The PP therefore encompasses self-interest – for this is undoubtedly a good – but is not confined to it. Indeed, the threatened good might be something incomprehensible from the standpoint of the self-interest of someone living comfortably in the developed world: the vital interests of people of the far future or the global poor, the survival of economically "worthless" species, the traditional cultural practices of indigenous peoples, and so on.

Adaptation and mitigation

Given the importance of precaution, what exactly should we do in order to avoid climate catastrophe? Well, it is obvious that we are going to have to adapt, and in many ways already are adapting, to the myriad changes climate change is bringing about. "Adaptation" is the general term for any scheme aimed at helping us cope with the anticipated effects of climate change on society. Here is the IPCC's slightly more technical definition of the term:

Adaptation is the process of adjustment to actual or expected climate and its effects. In human systems, adaptation seeks to moderate or avoid harm or exploit beneficial opportunities. In some natural systems, human intervention may facilitate adjustment to expected climate and its effects.[6]

Building sea-walls to hold back the rising tide or loosening immigration policy to allow the absorption of climate refugees are examples of adaptation. As these examples indicate, the concept is quite broad, applying to human development, livelihood security, disaster-risk management, ecosystem management, institutional reform, land-use planning, urban infrastructural development and more. The means by which these factors are managed range from laws to engineering practices, from policy changes to technological advances and behavioural nudges.[7] Moreover, it is difficult to make general statements about the challenges of adaptation because adaptation measures are a response to risk assessment and risk is not evenly distributed over the global population (not to mention across generations).

Nevertheless, we can say that the main goal of adaptation measures is to build resilience in communities so that they are able to cope better with inevitable climatic changes. Accordingly, the IPCC has identified principles for effective adaptation. Here are just a few of them:

- Adaptation is place- and context-sensitive, with no specific approach that is applicable to all regions or communities. For example, because of drought-stress in many of its rural regions, sustainable urban development is a primary concern for many African nations. By contrast, innovative work practices to reduce outdoor work will be essential in many parts of Asia in order to cope with the increased risk of heat-related mortality. All such measures respond to assessment and vulnerability to change among members of a population.
- Successful adaptation depends on values, objectives and risk assessments. The IPCC points to the diversity of values across societies as a source of knowledge about how to manage adaptation. In particular, it highlights the importance of indigenous, local and traditional ways of managing land and resources.
- There are many impediments to successful adaptation. These include, but are not limited to, financial constraints, competing values, absence of leaders and advocates, and limited tools for implementation of adaptation measures. Maladaptation can also occur through poor planning. This often involves overly short-term thinking.[8]

Let's note three key points here. First, it is striking that, according to the IPCC, values-diversity can be a source of either poor or effective adaptation. This is surely correct. It is important to highlight it so that we don't make the mistake of either overvaluing or undervaluing diversity and disagreement. We overvalue it insofar as it leads to policy paralysis, and we undervalue it when we exclude or downplay voices that ought to be heard in policy deliberation (for example, indigenous voices). Second, we must always be wary of maladaptive practices masquerading as adaptive ones. A lack of such awareness might allow our choices to be captured by vested interests. For example, the fossil fuel industry might argue for "adaptation measures" – for example, offshore oil rigs able to withstand more intense hurricanes – that may have the effect of locking in our dependency on oil and gas for generations to come. Finally, adaptation can be very costly, which raises the important question of who should pay for it in countries that bear minimal or no responsibility for climate change. We will return to this issue in Chapter 4.

Intelligent adaptation to climate change will be crucial, but it is an incomplete response. For one thing, the idea of adaptation tends to be interpreted in narrow technological terms. Former U.S. Secretary of State (who was also once the CEO of Exxon-Mobil) Rex Tillerson has said that climate change is "just an engineering problem."[9] Such technological optimism is probably unwarranted in this context. Of course we are an "innovative" species, but nothing we have accomplished in our history provides evidence that we are capable of responding in a purely technological manner to the challenges of feeding 10 billion people in a world with atmospheric CO_2 concentrations of, say, 750 ppm or more.

To whatever extent it is possible, *avoidance* of this outcome is therefore a better option. This is known as "mitigation." It effectively means moving *away* from RCP 8.5 and *towards* RCP 2.6 by reducing our CO_2 emissions drastically in the short- to medium-term. In the language of the IPCC, "mitigation" refers to any "human intervention to reduce the sources or enhance the sinks of greenhouse gases."[10] Sink-enhancement includes afforestation, sustainable forest management, reduction of deforestation, cropland management, grazing-land management, and enhancement of organic soils.[11] As important as sink-enhancement is, by itself it has limited potential to meet the challenges we face. In general, the problem with it has to do with scalability or with the conflicts it introduces in land-use priorities. This can be seen most clearly with afforestation. Afforestation on a scale large enough to be an appreciable CO_2 sink would necessarily encroach on land currently used for agriculture. But then how would we feed a rising population?

Or take enhancement of organic soils. One version of this is a technique of soil management originating with ancient Amazonian cultures. It involves the creation of biochar through pyrolysis. Instead of allowing the carbon stored in agricultural waste to rot in the open air and be released to the atmosphere, it is burned in an oxygen-free oven and ultimately returned to the soil. This can lock the carbon contained in the biomass into the soil for thousands of years. The soil this produces is rich and lovely and there's no release of CO_2 into the atmosphere from decaying biomass. This process is currently being researched as a way of sequestering carbon, and we can certainly hope that in the future it becomes a staple of agricultural practice. But it is unlikely to be available to us at the proper scale for decades or more, and even if it were it would address only a small percentage of emissions.

This brings us to reducing the sources of greenhouse gases, the second broad mitigation strategy. There are two principal means of doing this. The first is through the reformation of agriculture, aimed especially at regulating the production of methane from cattle. Ruminating animals like cows create methane in the process of digestion, which is then released to the atmosphere when the animals fart or belch. Methane, as we saw in Chapter 1, is an especially powerful greenhouse gas. According the U.N.'s Food and Agriculture Organization, there are now around 1.5 billion cows in the world. Indeed, the U.N. estimates that our livestock are responsible for as much climate change as the entire global transport industry.

Moreover, ranchland does not come cheap in ecological terms. Usually it is created through deforestation, meaning that even more greenhouse gases are produced when the carbon stored in trees is suddenly released into the atmosphere as the trees are cut down. With respect to freshwater use, land use, grain-feed use and greenhouse gas emissions, cattle ranching is one of the most inefficient methods of food production humans have ever devised. And people in the developed world eat enormous amounts of beef: the average American consumes nearly 170 pounds of it every year. Unfortunately, as the global middle class expands, overconsumption of beef appears to be intensifying. As people get richer, they seem to want more burgers and steaks (among other things, like cars and phones).

The second means of reducing greenhouse gases targets fossil fuel combustion directly. About 78% of the total GHG emissions increase from 1970–2010 came from fossil fuel combustion.[12] This combines emissions from transportation, industry, electricity and heat production and buildings. This total must be reduced rapidly if we are to move away from RCP 8.5. How rapidly? To have a 50% chance of keeping temperatures *below* 2°C by 2100 – the stated goal of the Paris climate agreement in 2015 – we must cut GHG emissions by more than 50% by 2050 and eliminate them altogether by 2100. Otherwise put, the goal is to have the total stock of atmospheric CO_2 peak at 450 ppm and then bring it down closer to 350 ppm (recall that it is currently well past 400 ppm). If we are going to achieve this, emissions must peak very soon – probably by 2025 or 2030 – and decline swiftly thereafter.[13]

However, as aggressive as these targets are they describe only the "coin-flip" scenario. Given the threats of climate change we might understandably want better odds than that. If we do, our cuts to GHG emissions must be even more aggressive than the ones just mentioned, on the order of 80% by 2050, with total elimination – a carbon-neutral global economy – by 2070. Now, if we are going to be non-idealists here, we must recognize that changes on this scale will come about only through deliberate manipulation of the global energy market. There's too much carbon left to burn to permit unchecked market forces to run down the supply until fossil fuels price themselves out of the global energy market. The reserves of fossil fuels on the balance sheets of the world's biggest publicly and privately owned oil and gas companies, if extracted and burned, would tip the planet into climate chaos. The only rational option therefore is for governments to *force* fossil fuels out of the energy market by taxing them heavily while investing robustly in renewables.

No economist should object to this, since it is at bottom nothing more than internalizing the currently externalized costs of burning fossil fuels. It is an attempt to align the price of these commodities with their real social and environmental costs, something the market by itself has clearly failed to do. However, there are ways to resist this conclusion. One might suggest that in order to combat climate change effectively we should instead (a) get a better grip on population control; (b) overthrow the growth imperative of modern capitalist economies; or (c) increase the efficiency of the technologies of carbon capitalism. Were any of these proposals sufficient to meet the climate challenge, there may be no need to focus obsessively on cutting greenhouse gas emissions through taxes or regulations. Let's look at these challenges next.

Three drivers of climate change

Economists have attempted to quantify the primary drivers of environmental impact generally and greenhouse gas emissions in particular. The most general approach is the I = PAT formula, according to which our environmental impact (I) is the product of our population (P), affluence (A) and technologies (T). The Kaya formula, named after the Japanese economist Yoichi Kaya, applies this to GHG emissions. The three main drivers here are population, economic growth (GDP per person) and technology (CO_2 per dollar of GDP). If we want to reduce emissions we may need to lean on one of these drivers, or some combination of them. The first involves acting aggressively to reduce fertility rates globally, the second to curb economic growth, the third to increase the efficiency of our energy-hungry technologies.[14]

Population

From 1979 to 2015 official state policy in China allowed for only one child per family. By some estimates this resulted in 400 million fewer births than would have occurred without the policy. But even if the policy had some effect on Chinese emissions in this period there are serious reasons to reject adopting a similar policy on a global scale. In China, the one child policy has produced unforeseen negative side effects, most notably a huge gender imbalance. In a society that values boys more than girls, the latter were often killed at birth by parents who wanted their only child to be a boy. This result would not necessarily be repeated everywhere the policy was implemented, of course, but it should make social planners extremely wary.

More generally, there is a political and cultural feasibility constraint that likely makes this option unworkable. In most places in the world, certainly in democratic countries, having children is considered a fundamental human right. Any attempt by a democratically elected government to curb this right would likely be met with severe resistance. In any case, we should be skeptical of the claim that population *per se* is the real problem when it comes to drivers of climate change. The bigger worry is overconsumption and this is a much graver problem in the developed than the developing world.

Over 95% of the growth in population from now until 2050 will be in Africa and Asia, regions of the world that are very low on the consumption – and therefore also emissions – scale. This is because the rest of the world has already gone through or is in the process of going through the demographic transition (examined in Chapter 1). The two major causes of reduced birth rates are the general wealth of the citizens and the education of its women. Greater wealth generally means a more diversified and urbanized economy, providing wider opportunities for decent work and taking pressure off rural households to procreate in order to have more hands to work the land. The education of women, for its part, both provides women with access to the diversifying job market and empowers them to resist patriarchal demands for early marriage.

In short, we are not going to force population reductions through heavy-handed governmental regulations. This is in any case a dubious strategy for reducing emissions if we don't halt overconsumption, which, again, is the real problem. This is a crucial insight. Pointing to population as the main source of our climate woes can have the effect of diverting our attention away from the consumption habits of most people in the developed world, instead blaming climate change's main victims – Africans and Asians – for the problem. For those people, this adds insult to injury. If we resist this temptation we might be forced to ask what kinds of assumptions about our economy are behind those developed world consumption patterns. This brings us to our second driver.

Economic growth

Since about 1945, the global economy has grown at an astonishing rate. One of the reasons for endorsing the notion that we are now in the **Anthropocene** (a concept examined in Chapter 6) is that the data show clearly that at this point in our history we really did begin to have an outsized effect on the Earth system. This period is referred to as the **Great Acceleration.** It is broken down into Earth system trends and socio-economic trends. The first covers such phenomena as CO_2 concentrations, ocean acidification, tropical forest loss and amount of domesticated land; the second covers things like fertilizer consumption, paper consumption, construction of large dams, expanded transportation networks and increased urbanization. Every Great Acceleration graph depicting the development of these phenomena has the same shape: a steady, linear line from 1750 to 1945, followed by a very steep curve from 1945 to the present.

Underlying all of these trends is economic growth, measured by GDP per person. Between 1900 and 2008 GDP per person increased by a factor of six, from $1,260 to $7,600. World GDP increased by a factor of 25 in this period, from $2 trillion to $51 trillion (adjusted for inflation).[15] Of course, the relationship between GDP increases on the one hand and other socio-economic and Earth system trends on the other is complex. Economic growth does not simply cause the construction of large dams, for example, but is also caused or sustained *by* such construction. Causation among all these phenomena is multi-directional. Nevertheless, in any complex system some things are more causally significant than others. An economy can function robustly in the absence of particular kinds of infrastructural development but any such development on a large enough scale *requires* a robust economy. For some economists and politicians, this means an ever-*growing* economy.

This is why there is a perceived growth "imperative" in most societies today. And of course economic growth is still powered almost entirely by fossil fuels. Hence the connection between growth and emissions. What are the chances of addressing climate change by challenging the economic growth imperative? Noticing the obvious fact that infinite growth is not possible on a planet of finite resources, some economists have argued in favor of a no-growth or steady-state economy. This concept is not outlandish. But implementing it in the short- to medium-term on a global scale is probably even more daunting than seeking to curb population growth directly.

The perceived need for perpetual growth is a cornerstone of capitalism, and capitalism is a deeply entrenched aspect of global culture. The culture critic Frederic Jameson once said that it is easier to imagine the end of the world than the end of capitalism. For better or worse, he may be right about that. In the time-frame that matters to us here, we are probably not going to see a move to a steady-state or no-growth global economy. And if the developing world is to find its way out of the poverty in which much of it is mired, this may be undesirable for now. It is one thing for (some) citizens of the North to dream of the end of economic growth, but the billions of people currently living without electricity might view things differently.

It does not follow that we should not work to reform capitalism in dramatic ways, or that we should abandon efforts to construct an economic system based on a more sustainable principle than that of endless capital accumulation. In fact, climate change forces us to ask fundamental questions about what the economy is for and how it can be manipulated to promote genuine flourishing among humans and between humans and other living things. But what *does* follow from the deeply-entrenched character of capitalism is that *for now* we are probably confined to harnessing, rather than overturning, market forces. This has already been done in the sorts of creative fusions of socialist and capitalist systems found both in Scandinavian countries and, in a different way, in China. The rest of the world would do well to look to these countries as models in this area. Remember, we must confine ourselves to a *transitional* climate ethics. We need to know what to do in the world as it is right now, even if we also have our eyes on a more idealized world order. This is one more expression of the commitment to non-ideal theorizing.

But having said all this, let's err on the side of caution on this issue. Let's say that economic development is a good thing for everyone. It brings people out of poverty and helps protect things we value. The main question is just this: can purely material development happen without perpetual economic growth? If it can, then let's challenge the growth imperative robustly. If it can't, then we need to ask harder questions about how much longer the global economy can grow and to whom the benefits of that growth should chiefly go. It's safe to leave the first question – about whether purely material development can happen without growth – to the economists. But the second one about distributing the benefits of growth is purely philosophical.

This brings us to the role of technology as a driver of our problems. If inefficiency drives climate change, then perhaps the whole problem can be addressed through efficiency improvements. Since firms already engage in perpetual efficiency upgrades as a matter of course, it's been characterized as a solution to the problem that is friendly to capitalism. As we will see, however, it has its own problems.

Efficiency

Pursuing efficiency is about getting better at converting the inputs of some process into outputs. A process is more efficient than an alternative if it uses fewer inputs than the alternative to produce the same, or a higher, output. There are a number of ways to think about efficiency, but for our purposes the most important one is the notion that we can "decouple" economic output from CO_2 emissions. One way to measure this is in terms of CO_2 emissions per dollar of GDP. If GDP is being generated with fewer and fewer CO_2 emissions over time, we can say that the economy is becoming *decoupled* from CO_2 emissions and is thus becoming more efficient. Sometimes the same point is expressed as an "intensity-reduction" goal: a process is more efficient than an alternative if it involves a less intense use of resources than the alternative. It's important to recognize that the global economy has managed to achieve steady decoupling at a more general level of material intensity over the last 40 years or so. We now use a lot less biomass, fossil fuel and minerals *per dollar of GDP* than we did before. In fact, during this period the material intensity of the global economy dropped by a remarkable 33%.[16]

Can we decouple the global economy from CO_2 emissions in time to avert climate disaster? Not likely, alas. The economist Tim Jackson has done some calculations to try and determine how much carbon intensity reduction would be required in order to keep atmospheric concentrations of CO_2 at 450 ppm by 2050. Granting for the sake of argument that this is an adequate target, we could achieve it through efficiency improvements alone only if the carbon intensity of our economy were reduced by a factor of nearly 130. If we extend the projection out to 2100, we would, says Jackson, need to see "a complete decarbonization of every single dollar." And if we seek to cap atmospheric carbon at 350 ppm, which is what most scientists consider to be a safer target than 450 ppm, we would effectively need to have "negative emissions." That is, every dollar of GDP would – somehow – need to reduce atmospheric CO_2. [17]

Efficiency improvements are often worth pursuing. But we should underline three skeptical points about this approach to our problem. First, the numbers just cited indicate clearly that, at this point, such purely technological solutions exist mostly in the realm of fantasy. We simply cannot reduce carbon intensity quickly enough to avert climate disaster. Second, even if we were making steady progress on efficiency in some area there is the problem of the "rebound effect." In short, people often react to these improvements, which can make energy or consumer goods cheaper, by consuming more of the same good than before or by diverting the savings into consumption of other goods which might not be produced as efficiently. The result is a net increase in consumption – anywhere from 10% to 100% more – which can swamp the gains made by the efficiency measures. [18]

This brings us to the third point. Given these two large problems we should be mindful of the ways in which efficiency arguments are used ideologically by vested interests. For example, defenders of the tar sands in Alberta, Canada often point to the gradual reduction of carbon intensity in the process of extracting the tar – which *has* happened – as a prop for the claim that this product is "clean" and should be regulated no further by governments. In fact, so goes the argument, tar sands operations should be expanded since they generally deploy the most efficient extraction technologies in the industry. That is climate change business as usual masquerading as environmental conscientiousness through strategic deployment of the language of efficiency.

Together, these three points should remind us that finding climate solutions that are "friendly to capitalism" is not an end in itself. Working through market mechanisms is desirable only if it delivers the goods, in this case in the form of steep emissions reductions. Overemphasis on removing inefficient technologies can blind us to the need for more radical measures. It can be a way of deceiving ourselves into believing that we are doing something important for the climate when in fact nothing has changed, or the "improvement" has even worsened the problem (this is exactly what happens with the rebound effect, for example). For this reason we should be extremely wary of efficiency arguments in the area of environmental regulation generally and climate change policy in particular.

The more general point of this section has been to suggest that we should probably not reduce the complex problem of climate change to the three drivers identified in the Kaya formula. It's not just about overpopulation, capitalism's problematic growth imperative or inefficient technologies. Once we appreciate this, we should be able to see that there really is no alternative to rapid reduction of CO_2 emissions on the order outlined in the previous section and that this is likely to happen only if governments actively price fossil fuels out of the global market. This does not entail abandoning the pursuit of other measures or ideals – building resilient adaptation, keeping fertility rates in check, improving efficiency, robustly researching and developing renewable energy technologies, building the steady-state economy – but these are all, at best, supplements to the immediate goal of responsible climate policy: rapid reduction of CO_2 emissions.

That is, what we mostly need is *aggressive mitigation* in the form of binding emissions reductions targets. It's no accident that this has been the main focus of climate diplomacy over the past few decades. Let's look at a few highlights of this history.

From Rio to Paris

By establishing the FCCC, the Rio Earth Summit set out a grand vision for addressing climate change. As we have seen above, the FCCC mandates an annual Conference of the Parties (COP) to work out the terms of agreements and protocols – like the **Paris Agreement** (2015) or the **Kyoto Protocol** (1997) – for dealing with climate change. The objective of the convention and its supporting institutional structures and legal arrangements is worth quoting at length:

> The ultimate objective of this Convention and any related legal instruments that the Conference of the Parties may adopt is to achieve, in accordance with the relevant provisions of the Convention, stabilization of greenhouse gas concentrations in the atmosphere at a level that would prevent dangerous anthropogenic interference with the climate system. Such a level should be achieved within a time-frame sufficient to allow ecosystems to adapt naturally to climate change, to ensure that food production is not threatened and to enable economic development to proceed in a sustainable manner.[19]

This statement contains three concepts that have been, in one way or another, at the heart of negotiations since it was made. The first is that GHGs need to be "stabilized" before they can interfere with the climate system in dangerous ways. This means that countries must work together to mitigate the problem of climate change. Indeed, it places mitigation measures at the heart of international climate policy, as we have suggested should be the case. The second is that mitigation needs to happen in such a way that adaptation to the inevitable effects of climate change is as painless as possible.

The third is that all of this must happen without interfering with the right to economic development of the developing world. To assert that we have arrived at no consensus about how to achieve these three goals after more than twenty COP meetings would be to understate the point. How do we explain the failure? Predictably, there is not much agreement on this question either. Any explanation of the failure is bound to be partial, but it is possible to highlight some of the most important moments in this sorry history.

One of the key commitments of the FCCC is that Parties will assume burdens to address climate change on the basis of **common but differentiated responsibilities (CBDR)**.[20] This seemingly innocent phrase was to become a lightning rod for differing interpretations of what individual countries were required to do under the terms of the FCCC, or any of the protocols, treaties or mandates it might spawn. Broadly, there are two such interpretations. The first is that the rich countries should do all the work, at least in the short term. This places a stress on the concept of "differentiation" in CBDR. The second, which stresses the concept of what is "common" in CBDR, is that everyone should have to do something right from the beginning of the commitment period.

To help us appreciate the complexity of the issues here, let's look in turn at a few significant features of three key COP meetings: Berlin (1995), Durban (2011) and Paris (2015).

COP I: Berlin, 1995

The first of these was also the very first COP after the FCCC entered into force, and from it emerged the Berlin Mandate. The Berlin Mandate proposes a hard and fast distinction between developed and developing countries, suggesting that the developed countries – so-called Annex I countries – should be the ones to take on the burden of reducing GHGs while the developing countries could continue to emit without limit, at least for a while. This notion was encoded formally in the Kyoto Protocol two years later (1997). There were big differences among Annex I countries in terms of what they were required to do under Kyoto but all of them had to engage in emissions cuts that would inevitably be costly for them.

How costly? Kyoto has been portrayed by some of its detractors, like the former Prime Minister of Canada Stephen Harper, as a job-killing, economy-destroying, quasi-socialist scheme designed to suck money away from rich countries and transfer it to poor ones. But in fact, the demanded cuts were relatively modest. Annex I countries as a group agreed to cut emissions by 5.2% by 2008–2012 from a 1990 baseline. The United States' share of the cuts was slightly steeper than this at 7%. Opposition to the Protocol among American lawmakers was nevertheless fierce. American President Bill Clinton signed the Kyoto Protocol but declined to submit it to Congress for ratification, realizing that it would never be approved by that body.

In fact, at roughly the same time the Kyoto Protocol was being hashed out, the U.S. Senate adopted the Byrd-Hagel Resolution, which stated the

American position on the issue of differentiated responsibilities succinctly. The Resolution, which passed unanimously, says that the U.S. will not adopt any treaty or agreement which would:

> mandate new commitments to limit or reduce greenhouse gas emissions for the Annex I Parties, unless the protocol or other agreement also mandates new specific scheduled commitments to limit or reduce greenhouse gas emissions for Developing Country Parties within the same compliance period.[21]

The Senators went on to justify this position by asserting that adopting the proposed emissions cuts would likely result in job losses, trade disadvantages and increased costs of energy and consumer goods in the U.S.

COP 17: Durban, 2011

The battle lines were thus drawn, the ultimate result of which was the spectacular failure of COP 15 in Copenhagen (2009). Much has been written about COP 15 in an effort to determine who was to blame for its failure. But whatever the source of the failure it is important to highlight some of its more disastrous implications for future COP meetings. Let's focus, for example, on what is arguably *the* key feature of COP 17 in Durban (2011). Negotiators in Durban, frustrated by the Copenhagen debacle, finally turned their backs on the Berlin Mandate's interpretation of CBDR (which, again, stressed the notion of differentiation over that of commonality). They urged *all* Parties to accept responsibility for emissions reductions within the same compliance period, i.e., right from the start.

One way to understand the stress on differentiation is that it embodied the developing world's sense of climate equity: as a matter of basic fairness the developed world should act first because they are largely responsible for the problem. The new stress on commonality rather than differentiation was therefore a rejection of such equity concerns. This was expressed clearly by the chief American negotiator Todd Stern. "If equity's in," said Stern in Durban, "we're out."[22] The rest of the world reluctantly bought into the position. At bottom, global capitulation to the Americans was the product of brute political realism. Given Byrd-Hagel, the world realized that the U.S. was not going to budge on emissions cuts unless the developing world, especially China, joined the effort right away. For its part, the European Union knew that a deal without the U.S. would be ineffectual and also damaging to its own economic interests, since in this case the E.U. would have to pick up the slack from a missing-in-action U.S.[23]

Durban did not produce agreement among countries on the important issue of emissions reduction targets, but it is nevertheless significant for two reasons. The first is that it enshrines the commonality-inflected CBDR interpreted so as to meet the requirements of the Byrd-Hagel Resolution and thus, hopefully, secure the participation of the U.S. in an international agreement on climate change. The second is that it set the policy terms for what many consider to be a radical departure from previous COP meetings, the Paris Agreement at COP 21 (2015).

COP 21: Paris, 2015

There is sharp disagreement among commentators about the merits of the Paris Agreement. Some dismiss it as hopelessly ambitious while others think of it as a genuine game-changer. We cannot settle that dispute here, but because the Agreement does offer an undeniably distinct approach to the issues compared to previous COPs we will look briefly at it. There are two main differences to highlight: the first is substantive, the second procedural.

The substantive issue is a commitment to "strengthen the global response to climate change" by:

> [h]olding the increase in the global average temperature to well below 2°C below pre-industrial levels and pursuing efforts to limit the temperature increase to 1.5°C above pre-industrial levels, recognizing that this would significantly reduce the risks and impacts of climate change.[24]

This is an immensely ambitious goal, by far the most aggressive target ever agreed upon at these meetings. Of course, we know from bitter experience that there is a chasm between commitments like this on the one hand and their ratification and implementation by national and sub-national legislatures on the other. Nevertheless, the Agreement has received the required number of signatures to go into force, so there appears to be some groundswell of support for it. Everything, of course, depends on how the goal is going to be achieved.

This brings us to the procedural difference between Paris and all previous agreements. The previous approach had been top-down, i.e., a global emissions reduction level had been set and each country was then assigned a share of the total. Many considered this approach to be unworkable because it was insensitive to the political and economic realities operative in particular countries. By contrast, Paris enshrines a "pledge and review" system. Negotiations leading up to Paris had every country work on a **Nationally Determined Contribution (NDC)**, constructed from the ground up by each country in the light of its own political and economic realities. The NDC commits each country to reduce its carbon emissions by a specified amount within a specified time-frame. At the end of this time, the pledge is reviewed by other members and ratcheted-up. It's meant to be a kind of upward emissions reduction spiral, with a new or updated climate plan pledged every few years, then reviewed, then updated again in the light of international scrutiny.

Does Paris represent a real breakthrough? There are reasons for skepticism. The first has to do with the weak mechanism for promoting compliance among the Parties. The requirement specifies only that a committee will be set up "that shall be expert-based and facilitative in nature and function in a manner that is transparent, non-adversarial and non-punitive."[25] That sounds like pretty much the diametric opposite of a "binding treaty with teeth." The hope seems to be that the pledge and review system will all by itself promote compliance through the operation of something like an international shame system. Second, it is unclear how all those NDCs will be coordinated so as to reach the 1.5°C target. So far there's a significant emissions gap between the NDCs and the target.[26]

A third reason for skepticism is ongoing American intransigence. The world plainly needs the U.S. to play along, but the Trump administration's withdrawal from Paris makes this unlikely and thus makes the Agreement considerably less forceful. As with Byrd-Hagel, the U.S. is once again holding the rest of the world hostage on this issue. It is worthwhile reflecting on the audacity of the American position. As we have characterized it here, the U.S. moved the whole world, by force, away from the accepted understanding of CBDR. This was a necessary condition of American participation in any climate regime. Having secured this major concession from virtually everyone else, the U.S. is, it appears, now unwilling to participate at all. Trump, it should be noted, has waffled about this, noting that the U.S. would stay in the agreement if it were more "fair" for the U.S. Clearly, the goalposts regarding "fairness" are constantly being shifted to suit American purposes. No meaningful deal on climate change is likely to emerge where there is so much bad faith on the part of one key participant.

Dale Jamieson, writing before the Paris Agreement, asserts that "climate diplomacy will increasingly become a zombie exercise," and that because of this the "Rio dream is over."[27] This may be too harsh, but not by much, especially in the age of Trump (and Trumpism, which will extend well beyond one man's reign). By clarifying the 1.5°C target, Paris probably achieves the most we can expect of an international climate agreement. For the first time, we have a target that requires very robust mitigation efforts, especially on the part of developed countries. This alone can be used to expose and shame the world's climate laggards. That is surely an improvement over the results of previous COPs.

Chapter summary

This has been a wide-ranging chapter, aimed at getting a firm sense of what policy measures are required to address the threat of climate change and what principles underlie such policies. We began by examining a principle which has been thought to be at the heart of the global commitment to limit environmental degradation so that future generations have a livable planet: the precautionary principle. Next we asked what specific policies we are looking to justify when we do climate ethics at the level of international policy. We focused on adaptation and mitigation. This brought us to an examination of three key drivers of climate change: population, the economic growth imperative and inefficient technologies. The point here was to show that while it is important to address all these issues, we should not thereby abandon the focus on mitigation through carbon reduction. That goal has been the primary focus of climate diplomacy since 1992, so we closed the chapter with a brief look at some of the highlights of this history.

Questions for discussion

1 Do you think the precautionary principle escapes the charge of being either banal or incoherent? If so, how?
2 What are some of the dangers of abandoning the effort to mitigate climate change through emissions reductions by focusing instead entirely on adaptation?
3 Is there any chance of addressing climate change exclusively through efficiency improvements in our technologies, perhaps combined with efforts to reduce the global fertility rate?
4 Do we need to challenge capitalism's growth imperative in order to address climate change? Is this feasible?
5 Is the Paris Agreement likely to result in a substantial change of course in the international effort to combat climate change? Why or why not?

Suggested reading

Dale Jamieson, *Reason in a Dark Time: Why the Struggle against Climate Change Failed and what it Means for our Future* (Oxford: Oxford University Press, 2014), chapters 2 & 7. A bracingly skeptical and detailed survey of the history of climate diplomacy.

Cass Sunstein, *The Laws of Fear: Beyond the Precautionary Principle* (Cambridge: Cambridge University Press, 2015). A lucid and thorough examination of the precautionary principle.

United Nations Framework Convention on Climate Change (FCCC). Available at: http://unfccc.int/files/essential_background/background_publications_htmlpdf/application/pdf/conveng.pdf. The foundational document of international climate diplomacy.

Notes

1 *United Nations Framework Convention on Climate Change* (FCCC), article 3.3, p. 9, http://unfccc.int/files/essential_background/background_publications_htmlpdf/application/pdf/conveng.pdf.
2 Cass Sunstein, *The Laws of Fear: Beyond the Precautionary Principle* (Cambridge: Cambridge University Press, 2015), 14.
3 Sunstein, *The Laws of Fear...*, 34.

4 Henry Shue, "Deadly Delays, Saving Opportunities: Creating a More Dangerous World?" in Stephen M. Gardiner, Simon Caney, Dale Jamieson and Henry Shue (eds.), *Climate Ethics: Essential Readings* (Oxford: Oxford University Press, 2010), 146–162.

5 Neil A. Manson, "Formulating the Precautionary Principle," *Environmental Ethics* 24, 2002, 263–274.

6 IPCC 2014, *Working Group II (WG II): Impacts, Adaptation and Vulnerability, Part A: Global and Sectoral Aspects*, 5.

7 IPCC 2014, *WG II: Adaptation...*, 27.

8 IPCC 2014, *WG II: Adaptation...*, 26–28.

9 Quoted in Matt Daily, "Exxon Chief Calls Climate Change Engineering Problem," *Reuters*. http://www.reuters.com/article/us-exxon-climate-idUSBRE85Q1C820120627 (June 27, 2012), accessed June 6, 2017.

10 IPCC 2014: Summary for Policymakers. In Edenhofer, O., R. Pichs-Madruga, Y. Sokona, E. Farahani, S. Kadner, K. Seyboth, A. Adler, I. Baum, S. Brunner, P. Eickemeier, B. Kriemann, J. Savolainen, S. Schlömer, C. von Stechow, T. Zwickel and J.C. Minx (eds.), *Climate Change 2014: Mitigation of Climate Change. Contribution of Working Group III to the Fifth Assessment Report of the Intergovernmental Panel on Climate Change* (Cambridge, United Kingdom and New York, NY, USA: Cambridge University Press, 2014), 4.

11 IPCC 2014, *WG II: Adaptation...*, 24.

12 IPCC 2014, *WG II: Adaptation...*, 6.

13 Romm, *Climate Change...*, 154.

14 Andrew Dessler and Edward A. Parson, *The Science and Politics of Climate Change: A Guide to the Debate* (Cambridge: Cambridge University Press, 2011), 126.

15 Rob Dietz and Dan O'Neill, *Enough is Enough: Building a Sustainable Economy in a World of Finite Resources* (San Francisco: Berrett-Koehler, 2013), 17.

16 Dietz and O'Neill, *Enough is Enough...*, 37.

17 Dietz and O'Neill, *Enough is Enough...*, 37–38.

18 Dessler and Parson, *The Science and Politics...*, 128–129.

19 *United Nations Framework Convention on Climate Change*, 1992, article 2, p. 9.

20 UNFCCC, article 3.1, p. 9.

21 Quoted in Jamieson, *Reason in a Dark Time...*, 41.

22 Quoted in Chukwumerije Okereke and Philip Coventry, "Climate Justice and the International Regime: before, during and after Paris," *WIRE's Climate Change* 7, 2016, 834–851 (838).

23 Okereke and Coventry, "Climate Justice...," 838.

24 United Nations, *Paris Agreement*, 2015, article 2(b), p. 2. https://unfccc.int/files/essential_background/convention/application/pdf/english_paris_agreement.pdf.

25 U.N., *Paris Agreement*, article 15(2), p. 12.

26 Climate Action Tracker, 2015, accessed September 1, 2017. http://climateactiontracker.org/news/222/emissions-gap-how-close-are-indcs-to-2-and-1.5c-pathways.html.

27 Dale Jamieson, *Reason in a Dark Time: Why the Struggle against Climate Change Failed and what it Means for our Future* (Oxford: Oxford University Press, 2014), 59.

4   International justice

Introduction

International climate diplomacy, discussed in the previous chapter, has been strongly influenced by our varying conceptions of what a just solution to the climate crisis might look like. It's now time to look more carefully at the concept of climate justice. In the next chapter we do so from the standpoint of relations between generations. Here we do so from the standpoint of relations among currently existing people and the countries to which they belong. We begin with an analysis of the connection between climate change and human rights, before moving to a consideration of the nature of climate justice and why so many in the developed world have resisted justice-talk in this area. Next, we examine climate change as an example of the tragedy of the commons. This brings us to a detailed analysis of some important principles of climate justice, with a focus on the polluter pays principle. We close with an examination of the right to development and its problematic connection to the imperative to curb global carbon emissions radically.

Climate change and human rights

One of the most powerful conceptual tools we have for countering the sort of unchecked political power that can result in widespread harms to people is that of rights. Michael Freeden defines rights this way:

> [A] human right is a conceptual device, expressed in linguistic form, that assigns priority to certain human or social attributes regarded as essential to the adequate functioning of a human being; that is intended to serve as a protective capsule for those attributes; and that appeals for deliberate action to ensure such protection.[1]

What are the human attributes that rights are meant to protect? Those that are required for us to live flourishing lives. Under this heading we might invoke some of the "capabilities" highlighted by Martha Nussbaum: life, bodily health, bodily integrity, affiliation with others, emotions, practical reason, play, control.[2] We need not agree that all of these items belong on a list of the capabilities whose developments provide the foundation for human flourishing, and which ought therefore to be protected by rights. We may decide to be more parsimonious, perhaps including only life, bodily health and integrity and affiliation with others. Or the list could be longer. Whatever its precise content, the list specifies our "vital interests," those capacities without which humans cease to live a fully human life. Rights are meant to protect vital interests so construed. They are claims made against other humans as well as political authorities.

Characterizing rights as socio-political *claims* points to their origin in deontological conceptions of human dignity and fundamental equality. People may have positive or negative rights, or both. As Freeden describes rights claims, for x to claim A from y as a matter of **positive right**, is for y to have a duty to provide x with A. On the other hand, if x has a **negative right** to be free of interference from others with respect to A, then y has a duty to forbear interfering with x in this area.[3] So there's a whole constellation of moral concepts at work here: duty, dignity, equality, flourishing and interests. The notion of rights is philosophically rich in this sense. It gets the idea of flourishing and vital interests from Aristotle, that of dignity from Kant, that of protection against the arbitrary exercise of power from Mill and Rawls, and more. Largely because of this richness, the notion has a great deal of rhetorical force in our culture. In one form or another, it has been employed very successfully in the cause of human emancipation for centuries (the civil rights movement, for instance).

The doctrine that best encapsulates this conceptual richness is **moral cosmopolitanism**. Cosmopolitanism itself has a long history in philosophy, with origins in the thinking of the fourth century BCE Cynic, Diogenes. Legend has it that when asked where he was from Diogenes replied, "I am a citizen of the world." The moral cosmopolitan holds that we are all citizens of the world, and that our connection to all other humans is more basic than our connection to members of smaller groups: family, compatriots, co-religionists, etc. This idea turned morality on its head. In Diogenes' day, many believed just the opposite: that our moral duties begin – and possibly end – with the relatively small groups to which we belong. There are still many who believe this, though the number of cosmopolitans among us is surely larger than it was in the fourth century BCE.

At bottom, this is a dispute about who *counts* morally, a question that will resurface often in this chapter (and beyond) in one guise or another. The moral cosmopolitan ideal is universalist and egalitarian. Universalism is the idea that everyone counts morally in virtue of being a person, while egalitarianism is the view that every person counts for the same. Moral cosmopolitanism is most clearly expressed, in the modern era, in Kant's moral philosophy – deontology – which puts the dignity of rational human nature at the center of our conceptions of value. For Kant, we must treat all other agents with respect insofar as they are actually or potentially *autonomous*. That is, to the extent that they are capable of setting ends for themselves and finding the means to achieve those ends, our duty is to allow this capacity to unfold on its own terms in each individual. Kant argues, moreover, that autonomy is a foundational value: without it, none of the other things we value have genuine worth. Deontological moral cosmopolitanism is ideally suited to provide a foundation for human rights because rights protect the capacity for autonomy thought of in this very broad sense. Now let's bring these somewhat abstract ideas back to climate change.

Simon Caney shows that climate change poses a clear threat to life, health and subsistence and thus violates the rights of its victims on that score alone. This is quite a slim list of rights-violations, but Caney's point is to show that even someone who is a minimalist about rights should accept the notion that strong action on climate change is required. That is, Caney invokes only negative rights and no positive rights.[4] Since it threatens to deprive people of life, basic health and subsistence, climate change is an *interference* in people's lives, the ultimate effect of which may be to render them incapable of flourishing in a uniquely human way. You can't be fully autonomous, in Kant's sense of the term, if your time is devoted overwhelmingly to fighting just to stay alive. Since almost everyone believes that governments should not violate these negative rights (whatever they think about positive rights) the argument has broad appeal.

If we want, we can add some of Nussbaum's capabilities to the list of things threatened by climate change – economic rights and solidarity-based rights are very important in Europe and Asia, for instance – but the point is that we do not require appeal to these capabilities and rights in this case. If nearly everyone agrees that negative rights are morally inviolable, and that climate change is a clear threat to them, then we should be able to achieve broad consensus on strong mitigation measures. Moral cosmopolitanism in the form of a commitment to protect human rights, and the associated capacity for richly autonomous choice, is thus very far-reaching in this application.

The discourse of human rights is also difficult to disavow sincerely. Most of us are already committed to it, to some degree. We believe that people deserve protection from the arbitrary exercise of power over them. Most people endorse the general thrust of documents like the UN Charter of Human Rights, which recognizes a broad range of protections for all humans from the threats posed to their vital interests by governments. If this is correct, and given the clear threats posed to such interests by climate change, which is itself caused by governments (mostly in the developed world), it is natural to frame climate change as a rights issue. And if climate change is a rights issue, then it is also preeminently a justice issue, because the protection of human rights has always been seen as a matter of justice. Let's turn next to this crucial topic.

The ideology of business as usual

Justice is, fundamentally, about the proper distribution of benefits and burdens within a political community. If we take justice seriously, then we are concerned to avoid, as much as we can, the harm that comes from the maldistribution of vital material and social goods. So to say that we care about justice means that we will seek to (a) establish fair procedures in relevant institutions, such as the judicial system (**procedural justice**); (b) allocate essential and scarce resources fairly (**distributive justice**); and (c) compensate those who have been unfairly harmed through some previous mal-distribution (**corrective justice**).

In the rest of this chapter we will be concerned mainly with distributive justice and corrective justice. Distributive justice is forward-looking, while corrective justice is backward-looking. In our case, distributive justice is about how to allocate the costs of climate cleanup among the countries of the world. Another way to put this is in terms of how we allocate the remaining fossil fuel stock if we decide to constrain its use significantly. Since it is, as things stand in the global economy, expensive to run an economy without the use of fossil fuels, moving away from them swiftly will be costly, at least in the short term (i.e., until renewables are able to supply the base-load power we require).

Decisions like this about the just distribution of costs and burdens will be made, in large part, by reference to claims about corrective justice. It is because some countries have benefited more than others from carbon-intensive industrialization that they must bear a disproportionately large share of costs and burdens to clean up the mess this development has caused. There is thus an important connection between the two kinds of justice – distributive and corrective – in the case of climate change.

But we are jumping ahead just a little. Let's begin with a more basic question, already alluded to in the discussion of rights. Since justice concerns distributing benefits and burdens within a political community we might ask who counts here. What are the boundaries of a political community? The cosmopolitan answer is: anybody whose vital interests are affected by that community's actions. The scope of justice therefore obviously depends on what resources or goods we are talking about. If it's access to a national health care plan, then the group in question comprises citizens of that nation. Things can get tricky when questions are asked about differential contributions to the plan based on levels of wealth among the nation's citizens or about the access claims of immigrants, temporary workers, migrants and so on. But these are special issues and cases within a relatively well-circumscribed system of collective organization.

In other words, in most cases the group that is relevant to concerns about justice will be contained within the boundaries of a specific political territory. Nobody asks whether or not citizens of Lithuania, living in that country, ought to have access to Sweden's health care plan. This is because the vital interests of Lithuanians are in no way affected by the decisions made by Swedes about how much of their national budget should be allocated to health care provision rather than, say, national park maintenance or the military. The issue is entirely contained within the political boundaries of Sweden. However, there are obviously issues that can cross national boundaries and whose resolution therefore has implications for justice or fairness among territorially dispersed people.

Carbon pollution is one of them. It respects no political boundaries. CO_2 pouring from a coal-fired power plant in China and making its way into the atmosphere can become a problem for Peruvian farmers coping with drought. But modern economies still require access to fossil fuels: we are not going to switch the carbon economy off tomorrow. In short, we *require* something whose use we must also *constrain* dramatically and eventually phase out altogether. That is the nub of our challenge. The most important questions for international climate diplomacy therefore have to do with who should get access to a common resource (and how much of it they should get), in this case the absorptive capacities of the atmosphere and other global carbon sinks.

We need an agreement to regulate our sink-filling activities, but as we saw in Chapter 3 this has been damnably difficult to achieve. The point to emphasize here, however, is that it is a quintessentially *international* issue (also, of course, an intergenerational one, but we will come to that in the next chapter). That is, it requires an agreement among all countries of the world in order to be effective. Effectiveness here refers chiefly to avoiding carbon "leakage" from one jurisdiction to another. If there were ten countries in the world and nine of them signed a treaty to reduce carbon emissions dramatically, firms in those nine countries would likely relocate to the tenth (unless they were forced or paid to refrain from doing so), where they could emit to their heart's content. Net carbon pollution would not be reduced in this case.

What we have said so far implies that the decisions of any single country about its domestic energy policies can draw in people from beyond its borders. In other words, just because the atmosphere is a vital but scarce global public resource, such people count morally in a way that ought to affect the deliberations of those making the policies. How should we understand this philosophically? Some have denied that such claims have any weight because they violate a basic principle of state sovereignty. Ever since the treaty of Westphalia in 1648, which ended the Thirty Years War, the default assumption in international affairs has been that individual nation-states ought not to be interfered with by outside powers in matters of "domestic" policy (including, let's suppose, energy policy). This made a great deal of sense at the time, since that war was terribly destructive and was both caused and prolonged, to a significant degree, by the Catholic Church's meddling in the internal affairs of European countries.

Of course, the principle is still relevant. It is enshrined in the U.N. Charter, providing a strong presumption against interference by one country in the internal affairs of another. But climate change looks like an issue that defies the logic of state sovereignty with respect to decisions about energy policy. Sometimes, state policies can cause harms that are morally impermissable because they violate the rights of *outsiders*. Consider Henry Shue's description of the four conditions that define a prohibited type of harm to outsiders that may be caused by a state's policies:

- The policies can harm people outside the territories of the state making the policy decisions
- The governments of the affected states are powerless to block these decisions
- The vital interests of people are undermined by the policies
- There are less harmful alternatives available to the state making the decisions[5]

Shue goes on to show that all four conditions apply to countries like the U.S. with respect to decisions about energy use. The four conditions are necessary and jointly sufficient to establish that the harm in question is morally impermissable. There's no need to belabor the first three points. We have ample evidence that the profligate use of fossil fuels causes harms across borders, that the governments of affected countries cannot stop this from happening, and that vital interests are at stake. But let's spend some time with the fourth condition, because it is more complex than it might at first appear to be.

In the case of the U.S. we saw in Chapter 3 that the dogged refusal to move away from fossil fuels has come largely in the form of erecting obstacles to a robust and binding global treaty aimed at reducing emissions. But it is also manifest in the unnecessarily slow pace of research and development of renewable energy sources. This has everything to do with the extent to which the government of the U.S. is captive to the Big Oil lobby. But, again, the point also applies, albeit to a lesser degree, to most other countries in the developed world. Canada, for example, has lurched between talking tough about emissions reductions while doing nothing about curbing them and outright denial of the problem. The same pattern, with a few twists, has been evident in Australia over the last few decades.

We could say that this is simply another example of the naked exercise of geopolitical power. But let's try to be a bit more charitable and construct a plausible rationale for this behavior. What if a party – a particular nation-state – accepts that the first three of Shue's conditions apply to it but that the fourth does not? This is a good way to frame a common mode of justification for business as usual. That is, the claim is often made, in one form or another, that there are no feasible alternatives to business as usual. The harms are not denied in this case, but they are deemed excusable because it is *necessary* to behave this way in order to protect goods that are equal to or superior in value to the ones under threat by the harms. Is this appeal to necessity convincing? Not very.

As Judith Shklar has argued such appeals are a "staple item of ideological discourse everywhere."[6] Ideology is a tool used by vested interests to maintain power. More specifically, it refers to any set of instruments – from moral arguments or divine commands to the control of media sources – whose function is to "justify" the current arrangement of social, economic and political relations. One strategy for accomplishing this is to claim that the arrangement being defended, although it undoubtedly benefits those at the top, is also good for everybody else. Consider in this context the arguments of fossil fuel companies that what's great about their products is that we *all* benefit from them, an argument that conveniently leaves out the fact that those on top benefit far more than anybody else.

The somewhat grandiose philosophical way to make the point is that ideology portrays the partial or particular as the universal. Arrangements that are in place chiefly to serve a minority are cast as being universally beneficial. Now of course it is possible for an arrangement – an economic arrangement, for example – to be both unequal and to everyone's benefit compared to some feasible alternative. For instance John Rawls presents a powerful argument to the effect that some economic inequality can be morally justified.[7] On the assumption that some people work hard to get ahead of others, and if an arrangement of enforced equality would dampen this incentive, it may be better to allow for some inequality. This would be the case if those at the bottom of the economic order were better off than they would be under strict equality because the incentive to get ahead had allowed for the generation of greater net wealth in the society as a whole – much of which is then redistributed downward through taxation – than the alternative would have done.

Whether Rawls' argument works is not our concern here. The point is that if it does it is largely because those on the bottom *really are* better off than they would otherwise be and so can, in principle, consent to the arrangement in full knowledge of the workings of the whole economic structure. The justification is therefore *not* ideological. But the same cannot be said of the attempt to justify the perpetuation of the global fossil fuel regime. Although the citizens of, say, Saudi Arabia or the U.K. might assert that this regime is good for everyone, this is probably because they are wearing the ideological blinders that are standard issue for those at the top of the economic heap. But we may get a different answer from a citizen of St. Martin. In September, 2017, Hurricane Irma destroyed 95% of that country's infrastructure. Would this person likely agree with the notion that the continued use of fossil fuels is "necessary"? What about people of the future, whose whole world might be ravaged by catastrophic climate change?

Some in the developed world might defend the alleged necessity of business as usual by claiming that it is simply too costly to address climate change robustly. As we saw in the previous chapter, however, Nicholas Stern's calculations belie this claim.[8] Stern, recall, argues that we can do the job of climate mitigation for a cost of 2–4% of global GDP per annum. To put this in perspective, that figure is close to what is spent on the military every year ($1.57 trillion in 2016). Since climate change is emerging as a significant security threat across the globe, it might make sense to divert as much money to preventing *it* as we already do to coping with other military threats.

One way to appreciate what is at stake here is to focus on the percentage rather than the total it represents. This is because the total can look very daunting when we are talking about large sums – you want us to spend over a trillion dollars a year on climate change?! – though 2–4% of *any* sum is relatively easy to mobilize in virtue of the financial flexibility supplied by the other 96–98%. If I want to buy a new house whose mortgage costs 2–4% more than my current house, I can probably manage this fairly simply by cutting something else – like my monthly cable bill or my somewhat extravagant grocery bill – that represents about that much of the budget. Indeed, this example makes it clear that adjustments like this can often be made with very little pain at all, at least after a short transition period. But if the point holds for a household budget then it does for a global budget as well. The vast difference in quantity of money in the two cases makes no logical difference at all.

In short, the amount of money the rich would have to pay to fix the problem of climate change is not onerous. It is a tiny portion of global GDP and is therefore a reasonable burden to place on them. Developed countries should not therefore oppose meaningful measures to address climate change on the grounds that they are too costly. But there is likely a darker truth here. What if our reluctance to incur high costs in order to deal with climate change is, at bottom, simply a refusal to tolerate *any* downward pressure on our current lifestyle?

On the eve of the Rio Summit in 1992, George H.W. Bush responded to critics of American consumption patterns by asserting that the American way of life is not up for negotiation. In saying this Bush may have been expressing the views of many people in the developed world, not just Americans. His comments at least have the virtue of honesty. For when we invoke "job-destroying environmental regulation," our "need" for more and more oil as well as the infrastructure to transport it, the way we push for emissions reduction targets that are insufficient or that we have no intention of implementing, aren't we really agreeing with Bush Sr.? What's allegedly necessary here is our current lifestyle *just as it is.*

Unlike my move to a better house, measures that would result in a genuine cleanup of our climate problems are perceived by many people in the developed world as a pure cost, and are considered intolerable for this reason. It is crucial to recognize the extent to which this basic psychological reality has infected our ability to assess the moral situation in an objective manner. Gardiner has encapsulated this sort of worry in the notion of "moral corruption": the temptation, as he puts it, to "distort our moral sensibilities in order to facilitate the exploitation of our global and intergenerational position."[9] Moral corruption is a difficult thing to counter because it is largely non-rational in character. Addressing it fully therefore goes beyond what philosophy can do.

But philosophy is not impotent here. One of the things it can do is show us how it is that our actions are undermining the vital interests of others, and then hope that this insight motivates people to change their behaviors. That is, philosophy can help clarify the "who counts?" question. One of the benefits of doing this is that it can aid us in reassessing the alleged unquestionability or necessity of some of our behaviors. It can help us see through the fog of ideology created by business as usual. If these behaviors undermine the vital interests of others then maybe they are not so necessary after all, or maybe we should at least entertain the possibility that morality requires some sacrifice from us in this area. Let's look next at the form this sacrifice might take when it comes to cleaning up the climate change mess.

The tragedy of the commons

Climate change is a massive collective action problem, but these come in different forms. For example, in Chapter 7, we will see how prisoner's dilemma-type scenarios work at the level of individual consumption choices, thus making the choice to adopt a high-carbon lifestyle look rational. In the area of international climate diplomacy the tragedy of the commons is probably a better example of a collective action problem. The idea is straightforward. A number of parties share an ecologically sensitive natural resource of some kind, whose exploitation provides something of material value to them (e.g., food or fiber). At various points each commoner must make decisions about whether or not to increase his level of exploitation of the resource at the economic margin. Garrett Hardin, the originator of the trope, imagined sheep herders co-managing a grassy commons and wondering at the end of some fiscal period whether or not to add another sheep to the flock.

Faced with this choice, each commoner reasons as follows:

1 The economic benefits of my continued exploitation of the commons accrue to me alone.
2 The degradation of the commons – the cost of my increased exploitation – will be spread among all members of the collective.
3 So, the benefits to me of my continued exploitation of the commons exceed its costs to me.
4 Therefore, I should engage in continued exploitation of the commons.

If every member of the collective reasons this way, the result is the ruination of the commons. Two further points are worth underlining. The first is that the trope is compelling partly because our commoners need not deny the reality of environmental degradation. They are not irrational in *that* way. The second is that another motivating force for them is the desire not to be left behind in the race to become wealthy. Wealth is seen by the commoners as a zero-sum game: one party's gain is always another's loss. If the others continue to exploit the commons and I refrain from doing so, then they will get ahead of me in the all-important job of wealth creation. Status anxiety is an important source of collective irrationality.

If anything these two features of the situation make its resolution even more difficult than it would otherwise be. The first implies that simply showing the commoners the facts about the likely environmental effects of their decisions will not be sufficient to cause a change in behavior. They already understand the facts. The second implies that some non-rational factors – the desire for improved social standing, attraction to the material goods that wealth brings, and so on – are at work in their decisions. It can be very difficult to dislodge or alter such motivational forces.

How does the trope apply to our problem? Think of individual countries reasoning about whether or not to continue the practice of fossil fuel-based economic development for one more fixed period of time. Nobody need deny the facts about climate change (though of course many do, as we'll see in Chapter 8), but the urge to get or stay ahead of the rest of the pack means the temptations of continued exploitation are hard to resist. So, the emissions reduction targets are set too low or, even if they are adequate, the measures are never implemented at national or sub-national levels. The result is the ruination of the atmospheric commons.

These problems are not in principle irresolvable. Where there is rough equality of power and resources among the commoners the latter will devise means – institutional structures, norms of conduct, policing mechanisms, and so on – for avoiding them or resolving them as they arise. More specifically, as Vanderheiden argues, such problems are easiest to resolve when three conditions are satisfied. The first is that all parties are equally responsible for the harm-causing activities; the second is that all parties are equally affected by the harm; and the third is that all are equally capable of addressing it.[10] *The* fundamental problem with international climate diplomacy is that none of these three conditions apply in this area. There is a pronounced rift among nations of the world – broadly, the developed and developing worlds, or the global North and the global South – with respect to historical responsibility for climate change, vulnerability to its worst effects and the capacity to do something about it.

These considerations would seem to make the issue of justice unavoidable. To clarify this claim, let's come back to the Paris Agreement. It might be thought that the pledge and review system enshrined in the Paris Agreement finally puts to rest the notion that there should be any disparity among the nations of the world when it comes to mitigation burdens. But that is obviously not the case. On any scenario that is likely to be both fair and effective, developed countries will have to act more aggressively than developing countries, especially in the short term.[11]

Recall Todd Stern's claim in Durban that the U.S. will be no part of an international climate agreement that invokes considerations of equity. What precisely did he mean? That every country should do exactly the same in terms of burden sharing? If generalized beyond the stance of the Americans, that position is clearly unworkable. No Indian official will accept a proposal from her Australian counterpart that the emissions reduction burdens of the two countries should be literally equivalent over, say, the next 20 years. In other words, though it has lost some prestige vis-à-vis the concept of commonality, differentiation must remain a central component of any acceptable agreement about burden sharing in this area. And this means that, whatever Todd Stern and his political masters believe, equity is still very much "in."

It is common to talk, as we have been so far, about the atmosphere's absorptive capacity in terms of a sink or bathtub metaphor. The idea is that it is a container with a finite capacity to hold some problematic substance, in this case CO_2. The container can be overfilled with the substance, with potentially dire consequences. Another metaphor employed in this area is that of a carbon budget. On this understanding, we are allowed to spend only a certain amount of our fossil-fuel capital if we want to avoid blowing the climate budget. Either way we put the point – in terms of a sink or a budget – the key idea is that we need to restrain our emissions. This implies, of course, that we can continue to emit at *some* level in the short term as we work towards the ultimate goal of a carbon neutral global economy. Here is where the justice question emerges.

Suppose we determine exactly how much carbon can be released to the atmosphere over the next few decades so that the sink's capacity is not breached and the budget is not blown. We could then create a corresponding number of emissions permits. But how do we distribute them among all the people of the world as well as generations to come? We'll postpone the question of future generations until the next chapter and begin to ask the one about the present generation by noting an important distinction. Whether we talk about sinks or budgets we can always ask whether we should distribute permits on the basis of the total sink (or budget) or what remains of it at the point at which we begin the task of distribution.

On the assumption that everyone deserves an equal share of this vital resource, the first approach would mean that the countries bearing historical responsibility for loading the atmosphere with carbon – the developed world – will have used a good deal of their share already. On the second approach, by contrast, the remaining budget would be split more or less equally among all countries. The first approach would therefore require very aggressive reductions by countries of the developed world, while the second would be much less onerous for them. These two broad approaches to the distributional problem define the parameters of the justice issue.

Three principles of climate justice

It should come as no surprise that representatives of developed countries have tended to downplay historical responsibility. But are they justified in doing so? The main theoretical prop used to support the idea that historical responsibility matters is a principle of corrective justice known as the **polluter pays principle (PPP)**. The PPP has a great deal of intuitive plausibility. Most people agree with the basic notion that we are responsible for fixing the things we ourselves have broken. Insofar as the breakage imposes unjustified costs on others we owe those people something by way of compensation or correction.

Because they industrialized first and industrialization has always correlated strongly with the burning of fossil fuels, nobody disputes the fact that developed countries are responsible for the lion's share of the current stock of atmospheric CO_2. This is especially clear if we count historical emissions on a per capita basis. Using that measurement, the U.S., Belgium, Luxembourg and the U.K. are the top emitting countries from 1850 to the present. The only real dispute is whether or not this fact matters morally. According to the PPP, it not only matters but is decisive. Countries like these ones should therefore take on a disproportionately large share of the burden of climate change cleanup. But this way of putting the point invites two broad objections to the PPP.

First, if we are talking about responsibility for emissions going back as far as 1850 and asking the present generation to pay up, then we have in effect abandoned the polluter pays principle. This is because present citizens are not in fact those who caused the pollution in 1850 (and subsequent years). According to Simon Caney, making these people pay for those emissions therefore "violates the PPP."[12] We might respond to this worry by arguing that members of the present generation *benefit* from those past emissions – since they clearly benefit from their countries' accumulated wealth – and that they should pay up for this reason.[13] As Henry Shue puts it, people can clearly prosper materially by being "participants in enduring economic structures."[14] This may implicate them in the harms those structures have caused historically. But notice that we have introduced a second principle of justice here: the **beneficiary pays principle (BPP)**. It is importantly distinct from the PPP.

Some might object to the BPP because they believe that inheriting the burdens of their ancestors is unjust. After all, they were not consulted about the evidently fateful decisions of their ancestors.[15] But they cannot plausibly deny that they benefit from the structures about which Shue is speaking, and this might matter morally if the harms produced by the structure are grave enough. This is the same sort of concern evident in the debate in the U.S. about reparations for slavery. The debate is by no means closed, but surely we can appreciate the force of the claim that African-Americans are entitled to some form of compensation for the harms visited on them by the institution of slavery. And anyone who benefited from that institution is morally obligated to provide the compensation.

What form such compensation takes is a difficult question – it can range from cash payments to formal apologies or more amorphous gestures of reconciliation – but some formal acknowledgement of the harm of slavery by current beneficiaries of the system is surely in order. This brings us to the second criticism of the PPP, one that also applies to the BPP.

We might want to claim that historical emissions do not matter morally because past generations were excusably ignorant of the effects of fossil fuel-based consumption.[16] The idea here seems to be that their ignorance of what they were doing gets them off the hook morally and that this innocence then transfers down the generations to present beneficiaries of their activities. This is dubious, to say the least. Of course ignorance *can* sometimes be an excuse for harm-causing action. If I offer a thirsty stranger a glass of water from my tap, not knowing that a malefactor has poisoned the local water source, my ignorance of the latter's actions excuses me from any moral blame for whatever harm comes to the stranger as a result of accepting my offering. But when it comes to climate change excusable ignorance does not extend indefinitely into the past.

Americans, for instance, knew about the possibly deleterious effects of climate change as early as 1965, when President Johnson delivered a Special Message to the Congress on Conservation and Restoration of Natural Beauty warning about it.[17] But even if we (generously) overlook 1965, the importance of 1988–1994 looms large. Among other developments on the climate awareness front, that six-year span saw (a) James Hansen's dramatic Congressional testimony to the effect that we should stop "waffling" about the reality of climate change; and (b) the FCCC's call to prevent "dangerous anthropogenic interference in the climate system."[18] Ignorance cannot plausibly be claimed after 1994, and GHG emissions have accelerated appreciably since then.[19]

But even if people in the developed world *could* plausibly claim ignorance of climate change right up to the present, this might not be decisive. That is, even in this case it might be correct to say that such people should be asked to shoulder a disproportionate cleanup burden. This, if true, would rescue the PPP (and the BPP) from the criticism we are considering. The key here is that people can be held *liable* for damages even if they are not at *fault* for them and liability does not depend on knowledge. Liability is about causal responsibility, while fault has to do with the much more complex notion of moral blame.

Here is how Vanderheiden understands this crucial distinction:

[J]ustice [requires] remedial responsibility or liability to be assigned in proportion to causal responsibility, measured by the degree to which various nations have contributed to the increasing concentration of atmospheric GHGs that cause the harm associated with climate change … [T]he polluter pays principle ... is concerned only with liability and not with the finding of fault.[20]

Causal responsibility is the key to this argument. Come back to my potentially harmful glass of water. If after drinking it, the stranger passes out on my front lawn it is plausible to say that I bear a special responsibility to help him out. Because I gave him the water it is up to me to call an ambulance, bring him to hospital or provide him with a place to lie down, call his family and so on. I'm liable for the harm that has befallen him even if I'm not at fault for it. If you are inclined to doubt this, compare my situation with that of, say, a neighbor across the street watching the whole thing transpire from her window. Owing to the distinct ways in which each of us is related to the causal story of the stranger's current predicament my duty to aid him seems more pressing than hers.

What does this have to do with climate change? As Vanderheiden goes on to show, China and India have roughly 40% of the world's population but have together contributed around 10% of the stock of atmospheric GHGs. The U.S., by contrast, is causally responsible for more than 30% of this stock while having a 5% share of global population. Strict liability, with no reference whatsoever to fault, dictates that the U.S. should therefore bear significantly higher mitigation costs than China or India.[21] Again, this is a claim only about causal or historical responsibility, not about blame. However, even if we confine ourselves to liability in this fashion, the issue gets muddy. This is because a liability criterion obliges *everyone* to bear the costs of reduction to the extent that they are responsible for emissions. But even very poor countries are responsible for some emissions. Should a very poor country – one whose emissions are devoted entirely simply to keeping its citizens alive, let's suppose – really be expected to incur climate cleanup burdens?

A further distinction can help us with this problem. We might distinguish between those emissions that are essential to survival and those that are frivolous or at least not essential. Driving a gas guzzling car, flying to Aspen for an annual ski trip and consuming expensive foods shipped from across the world are the source of "luxury emissions." Burning the fossil fuels necessary to send a child to school, cook a basic meal and keep the lights on in the house for at least a few hours a day are basic needs, and the emissions they generate are therefore "subsistence emissions."[22] Of course, there is bound to be some grey area here, some patterns of consumption that are not clearly about bare survival but do not quite fit the luxury category either. But that difficulty should not prevent us from employing the distinction to make the point that, by any reasonable standard, people should probably not be obliged to pay cleanup costs for subsistence emissions. In this case, the PPP and BPP dictate that a country is responsible for bearing some costs only *after* crossing the subsistence threshold.

There is one final wrinkle to add. Sometimes we can be morally required to provide assistance to people even though we are not at all responsible for the harm that has befallen them. We can see this by returning once more to the example of the tainted glass of water. If seeing the stranger collapse I fall into a faint myself, then that watchful neighbor now has a duty to step in and help any way she can. Why? Simply because a harm is occurring, the person causally responsible for it – me – is incapacitated and the neighbor is, by hypothesis, able to prevent the damage from escalating. Similarly, if a hypothetical country became wealthy without having generated any emissions in the process, it may be morally required to help poor nations struggling to cope with the effects of climate change. Why? Simply because the harm is occurring, those who should help out according to strict liability are not doing so, and it is able to help.

To complete our picture of the principles of climate change justice we thus need a third principle: the **ability to pay principle (APP)**. According to the APP, a country may be required to bear harm-reducing costs – in order to prevent the damage from escalating, or to compensate its victims, or both – even though it played no part in producing the harm. The reason for this is just as it was with my neighbor: they are able to help out and the responsible parties have not assumed their rightful burden.

The main worry about the APP is that in applying it we are surely punishing the virtuous. Can it really be *just* to require disproportionate work from those who have gotten wealthy without damaging the climate?[23] Of course, in the real world there are no countries that strictly fit this description. All wealthy countries got that way largely by burning fossil fuels. This means that they are strictly liable in accordance with their degree of responsibility for the current stock of atmospheric GHGs. This observation does not make the concern go away altogether. This is because even in a situation in which those required to help out are, to some extent, strictly liable, the APP can be invoked to require them to pay *more* than strict liability demands. This is an especially pertinent concern where some agreement has been worked out among countries to reduce emissions but some major emitter, or a large enough group of smaller ones, refuses to join the effort.

U.S. intransigence on Paris, for example, may oblige other wealthy countries to take on a larger burden than would be the case if the U.S. were doing its part in the international effort. In this case obliging some to do more than they would in a situation of universal compliance may seem like a bad bargain for those countries. This is another manifestation of what it means to do climate ethics in a non-ideal world, and we may simply have to bite the bullet here. It would have been better if everyone had done their fair share, but if refusing to pick up the slack left by the laggards comes at the cost of climate catastrophe, the more virtuous countries of the world may be morally required to do just this.

There is one more large issue to tackle in this chapter. Justice seems to require us to distribute the lion's share of whatever space remains in the carbon sink to those most in need of it, namely countries of the developing world. Let's explore the complexities of this claim.

The right to development

Consider, to begin, two interesting facts about India. First, its coal reserves are huge. The India Coal Company is the largest single producer of coal in the world, with assets of around (USD) $16 billion. Second, more than 300 million Indians have no electricity. Clearly, India could engineer its way out of poverty relatively simply by building coal-fired power plants at a rate similar to that of China in the 1990s and 2000s. The only problem is that it would wreck the climate in doing so. Everyone therefore has an interest in persuading India not to go down this path, but it can hardly be argued that it ought to tolerate widespread poverty among its citizens either. The point extends beyond the case of India to the developing world generally. They have a right to develop but we must also avoid dangerous interference in the climate system. What should be done?

There's a genuine dilemma here. Athanasiou and Baer put it this way:

> We cannot hope to find justice in a world where the poor come to live as the rich do today, for there is not world enough. There will have to be some other kind of solution. There will, indeed, have to be new dreams on all sides, and the rich, in particular, will have to make those dreams possible by learning to share.[24]

The atmosphere's absorptive capacity, we have seen, is finite and the sink is filling fast. Assume for the sake of argument that we are very serious about avoiding climate catastrophe and that this means bringing our emissions down dramatically in the coming decades. If the only way for poor nations to develop in the short term is by burning fossil fuels, then this means either (a) that they cannot develop; or (b) that their increases in emissions must be accompanied by even more dramatic cuts in the developed world.

Alternatively, we could push hard on the antecedent of this conditional and deny that the only path to development goes through fossil fuels. But that is probably unrealistic since renewable energy sources are unlikely to be scaled up in time to avert disaster. At the scale required to meet the world's energy demands these are technologies for the middle and farther futures. We should of course begin switching aggressively to them now (on the model of Germany), but also recognize that the relevant data here do not inspire optimism. Almost all of our energy – about 87% – still comes from fossil fuels, the remaining 13% split among nuclear, hydroelectric, solar and wind. This means that we are in the very early stages of the required energy transition. Compare this to previous transitions from one dominant energy source to another. According to David Weisbach, the transition from biomass to coal took approximately 130 years while the transition from coal to oil and gas took about 80 years.. We simply do not have this much time.[25]

That leaves us with options (a) and (b), above. Can (a) be justified morally? The arguments against it are daunting. Rawls has argued that people ought not to be deprived of goods necessary to live flourishing lives for reasons stemming entirely from bad luck. Nobody deserves to be deprived of access to adequate health care, for example, because she is born into an impoverished socioeconomic class in a society that has systemic issues of class discrimination. But option (a) would effectively trap billions of people in poverty forever, with no better justification. They would be denied the right to develop many of the capacities required to live full human lives simply because of the bad luck of being born in an impoverished nation in the age of climate change. That is a blatant injustice to those people.

Moreover, as Shue has shown, the original injustice of a world split between the rich and the poor can be "compounded" in two ways by climate change.[26] First, climate change will make poor countries even poorer as they scramble to pay for damage cleanup or, if this is too expensive, simply leave basic infrastructure – bridges, schools, electricity plants, houses, highways, etc. – to crumble and rot. Second, the injustice is further compounded by the fact that we in the developed world are causally responsible for the first compounding. It would be bad enough to refuse to assist the poor in coping with disasters that were entirely naturally caused but it is more unfair to refuse when we have brought the disasters to their doors.

We are evidently backed into a logical corner here. Option (b) is all that remains, but it will require the developed world to make appreciable material sacrifices in order to mitigate climate change as well as assist those in the developing world in the task of adaptation. To put the point starkly, for every tonne of carbon emissions originating in the developing world, the developed world must cut *more* than one tonne. It will also require us to share green energy technologies we have developed so that as much of the developing world as possible might leapfrog fossil fuels on the path to development.

Chapter summary

In this chapter we have examined one component of what many take to be the central ethical issue of climate change: the problem of justice. We began by showing how some philosophers have tried to couch the justice question in the language of human rights. This is a powerful rhetorical tool. Next, we tried to clarify how climate change is an example of a prohibited kind of harm perpetrated by some countries on others, and why people in the developed world might resist this sort of analysis. The next task was to characterize the climate challenge as an example of the tragedy of the commons. The point here was to demonstrate that a collective action problem like climate change is difficult to resolve mainly because of the skewed vulnerabilities of those affected by it. This brought us to the polluter pays principle, which appears to be cogent so long as it is supplemented in an appropriate way by two other principles: the beneficiary pays principle and the ability to pay principle. Finally, we looked at the connection between climate change and the right to development, noting the dilemma we face as we seek to combat the former while promoting the latter.

Questions for discussion

1   Explain the sense in which climate change is a human rights issue. Should we focus on positive rights or negative rights (or both) in making this kind of argument?
2   Is the polluter pays principle sufficient to establish strong duties on the part of the developed world to shoulder most of the costs of climate change cleanup? Do the supplementary principles considered here – the BPP and the APP – help make the case or do they undermine the PPP?
3   Explain the tragedy of the commons and how it helps clarify what is at stake in international climate change diplomacy.
4   Is business as usual propped up by the appeal to the "necessity" of the current way of doing things, as suggested in this chapter? How does Gardiner's notion of "moral corruption" clarify the analysis?
5   Is there a genuine dilemma between addressing climate change properly and promoting the right to develop of the world's poorest countries? What should be done and how do considerations of justice affect the issue?

Suggested reading

Steve Vanderheiden, *Atmospheric Justice: A Political Theory of Climate Change* (Oxford: Oxford University Press, 2008), chapters 2 & 3. A clear and informed analysis of the central philosophical issues surrounding the international climate justice issue.

Henry Shue, *Climate Justice: Vulnerability and Protection* (Oxford: Oxford University Press, 2014). A collection of Henry Shue's essays on climate justice. Shue's work is foundational in this area.

Stephen Gardiner, *A Perfect Moral Storm: The Ethical Tragedy of Climate Change* (Oxford; Oxford University Press, 2011), Part B. International climate justice is one the three "moral storms" structuring Gardiner's penetrating analysis of the issue.

Notes

1 Michael Freeden, *Rights* (Minneapolis: University of Minnesota Press, 1991), 7.
2 Martha Nussbaum, *Creating Capabilities* (Cambridge MA: Harvard University Press, 2011).
3 Freeden, *Rights*, 4.

4 Simon Caney, "Climate Change, Human Rights, and Moral Thresholds," in Stephen M. Gardiner, Simon Caney, Dale Jamieson and Henry Shue (eds.), *Climate Ethics: Essential Readings* (Oxford: Oxford University Press, 2010), 163–177 (164–165).

5 Henry Shue, "Introduction," in *Climate Justice: Vulnerability and Protection* (Oxford: Oxford University Press, 2014), 1–26 (12).

6 Judith N. Shklar, *The Faces of Injustice* (New Haven: Yale University Press, 1992), 74.

7 Rawls, *A Theory of Justice* (Cambridge, MA: Harvard University Press, 1971).

8 Nicholas Stern, *The Global Deal: Climate Change and the Creation of a New Era of Progress and Prosperity* (New York: Public Affairs, 2009), 48.

9 Stephen Gardiner, *A Perfect Moral Storm: The Ethical Tragedy of Climate Change* (Oxford: Oxford University Press, 2011), 8.

10 Steve Vanderheiden, *Atmospheric Justice: A Political Theory of Climate Change* (Oxford: Oxford University Press, 2008), 82.

11 Vanderheiden, *Atmospheric Justice…*, 66.

12 Simon Caney, "Cosmopolitan Justice, Responsibility, and Global Climate Change," in Stephen Gardiner, Simon Caney, Henry Shue and Dale Jamieson (eds.), *Climate Ethics: Essential Readings* (Oxford: Oxford University Press, 2010), 122–145 (127).

13 Caney, "Cosmopolitan Justice…," 128.

14 Henry Shue, "Global Environment and International Inequality," in Gardiner et al., *Climate Ethics…*, 101–111 (105).

15 Caney, "Cosmopolitan Justice…," 130.

16 Caney, "Cosmopolitan Justice…," 131.

17 Dale Jamieson, *Reason in a Dark Time: Why the Struggle against Climate Change Failed and What it Means for our Future* (Oxford: Oxford University Press, 2014), 20.

18 Jamieson, *Reason in a Dark Time…*, 34

19 Byron Williston, "Climate Change Ethics," *Encyclopedia of the Anthropocene*, edited by Michael Goldstein and Dominick DellaSalla. London: Elsevier, 45–52.

20 Vanderheiden, *Atmospheric Justice…*, 67.

21 Vanderheiden, *Atmospheric Justice…*, 71.

22 Henry Shue, "Subsistence Emissions and Luxury Emissions," in Shue, *Climate Justice…*, 47–67.

23 Caney, "Cosmopolitan Justice…," 137.

24 Quoted in Vanderheiden, *Atmospheric Justice…*, 70.

25 Stephen Gardiner and David Weisbach, *Debating Climate Ethics* (Oxford: Oxford University Press, 2016), 162–163. See also Byron Williston, "The Question Concerning Geoengineering," *Techné: Research in Philosophy and Technology* 21(2–3), 2017, 1–23.

26 Henry Shue, "The Unavoidability of Justice," in Shue, *Climate Justice…*, 27–46.

5   Intergenerational justice

Introduction

Matters of international justice comprise only half of the problem of what we owe to other humans in the age of climate change. The other half concerns what we owe people of the future. The current non-existence of such people adds significant complexity to the issue, but in outline the problems are the same in the two cases: how to distribute climate change costs and benefits across a population, in this case a population spread over several generations. How should we think about the interests of future people in our policy deliberations? Why should they count and how much? This chapter examines those questions. We begin with Gardiner's analysis of how bad things might get for future people under business as usual. Next, focusing on Parfit's non-identity problem, we examine why it is so problematic to say we wrong these people by continuing down this path. This brings us to a sustained engagement with a broadly contractarian approach to intergenerational obligations, rooted in the philosophy of John Rawls. We close with some skeptical reflections on this approach to the problem.

An "intergenerational arms race"

We can imagine a scenario in which the problem of international climate justice has been solved to the satisfaction of all current national governments. All have agreed on the interpretation of common but differentiated responsibilities, with developed countries taking the lead on emissions cuts while developing countries have been assisted in the task of bringing their citizens out of poverty. As Vanderheiden observes, by itself this outcome might nevertheless fall far short of the goal set in Paris of keeping the global climate to 1.5°C above the pre-industrial baseline. In other words, we might achieve full international consensus on the terms of a climate treaty and still blow the carbon budget.[1] To believe otherwise is to suppose, against a good deal of evidence to the contrary, that the current generation is robustly committed to protecting the interests of people of the future as opposed to appeasing present citizens.

To appreciate the truth in this, consider again collective action problems like the tragedy of the commons. A key premise of this trope, applied to the problem of climate change, is that all parties prefer the outcome in which "dangerous interference with the climate system" has been avoided. For reasons that should be obvious, climatic stability is in the interests of everyone involved. It is, we might say, collectively rational for everyone to cooperate, which in this case means crafting and abiding by the terms of an emissions reduction treaty. It is worth re-iterating the point made in the previous chapter that this kind of agreement is what makes such problems surmountable in principle.

There will always be a temptation for free riding in collective action scenarios. But so long as the parties involved agree to a system of enforceable rules governing the use of the relevant resources, disaster can be avoided. For example, a group of fishers harvesting fish stocks in an inland lake can agree to be bound by a system that effectively prevents free riding by any of them. This can allow the stocks to be harvested for the lifetime of the fishers, and perhaps their children's too.[2]

In other words, although the central problem with collective action problems is the gap between what is collectively rational and what is perceived to be individually rational, this gap can be overcome in particular cases, as with our fishers. However, all of this applies mainly to any present generation. A more difficult problem arises when we extend the analysis to "interactions" among generations rather than within them. Our fishers may have solved the problem of overfishing for a generation or two but nothing in their arrangement guarantees that the fish stocks will remain healthy for many generations to come.

In fact, there may be an inverse relation between the length of time covered by the agreement and the power it has to *constrain* the relevant actions of individuals. The shorter in time the agreement extends, the more motivation the fishers have to refrain from free riding, because they can harvest at a higher rate over shorter time periods. By contrast, if they were forced to consider the health of the fish stocks over a longer period – several centuries, for example – our fishers would need to constrain present harvesting more aggressively. The motivation to abide by the rules would likely wane in such cases, re-opening the gap between collective and individual rationality.

This is the complication that arises when we talk (metaphorically) of "interactions" among generations. Gardiner states the problem crisply: in these cases, "[i]t is collectively rational for most generations to cooperate: (almost) every generation prefers the outcome produced by everyone cooperating over the outcome produced by no one cooperating."[3]

Obviously, the "most" and "almost" in this formulation of the problem have introduced a significant new problem because the generation for whom the collectively rational solution is not the best one is *any present generation.*

Consider the possibilities applied to emissions reductions. A present generation – ours, for instance – might be living high on the hog with respect to its emissions and the consumption patterns that produce them. In what sense is it in the interest of this generation to curb its consumption? If it did so, it would be incurring a pure cost, the benefits being passed on entirely to people of the future. The same logic applies to a (future) generation suffering the ravages of climate change. As bad as things are for that generation, they would presumably be made worse by the decision to cut carbon emissions. For this generation too such cuts would constitute a pure cost, with the benefits being enjoyed entirely by people of their future. Sticking solely to the logic of collective action scenarios, where is the motivation to reduce carbon emissions supposed to come from in these cases?

The problem might get very bad. RCP 8.5, we have seen, involves no significant effort to get beyond fossil fuels in the short to medium term. For instance, if we were serious about ditching fossil fuels we would need to cease building infrastructure for them immediately, but we are not. To take just one example, the government of Canada is both championing the 1.5°C Paris target and expanding the system of pipelines carrying tar sands oil – among the most carbon-intensive fossil fuel products on the global market – from the country's interior to tidewater. This kind of decision is explicitly intended to extend the reign of fossil fuels for decades to come. Generalize the phenomenon and it is easy to appreciate the untenable position into which we are putting future generations. Climate disasters are going to become more and more intense, increasing the difficulty of adaptation. Any successful technological form of adaptation requires energy – try desalinating water, building seawalls or cooling apartment buildings without it – but this can only be supplied by fossil fuels if that's all we leave people of the future.

It follows that in coping with disaster future generations will make the situation even worse for those coming after them. The problem is iterated down the generations, intensifying for each one of them. For example, faced with a humanitarian disaster as its citizens die *en masse* from heat exposure, why should the government of India not turn to its abundant coal reserves in order to supply power for air conditioners in every household? This is what Gardiner calls the **intergenerational arms race**.[4] Every generation will have to burn more and more fossil fuels in order to cope with climate change disasters, thereby not just passing on the same problem to the succeeding generation but making it even worse for them.

Gardiner concludes that our refusal to adopt the measures that would forestall this outcome means that the relation between us and people of the future is a form of *tyranny*. Because they have been forced by the tyrannical present – us – to "attack" subsequent generations by burning fossil fuels to stay alive, future people apparently cannot be blamed for their actions. After all, they are only defending themselves, aren't they? And, although self-defence does not permit *anything* it gives agents wide moral latitude for action aimed at self-preservation.

This is a very harsh assessment of us, but it seems warranted. Tyranny describes the most extreme form of domination of one human by another or one group of humans by another. It is an arrangement that wears its wrongness, its injustice, on its face. But is it so obvious that our refusal to bear the costs of mitigation wrongs people of the future? What if that decision actually determines the identity of those people? In that case, shouldn't they be grateful to us – or at least not blame us – for our fateful decisions? These questions bring us to Parfit's famous non-identity problem.

The non-identity problem

The notion that future people might despise us for our actions and omissions has philosophical bite only if they are justified in adopting this attitude. They must be able to say, with warrant, that our current behavior wrongs them. Derek Parfit's **non-identity problem (NIP)** is often invoked to show that this is exceedingly difficult for them to do. The NIP is a conceptual puzzle that poses profound difficulties for everything from procreative ethics to energy policy. The problem has to do with the way in which some of our decisions in the present affect the *identity* of people born in the future, and how this, in turn, can change the moral quality of our relation to those people with respect to those decisions. To see the problem, notice a disanalogy between such cases and those in which our actions affect people who are distant in space. For instance, the consumer choices of people in the developed world can clearly affect the lives of those in the developing world. In choosing which brand of coffee to buy we might be either abetting a brutal dictator who exploits coffee farmers or supporting fair and sustainable coffee farming practices half way across the world.

To the extent that our actions can have such impacts, the merely spatial separation between us and the farmers is of no moral consequence.[5] It follows that we can in principle be criticized by those affected by our actions if the latter harm them. They can say, for example, that they are worse off by our actions than they would have been had we acted otherwise (or perhaps not acted at all). The truth of these claims is an empirical matter, but the possibility of such criticism clearly exists. But now imagine a situation in which our decisions affect the identity of the people whose lives they impact. That is, imagine that those people would not have existed absent these decisions. In this case, it is difficult to see how they can criticize us for our harmful choices. Apparently, they cannot say – as could our harmed coffee farmers – that they are worse off because of our decisions than they would otherwise have been. For our decisions were instrumental in bringing them into existence. The only other option *for them* is non-existence.

Let's see how the argument applies to energy policy. Parfit himself applies it this way, invoking a distinction between two policy choices, a risky policy (RP) and a safe policy (SP). Here is RP:

> Suppose that, as a community, we have a choice between two energy policies. Both would be completely safe for at least two centuries, but one would have

certain risks for the further future. If we choose [RP], the standard of living would be slightly higher over the next two centuries. We do choose this policy. As a result, there is a ... catastrophe two centuries later, which kills thousands of people.[6]

SP, by contrast, is the policy that would not have this outcome. Now, some of the details here do not exactly fit our problem. For example, the time-frame is off for the climate challenge and the idea that our choice is a stark either-or oversimplifies things somewhat (recall that the IPCC offers four scenarios). But the thought experiment nevertheless gets to the heart of the challenges we face in our climate policy.

The basic idea is that because such policy has the potential to pervade so many aspects of social life, it will change the procreative decisions many people make. Perhaps a government, choosing RP, decides to enhance coal extraction in some part of its territory. Lured by the promise of making big money in a relatively short period of time, a couple decides to put off starting a family for another year or two, so that the husband can go and work in the mines. The identity of people is the contingent product of the exact sperm and egg coming together at the moment of conception. This means that the child our couple would have conceived had the husband stayed at home will not be born, instead giving way to a different child born one or two years later. RP has altered the personal identity of our couple's progeny. Decisions like this will be made across the social spectrum and, just as importantly, will ramify down the years. Eventually – perhaps one or two centuries on – RP will result in a population that is entirely different from the one that would have existed under SP.

With this in mind, let's formalize the NIP as follows:

1   We have a decision to pursue RP or SP and we choose RP.
2   Because it is large-scale, the choice will ramify pervasively into the social world.
3   This will cause different people to be born than would have been born under SP.
4   The lives of the people born under RP will be worth living, meaning that people of the future have been benefited by being brought into existence.
5   Therefore, they cannot blame us for the quality of the world they have been bequeathed since the only other option for *them* – for example, the world under SP – is non-existence.

From the standpoint of its challenge to morality, there are two key assumptions of this argument. First, it adopts a person-affecting conception of morality. The attitude of blame that the person of the ruined future presumably wants to take up against the present generation depends on the notion that we have harmed *her*, but this is apparently just what she cannot say. Second, it depends on a comparative notion of harm. It makes sense to say that our future victim is harmed in the first place only if she is worse off than she *would have been* under some alternative scenario.[7]

Both assumptions have been challenged, so let's look at the challenges in order. We will also consider a third challenge, focusing on whether or not we can be sure that people's lives will be worth living in a climate ravaged world.

Person-affecting morality

Parfit himself defuses the NIP by rejecting the claims of person-affecting morality in cases like this. In its place he offers an impersonal principle of beneficence, to the effect that RP is a bad choice simply because it produces a world in which people are worse off than the population of the alternative world would have been.[8] We can presumably make this determination by looking at net levels of welfare in the two worlds. If it is lower in the world created by RP than it is in the world created by SP, then our choice of RP can be morally criticized. This world is bad even though it is not worse *for anyone.*

The problem with this response, as Parfit himself notes, is that it flies in the face of our intuitions, which are decidedly person-affecting in cases like this. Again, think of this from the standpoint of those suffering in a climate change-ravaged world. Insofar as they are inclined to criticize our decisions at all, it seems unlikely that the target of their moral anger would be our failure to bring into being people other than them. But that is what form their criticism would have to take if Parfit is right: even as their world was falling to pieces because of our choice, they would be forced to adopt the standpoint of the impersonal moral judge comparing net welfare levels in possible worlds. That seems like a bizarre portrait of how humans actually think.

To elaborate, consider Fiona Woollard's analysis of the NIP. Woollard thinks that Parfit's "solution" to the problem – the comparison of net welfare levels in the two possible worlds – fails because it "cannot account for our intuitions about our reasons to stop damaging the environment."[9] That is, although Parfit's solution would have us refrain from doing such damage, he misunderstands *why* we think we should refrain. And once we appreciate this, we will see that what we really care about is the harms our actions are bringing to future people. This argument, if successful, would help support our intuition that the person-affecting status of our actions is ineliminable. Woollard's point is based on an alleged distinction between two kinds of cases. In the first case, we are faced with a choice whether or not to refrain from polluting the planet. This is Parfit's choice between RP and SP. In the second case a volcano will erupt in 300 years, polluting the atmosphere with CO_2 and thereby causing many of the same hardships for humanity as would occur with our choice of RP.

The question is this: would our failure to seek out a way of averting the volcano disaster be morally equivalent to our choice of RP? For Woollard, the choice of RP would be morally worse than failing to avert the volcano disaster. The argument rests on the **Doctrine of Doing and Allowing (DDA)**, according to which, other things being equal, it is morally worse to perform immoral actions than to allow them to happen. The DDA is undoubtedly an element of commonsense morality. For example, in debates about euthanasia, we sometimes make a distinction between killing the patient and allowing her to die, suggesting that the former is impermissible, the latter permissible.

How can we use the DDA to show that we probably cannot abandon consideration of the manner in which our actions are likely to affect future individuals? The answer is that, according to the DDA, there is something especially bad about the world created by RP, precisely because we chose it rather than simply allowing it (or something morally equivalent) to happen. But we cannot appreciate what makes the choice of RP especially bad if we abandon the person-affecting consequences of it. Its special badness, we might say, is tied *essentially* to the effect it will have on persons. To test your intuitions here, consider how you would react to two possible time travellers from the future. One of them is coming from the world ravaged by the volcano, the other from the world ravaged by our choice of RP. They are travelling to the present to attack us, in the one case to prevent our choice of RP, in the other to force us to take steps to prevent the volcanic eruption.

Woollard claims that only one of the attacks is morally justified: the one from the future consequent on our choice of RP.[10] As Woollard herself recognizes, this thought experiment cannot *ground* the DDA because it presupposes the soundness of that doctrine. If we judge that one time traveller's enterprise is justified while the other's is not that is only because we have already decided that the DDA is an apt principle to invoke in this context. The fact that the DDA is an element of commonsense morality gives it *prima facie* weight in our moral deliberations, but it is surely defeasible. In the euthanasia case, for example, consequentialists simply deny that there is a morally important distinction between killing and letting die. What ultimately matters is that the patient's suffering is alleviated in as timely a manner as possible.

Since Woollard has not shown the DDA itself to be justified she cannot rely on it to undercut Parfit's solution to the NIP. Again, Woollard is employing the DDA to buttress the notion that we require the person-affecting description of, say, RP because without this description we will not appreciate what is really bad about that policy choice. But we can see why we need not assent to this claim given its shaky grounding in the DDA. In any case, what might get lost in this sort of discussion is the fact that Parfit's solution is probably strong enough to warrant robust policy measures in this area. So long as his solution clearly indicates that we should choose RCP 2.6 over RCP 8.5 – and it surely does – does it really matter that we may be logically prohibited from employing a person-affecting description of our choice?

The comparative notion of harm

Woollard is correct to add that many philosophers are not satisfied with Parfit's response to the first assumption, the one about morality being person-affecting. But in their critique of Parfit many of these philosophers instead attack the second assumption, the NIP's comparative notion of harm. The idea here, recall, is that when we say that someone has been harmed what we mean is that she has been made worse off than she would have been under some alternative scenario, i.e. one in which the specific harm-causing action had not been performed. If we are going to reject this notion, we need to be able to say that people can be harmed without being made worse off in the relevant sense.[11] Can we insert a *wedge* between the concept of harm and that of being made worse off?

Here's another thought experiment to help us find the wedge.[12] Suppose we choose RP, thus dooming a good portion of humanity in exactly 200 years' time to lives of terrible suffering and deprivation. Suppose also that there is a misanthropic and powerful, though not omniscient, demon. He delights in the prospect of our suffering and would be especially pleased if we brought it on ourselves through the choice of RP. But because he is not omniscient he cannot be sure that RP will do the trick. Just in case it fails to produce the effects he longs for, he has therefore decided to intervene in the climate system to produce effects identical to those he hopes will be caused by RP. As it turns out, RP brings the hoped-for disaster so the demon does not intervene in the climate system, instead delighting in what he takes to be the superior spectacle of humanity destroying itself.

In this example, future humans have been harmed by RP, but they have not been made worse off than they would have been had we not chosen this policy. This is because the demon was determined to visit exactly the same suffering and deprivation on humanity as RP would cause. So we have a dilemma. Either we say that harms can happen without the victims being made worse off than they would otherwise have been or that this is impossible and in cases like the one just rehearsed no harm has been produced. The idea that no harms have been produced in such cases seems outlandish. There is a direct causal link between RP and the sufferings and deprivations of people 200 years on. That the demon would have intervened in the climate system had RP not produced this result seems irrelevant. We are therefore apparently forced, or permitted, to reject the comparative notion of harm assumed in the NIP. This is a happy result since it allows us to focus on those harms themselves, which brings us to the third kind of response to the NIP.

Lives worth living?

The third response is to deny that the lives of most people in the future will be worth living if we adopt RP, here thought of specifically as RCP 8.5. Of course, this does not *solve* the NIP, because the premise about people's lives being worth living is simply part of the original hypothesis. However, the suggestion here has the virtue of bringing back down to earth a discussion that has become very abstract since Parfit first introduced it. In particular, the suggestion forces us to confront the NIP in terms of what our current climate forcing implies about our moral relation to people of the future. One way to approach the issue is to notice that, in choosing RCP 8.5 we may be bringing about a state of affairs in which the future population can be divided roughly into two groups.

The first are those who judge their own lives to be not worth living. In a stirring account of climate change in the 17th century, the historian Geoffrey Parker describes a world torn apart by repeated crop failures, flooding, war, disease and famine. This is Parker citing a local account of the suffering in Shandong, China:

> Many people held their lives to be of no value, for the area was so wasted and barren, the common people were so poor and had suffered so much that essentially they knew none of the joys of being alive ... Every day one would hear that someone had hanged himself from a beam and killed himself. Others, at intervals, cut their throats or threw themselves into the river.[13]

It is worth remarking that this period – the Little Ice Age, as it is called – saw a climate anomaly of just $-0.6°C$ relative to the period 1000–2000. This puts into perspective our current flirtation with an anomaly approaching $+5°C$ relative to the pre-industrial baseline.[14]

Many of our societies are more resilient and therefore better able to cope with the challenges of adaptation than were most societies in the 17th century (though Parker notes that the Japanese were able to cope quite well). However, (a) this adaptive capacity is not uniform across contemporary societies; and (b) the relatively large temperature anomaly we face will eventually produce challenges for everyone. Let's be honest: RCP 8.5 will eventually produce a world rife with existential despair. Surely, many people will judge that their lives are not worth living in this world, a judgment that might be entirely sincere whether or not they actually take their lives. These people will be able to point directly to our actions and accuse us of wrong-doing. In other words, the person-affecting account of morality fits these people just fine, in spite of the NIP.

This brings us to the second group, comprising those whose lives are worth living but who empathize strongly with the plight of those in the first group. To appreciate the difference between the two groups and to see how this relates to the NIP, consider Peter Strawson's discussion of resentment and indignation. These are both hostile moral attitudes we can take up in response to perceived wrongdoing, but they are importantly distinct. Strawson argues that resentment is a reaction to personal wrongdoing, whereas indignation is "vicarious," directed by third parties at perceived wrongdoers on behalf of those who have been wronged directly by them.[15]

Let us say that people in the first group can feel *justified* resentment against members of the present generation for adopting RCP 8.5, while people in the second group can feel *justified* indignation towards them for this choice.[16] This grounds the hostile attitude of (almost) everyone in the future to members of the generation that chose RCP 8.5. The only people it leaves out of account are the ones who have been only lightly affected and those who don't much care about the suffering of others. A minority, surely.

Further, it makes sense to say that the place our energy policy choices put us on the spectrum of 1.5°C to 5°C (in 2100) will determine the ratio of those in the first group to those in the second and also therefore, the ratio of justified resentment and indignation directed by future people at us. The worse the outcome, the more people will be directly affected, and so the more opportunity for resentment there will likely be. Unfortunately, the RCP 8.5 pathway, our current trajectory, will lead to a lot of ruined lives, and therefore plenty of scope for feelings of resentment directed by people who judge that their lives are not worth living towards those who brought this upon them.

In this section, we have canvassed three broad strategies for avoiding the conclusion of the NIP. It is important to do this because the problem is a powerful challenge to our intuitions about what we owe to future people. If it is correct, then future people have no basis on which to criticize our refusal to act meaningfully to avert climate disaster. Our actions do not wrong them, which means that they cannot blame us for what we do or fail to do. But if they cannot blame us, then aren't we off the hook morally? Of course, there are plenty of people in the present and near future whose identities will not be affected by our choices. With respect to these people, ordinary moral constraints surely remain in force here and these might be significant enough to warrant a move to RCP 2.6. In that case, the interests of future people – i.e., those whose identities our choices can help determine – will have been taken care of.

But we may not be content with this thought. We may think that we have direct duties to future people even if our choices affect their identities. In that case, we will need to lean on one of the three arguments examined here (or some combination of them), arguments meant to undermine the NIP, or at least blunt its force as applied to the problem of climate change. With respect to identity-affecting cases, we will, that is, need to argue (a) that person-affecting morality is suspect; (b) that the comparative notion of harm is suspect; or (c) that in the case of climate change the claim that the lives of future people will be worth living is suspect. Pushing back against the NIP in one of these three ways gives us a basis for moralizing our current behaviors in the right way. This allows us to raise the question of what precisely we should do for future people to help them cope with the effects of climate change. What do we owe the future?

The contractarian gambit

One way to think about this question is by appeal to contractarian moral theory. Contractarianism grounds our obligations to others in agreements we have with them. If I have hired someone to do a job for me, at a specific cost and by a specific date, then he is required to meet these terms and, if he does, I am required to pay him what we have agreed upon. Though useful as a paradigm case, one way in which this is oversimplified is that contractarian moral theory is, for the most part, idealizing. That is, it attempts to lay out what informed agents *would* agree to in conditions of ideal communication. That way, considerations that are extrinsic to the agreement – those stemming from various biases or power differentials among the contracting agents – can be weeded out. Though the theory has deep roots in the history of philosophy, John Rawls provides the most forceful modern version of it.[17]

Rawls thinks that the principles of justice governing our social lives must be derived from agreements among us. But the process by which we discuss these principles with a view to coming to an agreement about them must be designed in a way that negates the power of morally arbitrary facts about us, facts rooted in what Rawls calls "natural and social lotteries." How can we do this? Rawls answers by way of a thought experiment whose purpose is to underwrite the egalitarian moral principles of the participants – these are citizens of liberal-democratic societies – by eliminating from their deliberations all sources of unfair or biased reasoning. He calls the thought experiment the "original position" and the device employed in it the "veil of ignorance." Behind the veil of ignorance participants do not know anything about themselves that is the product of natural and social lotteries: their socio-economic position, their race, their gender, their age and so on.

Since these qualities are the sources of our biases, ignoring them helps the participants arrive at genuinely consensus-based principles of justice. Rawls argues that one of the things the participants will agree on is the **difference principle**, the idea that some economic inequality is to be tolerated so long as those on the bottom are better off than they would be under a system of strict economic equality (we referred to this aspect of the difference principle in our discussion of the ideology of business as usual, in Chapter 4). Beyond this, they will all agree that each should be entitled to many social goods: adequate wealth, access to positions of power and prestige in society and protection of the basic liberties. How does all of this apply to the matter of intergenerational justice?

Well, surely one of the things over which nobody has control is when he or she will be born. Surely a person's precise generational membership is the ultimate product of the natural lottery. So, shouldn't we make it one of the things about which participants are ignorant in the original position? We can see how helpful this would be in grounding strong duties of savings and conservation across generations. If I don't know which generation I belong to, then I would want to see to it that every generation was reasonably well-provided for by the generations preceding it in the temporal order.

In other words, it looks as though participants in the original position should be thought of as members of an intergenerational polity, whatever else they are. On the assumption that some generations are wealthier than others, but also that behind the veil of ignorance one does not know which generation one belongs to, participants should, it seems, endorse a policy of extreme environmental caution (among other things). This would effectively mean endorsing an intergenerational version of the difference principle. Even those on the bottom of the intergenerational heap would have access to whatever is required for them to live decent lives. Indeed, participants might allow for significant intergenerational inequality so long as each generation was better off this way than they would be under a system of strict intergenerational equality.

This, of course, entails that every generation must take steps to constrain itself with respect to behaviors that might degrade the material resources upon which every generation depends. The application to climate change seems obvious. According to Rawls, participants in the original position are not comprehensively ignorant. They know about the state of the world as well as the basics of science and economics. So they are aware of the problem of carbon pollution as well as the connection between GHG emissions and national wealth. Since for all they know they might belong to a generation suffering the effects of catastrophic climate change, should they not endorse strong mitigation measures?

Unfortunately, this is where Rawlsian contractarianism fails us, and the failure goes to the heart of all attempts to ground strong intergenerational duties in contractarian moral theory. For Rawls, while participants in the original position do not know what generation they belong to they do know that they are all members of the *same* generation.[18] This seems arbitrary, but it is not: it speaks to a deep feature of contractarian moral theory. The reason for restricting the moral gaze of the participants to members of their own generation is that contractarianism is premised on the notion of *reciprocity* among members of a political or social group.

Here we see the sense in which the whole theory is constrained by key features of the paradigm example, sketched above. The person I have hired is bound to me and I to him in ways laid out in the explicit contract we have brokered. Now that the contract is signed by both parties, we have a rough equality of power over one another: neither side can breach the contract's terms without penalty. It is this idea that our interests can be affected by the actions of others, and their interests by ours, that makes the metaphor of a contract between generations inapt. For the brute fact is that people in 2100 have no power over us. The implications for climate policy are far-reaching. To see why, let's return to the logic of the intergenerational arms race, examined above.

Suppose we are in the original position and we must deliberate about emissions reductions. As Vanderheiden points out, it is implausible that we would ever endorse such reductions no matter which generation we end up belonging to.[19] Remember, we know how the world works, broadly speaking, and so we understand the connections among carbon emissions, industrial development and the generation of material wealth. We 21st-century inhabitants of the developed world exist in a charmed time and place. Things have never been as good as they are right now and, if we don't change our ways soon, they probably won't be again for a very long time. We are living at the apex of industrial civilization. We forget about this sometimes, or simply fail to notice it in the first place. We assume that things must always get better, but this assumption is itself a peculiar psychological feature of historical apex-dwellers.

But now we find ourselves, by hypothesis, in the original position, knowing that such riches are an historical anomaly but deprived of the knowledge of whether or not we possess them. We must decide about emissions reductions. If we turn out to be rich we can probably afford such reductions, but why would we bother to incur the cost they entail? After all, according to Rawls, we are all members of the same generation. No other generation's interests count in our deliberations. If we wind up as citizens of the apex that is very lucky for us, but we would have literally no reason in this case to share our wealth with those to come. The real problem, however, is that the odds of being born in this generation are very low. The possibility of belonging to a poor, pre-industrialized or un-industrialized society looms large. Why gamble, since if it turns out that you belong to a generation needing to emit carbon in order to develop, your decision to place limitations on CO_2 emissions will prevent this from happening?

It seems to follow that, as far as contractarianism allows, we cannot justify the strong mitigation measures required to avert climate disaster. Vanderheiden concludes that Rawls has given us no way of grounding intergenerational duties in the difference principle and the value of moral equality it expresses.[20] But he has addressed the issue in other terms. Let's turn to that discussion.

Just savings

Rawls argues that generations do have future-spanning obligations, claiming it is right that "each [generation] receives from its predecessors and does its fair share for those which come later."[21] This is the basis of the **just savings principle**. Rawls is never very precise about what or how much should be saved according to this principle, but it must be an amount of capital and resources sufficient to preserve just institutions down the generations. Perhaps we can get a better sense of what the requirement is by looking at two distinct ways of criticizing it. The first criticism is that Rawls is asking for too much here, that in requiring us to do what it takes to preserve just institutions and their material prerequisites we are unduly or unjustly constraining the freedom of future generations to shape their own lives. The second criticism is that the requirement asks too little of us, that in particular it cannot account for strong duties of environmental preservation.[22]

The principle is too demanding

Some have argued that the just savings principle illegitimately ties people of the future to *our* conceptions of the good life. Why, it is asked, should we be so concerned to pass on our institutions rather than allowing future people the freedom to develop their own? It is important to remember that in talking of "institutions" here we are including the material embodiments of our conceptions of justice: in the case of liberal democracies, this means universal adult enfranchisement, regular and fair elections, a transparent and rule-bound judiciary, guaranteed protection of basic liberties, and so on. It also includes whatever stock of "natural resources" is required to keep the whole thing running smoothly. The commitment to maintaining the conditions of "justice" is meant to catch all of this.

The complaint here is that this constrains the choices of future people too much. If this were correct, it would follow that we should not be striving to embody our ideals of justice in relatively permanent institutions. As Janna Thompson has argued, however, we cannot help but foist all of this on future generations. This is because the commitment to justice is "lifetime-transcending":

> Justice is a lifetime-transcending ideal. The very nature of justice as a moral concept ... requires people to believe that their reasonable, well-debated beliefs about justice ought to be accepted by everyone, including their successors. When they construct institutions of justice they are bound to think that they are building something for their successors as well as themselves.[23]

It would be odd to think otherwise, to believe sincerely that although the institutions of justice we have inherited and cultivated are good for us, future people might legitimately consider them dispensable. And Thompson seems right about the reason underlying this belief: that there is something universal about the arguments we have been making since the Enlightenment concerning the bedrock ideals of liberal-democratic polities.

It does not follow that we should be complacent about these ideals. For example, they have enabled the rise of neo-liberal capitalism, an economic system that is in the process of destroying the biosphere, not to mention creating vast inequalities of wealth among people. It would be a good idea to figure out how the ideals became perverted to allow for this kind of development because this would tell us how to reform the ideals and thus make better institutions, including economic ones. In any case, what is of most importance to our discussion is that if we do think it worthwhile to preserve just institutions, we are also required to preserve the "natural resources" required to sustain them. If the institutions cannot function against the backdrop of a ruined biosphere, then we are morally obligated to avoid ruining the biosphere, whether or not this constitutes a "constraint" on future people. This leads us to the second broad challenge to the just savings principle.

The principle is not demanding enough

From the standpoint of the just savings principle, the duty to maintain the integrity of the biosphere is minimalist, meaning that it is probably compatible with significant environmental degradation so long as we can find technological replacements for what we degrade or use up (assuming we depend on it). The second worry about the just savings principle – captured in the claim that it is not demanding enough – is that it gives us no basis for opposing this trend. The biosphere, we might suppose, is super-abundant with life, most of which has no conceivable function in the preservation of institutions down the generations. Much of this superabundance is therefore dispensable in principle. Those who are alarmed by this conclusion argue that we need to go beyond the just savings principle to determine what must be preserved – "saved" – for future generations. Call this the "environmentalist" critique of Rawls.

Thompson argues that environmentalism thus construed is too exclusive a concern to expect special promotion by liberal-democratic governments.[24] It is not a value endorsed by a sufficiently broad swath of citizens. One of the key requirements of government in liberal democracies is that they must maintain *neutrality* among what Rawls calls the various "conceptions of the good" held by citizens. Ideally, this prevents the capture of government by narrow conceptions of the good, those held by theocrats for example. Similarly, Thompson believes that we cannot justify allowing government to be captured by the environmentalist conception of the good.

There are at least three possible responses to this argument. The first would reject the liberal-democratic approach to this issue, arguing instead that at least when it comes to something as important as biodiversity protection governmental neutrality is overrated. Second, we could accept the principle of neutrality but suggest that in failing to act robustly to protect biodiversity governments are in fact in violation of this principle. This is because the just savings principle depends on the view that only human interests count and that the rest of the biosphere is at best a resource for us. This position, it might be urged, itself implies a conception of the good, one moreover that is very congenial to the expansionist interests of neo-liberal capitalism. Why should we think it justifiable for governments to be captured by *this* conception and *these* interests but no others?

Third, it makes sense to say that because climate change is a threat to civilization itself, the moral imperative to undertake strong measures to mitigate it simply does not express a narrow interest. These are measures all of us would endorse were we to see the issue unobstructed by ideology. But the just savings principle is far too weak to support these measures. It is, Rawls says, a "natural duty" involving an obligation "to further just arrangements not yet established, at least when this can be done without too much cost to ourselves."[25] However, the invocation of subjective cost assessments is bound to produce mischief in the context of the climate crisis. For much of this and the previous chapter we have been emphasizing the ways in which citizens of the developed world tend to have a skewed view of costs.

Such skewing is likely to make us especially stingy in providing for future generations. The just savings principle licenses this stinginess, and will therefore permit the ruination of the global climate. To avoid this outcome, Rawls would need to provide an *objective* account of the distinction between reasonable and unreasonable costs. This he does not provide, and it is hard to see how he possibly could. For doing so would seem to require bringing future people into the original position so that their interests could be properly represented in the present.

Beyond the contract?

We seem to have arrived at an impasse. Contractarian theory is attractive because it provides a clear and compelling account of what motivates agents: they are signatories to an agreement with other agents, or at least they would be in ideal conditions, and their self-interest is furthered by abiding by the terms of the contract. But the theory looks too weak to give us guidance on a problem like climate change. Again, the problem is not just with Rawls, but with the very structure of contractarian moral theory as it applies to our relation to future generations.

Consider this remark by Mark Rowlands:

> Those who fall outside the scope of the contract fall outside the scope of civilization. They lie outside the boundaries of morality. You have no obligations to those who are significantly weaker than you. That is the consequence of the contractual view of civilization.[26]

Rowlands is talking about non-human animals here, but the point applies to future people just as well. They are powerless with respect to us, and this places them, in Rowlands' terminology, outside the bounds of civilization. The contractarian framing of the issue gives us permission to do anything we want to them. Let's close the chapter with two broad ways of responding to this problem. The first attempts to answer it by revising our thinking about who belongs in the "scope of the contract"; the second accepts the criticism of contractarianism, suggesting that we need a different moral theory to make sense of our intergenerational duties.

The first response to the challenge brings us back to Thompson's notion of "lifetime-transcending interests." Samuel Scheffler has made much the same point, arguing that we all have an interest in how the "afterlife" – his word for the future without us, not a different world to which we escape when we die – goes.[27] In particular, we have a reason to care about how our important projects are brought to fruition by future people. We might think of a church that takes several generations to build, or the search for a cure to cancer. Or take the interest in promoting justice. We might believe that this is an ongoing project, one that will never be fully complete but that will require the work of generation after generation. In these cases, we should say that a necessary condition for these projects to have meaning in *our* lives is that future people be able to continue them. It follows that we have an interest in seeing to it that they can do this, that their world is not so ravaged that our projects fall to the wayside as future people scramble to survive.

This thought may be sufficient to ground strong duties of mitigation in the present. It is crucial to see why. We may feel compelled to do this because *we need* people of the future, which means that some reciprocity has been brought to our relations with them. Without them, our projects would lose all point. If you doubt this, Scheffler argues, contemplate what certain knowledge of an asteroid strike in, say, 30 years would do to your investment in the kinds of projects just mentioned. Would you bother with any of them? Why? Because it reveals our dependency on the future, this thought can bring future people into the charmed circle of civilization, which is another way of saying that their powerlessness vis-à-vis the present has been diminished.[28]

These ideas may constitute the last, best hope for contractarianism with respect to finding a theoretical ground of our obligations to people of the future. But they might be deemed insufficient, which brings us to the second response to Rowland's challenge: to give up on this approach. If we do, it is probably because we cannot get around the problem of reciprocity in spite of what philosophers like Thompson and Scheffler have been urging. That is, we might think that the reciprocity between generations offered by reflections on the afterlife and lifetime-transcending interests is simply too shadowy a thing, not material enough, not translatable into the language of real-world *power* relations.

Or at least that it is not sufficient to motivate bold climate action, which is what we are interested in here. Fortunately we have theoretical options. We could, for instance, insist on a deontological approach to the problem, arguing that future people are (or will be) moral agents and thus are (or will be) worthy of respect. In refusing to mitigate we may be violating their rights. This thought can motivate meaningful constraint on our actions now. The fact that future people are currently non-existent and, more importantly given our focus in these sections, powerless with respect to us is morally irrelevant from the standpoint of deontology. In fact, deontology, expressed in the theory of rights, is in many ways a moral theory *for* the powerless and dispossessed. At least in comparison with contractarianism, it might for this reason be a good theoretical option for a sound intergenerational ethics.

Chapter summary

In this chapter, we have extended the analysis of climate change justice begun in the previous chapter by looking at how the topic encompasses future generations. We began by examining the possibility, introduced by Gardiner, that by doing nothing significant about the problem we might be setting in motion an intergenerational arms race. This was meant to emphasize the intergenerational badness of business as usual. Next, we took a step back and asked how it can be that we are capable of wronging people of the future at all. If our actions shape their identities and their lives are worth living, then we have not, it seems, made their lives worse than they would otherwise have been. This is because for those people the only other option was non-existence. We analyzed three ways of responding to this challenge. Rawls' contractarianism formed the backbone of the following two sections. We examined, in turn, his "original position" and "just savings principle" to see if either might provide the basis for strong intergenerational duties in the age of climate change. Finally, we asked about the adequacy of the contractarian model to the problem at hand, noting that its failures force us to either revise it or abandon it.

Questions for discussion

1   Explain the logic of the intergenerational arms race. Do you agree with Gardiner that generations that contribute to it – apart from ours – are acting out of self-defence?
2   Must morality be person-affecting? Discuss this question with reference to the non-identity problem.
3   Is Rawls justified in claiming that participants in the original position must be thought of as being aware that they all belong to the same generation, even if they do not know which generation it is?
4   Is the just savings principle theoretically well-grounded? Do we have a "natural duty" to save for future people, as Rawls supposes, and if so how far does the duty go?
5   Is it possible to ground duties to future generations in something like Thompson's "lifetime-transcending interests"? Can these interests be strong enough to do enough for future people to avoid climate disaster?

Suggested reading

Stephen Gardiner, *A Perfect Moral Storm: The Ethical Tragedy of Climate Change* (Oxford: Oxford University Press, 2011), Part C. One of Gardiner's three moral storms, and the most engaging aspect of his overall analysis. Seminal.

Samuel Scheffler, *Death and the Afterlife* (Oxford: Oxford University Press, 2012). An arresting attempt to show how we depend on future people to carry on our projects.

Derek Parfit, "Energy Policy and the Further Future: The Identity Problem." In Stephen M. Gardiner, Simon Caney, Dale Jamieson and Henry Shue (eds.) *Climate Ethics: Essential Readings* (Oxford: Oxford University Press,

2010), 112–121. This got everyone talking about whether, and how, our actions can wrong future people if they determine the identities of those people.

Notes

1 Steve Vanderheiden, *Atmospheric Justice: A Political Theory of Climate Change* (Oxford: Oxford University Press, 2008), 111–112.
2 Eleanor Ostrom, *Governing the Commons: The Evolution of Institutions for Collective Action* (Cambridge: Cambridge University Press, 1990).
3 Stephen Gardiner, *A Perfect Moral Storm: The Ethical Tragedy of Climate Change* (Oxford: Oxford University Press, 2011), 162.
4 Gardiner, *A Perfect Moral Storm…*, chapter 6.
5 Thomas D. Bontly, "Causes, Contrasts and the Non-Identity Problem," *Philosophical Studies* 173, 2016, 1233–1251 (1233–1234).
6 Derek Parfit, "Future Generations: Further Problems," *Philosophy and Public Affairs* 11(2), 1982, 113–172 (114).
7 Robert Huseby, "Person-Affecting Moral Theory, Non-Identity and Future People," *Environmental Values* 19(2), May, 2010, 193–210 (194).
8 Derek Parfit, *Reasons and Persons* (Oxford: Oxford University Press, 1984), 360.
9 Fiona Woollard, "Have We Solved the Non-Identity Problem?" *Ethical Theory and Moral Practice* 15, 2012, 677–690 (679).
10 Woollard, "Have We Solved…?" 680.
11 M. Hanser, "Harming Future People," *Philosophy and Public Affairs* 19, 1990, 47–70.
12 The example is mine, but similar examples of the point I'm making here abound in the literature. See, for example, David Boonin, *The Non-Identity Problem and the Ethics of Future People* (Oxford: Oxford University Press), chapter 3.
13 Quoted in Geoffrey Parker, *Global Crisis: War, Climate Change and Catastrophe in the 17th Century.* (New Haven: Yale University Press, 2013), epigraph.
14 Byron Williston, *The Anthropocene Project: Virtue in the Age of Climate Change* (Oxford: Oxford University Press, 2015), 6.
15 Peter F. Strawson, *Freedom and Resentment and Other Essays* (London: Routledge, 2008), 15.
16 Williston, *The Anthropocene Project…*, 163.
17 John Rawls, *A Theory of Justice* (Cambridge, MA: Harvard University Press, 1971).
18 John Rawls, *A Theory of Justice*, 285.
19 Vanderheiden, *Atmospheric Justice…*, 119.
20 Vanderheiden, *Atmospheric Justice…*, 119.
21 Rawls, *A Theory of Justice…*, 291.
22 Janna Thompson, *Intergenerational Justice: Rights and Responsibilities in an Intergenerational Polity.* (London: Routledge, 2009), 88.
23 Thompson, *Intergenerational Justice…*, 89.
24 Thompson, *Intergenerational Justice…*, 94.
25 Rawls, *A Theory of Justice…*, 115.
26 Mark Rowlands, *The Philosopher and the Wolf: Lessons from the Wild on Love, Death and Happiness* (London: Granta, 2008), 124.
27 Samuel Scheffler, *Death and the Afterlife* (Oxford: Oxford University Press, 2012).
28 Scheffler, *Death and the Afterlife*, 41.

6 Nature in the Anthropocene

Introduction

Nature often gets short shrift in philosophical treatments of the ethics of climate change. This is a pity because the damage we are in the process of doing to nature through unconstrained GHG emissions is just as morally problematic as the way our actions and omissions on this issue are affecting humans. In this chapter, we focus on the destruction anthropogenic climate change is wreaking on ecosystems and the non-human species that make them up. The chapter begins by asking why species and ecosystems matter morally. Why are they valuable? The discussion brings us to an analysis of what our duties of species preservation look like in the age of climate change. This is a difficult task because we are now in the Anthropocene, a new geological epoch defined by pervasive human influence in the Earth system. In the next two sections, we examine the permissibility of engaging in the sort of "activist preservationist" projects the new epoch seems to demand of us. This is followed by critical analysis of the claims (a) that the Anthropocene is a welcome moment in human history; and (b) that nature is at an end.

Why species matter

We have seen (in Chapter 1) that anthropogenic climate change poses a profound threat to many non-human species. What is at stake here from the standpoint of our values? In the history of environmental ethics, it has been common to argue that species and ecosystems – among other things – have "intrinsic value," a value entirely independent of the human. If the claim is just that the way these things matter is not reducible to how they serve human purposes, it is unobjectionable. However, if it means that these things are somehow *self-valuing*, then the claim is difficult to support. From the fact that the value of x is not reducible to how humans can use it, it does not follow that x's value cannot be captured by some other way in which *we* might value it.

Although some balk at the idea, it is hard to see how a world without humans would have any value in it at all, even though it contained lots of non-human life. Humans, as far as we know, are the only genuine valu*ers* in the universe, and we are therefore forced to ask about the value of species by reference to the modes of valuation we have at our disposal. As Jamieson points out, were we to attempt to describe the value of the world without humans, it seems like we would always refer back to one of these modes of valuation, in the process smuggling ourselves back into the picture.[1]

This is not meant to settle the issue but pursuing it any further would take us too far afield. So let's side-step it and instead ask candidly why we think species are valuable or worth preserving. We will look at three ways of understanding this.

Scientific value

The eminent evolutionary biologist Stephen J. Gould has argued that species are "nature's objective packages." For Gould, a duty of preservation flows directly from this conception of species. It's not entirely obvious what Gould means by this, but since he is speaking from the perspective of science, it seems likely that what he means is that species have value as potential objects of scientific investigation:

> By grasping the objective status of species as real units in nature (and by understanding why they are not arbitrary divisions for human convenience), we may better comprehend the moral rationale for their preservation. You can expunge an arbitrary idea by rearranging your conceptual world. But when a species dies an item of natural uniqueness is gone forever.[2]

Gould has surely hit on something important here. One of the reasons we generally shrink from the idea of expunging species is that they represent biological lineages (often) millions of years in the making. They have emerged victorious from the long struggle for existence and this very fact, we seem to think, should give us pause as we make decisions that are likely to impact them significantly. Other things being equal, surely the appropriate attitudes about them are awe and respect and the default behaviors towards them are constraint and care.

However, Gould's appeal to the objectivity of species does not get us very far, for two reasons. First, we might think very little of destroying a species that is deadly to humans. It is easy to sympathize with the human attempt to kill every last one of those multi-jawed space monsters in the *Alien* movies, for example. In this case, the objective reality of the species is not a sufficiently compelling reason to preserve it. The same point presumably applies to real-world threats to humans, like deadly bacteria.[3] Second, we may be faced with a situation in which an action required to save one species threatens another. Perhaps "rewilding" an area by re-introducing a predator species into it threatens a species native to that place, something lower down the food chain. In this case, both species are, of course, objective –both have scientific value in this sense – which means that this criterion provides no guidance for us. Clearly, we must look elsewhere for the locus of species value.

Economic value

The most natural place to begin is with our own interests. Species diversity is key to healthy ecosystems, acting as a kind of insurance policy for them. Because ecosystems are by definition highly interconnected networks comprised of biotic and abiotic elements, harms to ecosystems can cascade throughout them. Climate change, for example, might disrupt weather patterns in some region so severely that some population of a species has difficulty finding food. Perhaps because temperatures have risen, they awaken from hibernation a few weeks earlier than normal only to discover that their traditional food source has not yet appeared on the scene. This can make it difficult for the population to feed its young, causing many of them to die. If the problem persists for a few years, and the animals in question cannot migrate to a safer place quickly enough, the species may become extirpated in their current place.

The point here is this sort of phenomenon can reverberate throughout the entire ecosystem of which that species is a part, bringing the whole system perilously close to crashing. But biodiversity creates virtuous redundancies in such systems: when one species goes down there's another to fill its place and the system is preserved. Biodiversity is thus key to ecosystemic resiliency. Now, although we have a tendency to forget the fact, humans depend on healthy ecosystems for their very survival. Food, water, medicines, protection from storm surges, air quality, pest control and so much more – these are gifts to humans from healthy ecosystems. Recognizing this, economists have attempted to put a monetary value on biodiversity. But this area is rife with uncertainties, and uncertainty is generally fatal to accurate accounting.

For instance, decisions about biodiversity protection affect the life-world we pass to our descendants and such decisions therefore depend on what we think about the values of future people. Not only might future people find a use-value for the species whose value we discount, but they might also, or alternatively, find a reason to value it for non-economic reasons. Were they to learn about the way our activities led to the extinction of polar bears people of the future might be justly critical of us, even if they could point to no economic benefit to them deriving from the existence of this species. Moreover, since we have no idea how wealthy they will be, the prospect of determining accurately future generations' "willingness to pay" for biodiversity protection – which, if successful, would give us some indication of how much value *we* should ascribe to it on their behalf – looks hopeless.

Economic value is obviously important, but we should resist the erstwhile attempts of economists to convince us that it is the only game in town.

Aesthetic value

Darrel Moellendorf has argued that the loss of a species is bad in the same way that the loss of a "genre of art" is. It is the beauty of species – or more precisely of an individual member of a species insofar as it is "a good instance of its kind" – that is of utmost value to us, or ought to be.[4] There is no reason to deny the claim that we value nature generally because of its aesthetic qualities, but the approach has problems.

One reason for skepticism about it derives from what Glenn Parsons calls the "preservationist's dilemma." This has to do with the weight we ascribe to aesthetic considerations in our overall evaluations of what to do when our policy options threaten valuable natural places. Imagine a public building with a beautiful display of lighting, powered by coal extracted through the process of mountaintop removal. The process of extracting the coal has made the world uglier, in part by destroying the fauna and flora that used to live on the mountain. But what if most people judge that the beauty of the building's lighting outweighs the ugliness of the altered mountain landscape?[5]

With this example in mind, here's the dilemma. Either (a) aesthetic valuation is all we have to go on, in which case we will be hostage to people's shifting and often deplorable conceptions of beauty; or (b) in an effort to avoid this outcome we make aesthetic judgments subservient to other forms of valuation, such as moral evaluation. In the case of (b), according to Parsons, aesthetic considerations become mere "rhetorical" props for more basic kinds of valuation.[6] That is not necessarily a bad thing, but the champion of aesthetic valuation might have been hoping for something a little more substantive. In any case, option (b) is surely better than option (a), because of the possibility illustrated in the example just considered.

Perhaps we should simply give up on the notion that one kind of valuation is paramount. In other words, we should reject the idea that there is one basic and many non-basic forms of valuation when it comes to nature generally and species diversity more particularly. Why not be open-minded and pluralistic when it comes to valuing biodiversity? There are many ways to value species: economic, cultural, spiritual, aesthetic, philosophical, scientific and so on. And such values emerge from a large variety of groups: academic researchers, aboriginal groups, recreational enthusiasts, economists, policy makers, religious organizations, ordinary citizens and more. The more of these values we can invoke in the job of nature preservation the stronger will be the case for adopting the precautionary principle (PP) in this area.

In any case, with respect to minimizing the damage anthropogenic climate change is doing to nature many of the values just listed could converge on a single solution in the short term: as Sandler puts it, "mitigate, mitigate, mitigate."[7] However, since we are not doing this with the requisite urgency, in the longer term assisting species in adapting to climate change is both important and inevitable. Having examined why such assistance might be important – i.e., because it expresses our commitments to the value of non-human life, however this is expressed – let's focus on the more difficult claim that it is "inevitable." We begin with some geological stage-setting.

The Anthropocene

Climate change is unfolding against epoch-defining alterations in the planet's basic workings. We are re-ordering the biosphere. This insight was made possible by the rise and development of Earth system science, beginning in the 1970s. A key event here is the establishment, in 1986, of the International Geosphere-Biosphere Program. Its mandate was to:

> describe and understand the interactive physical, chemical, and biological processes that regulate the total Earth system, the unique environment it provides for life, the changes that are occurring in that system, and the manner in which these changes are influenced by human actions.[8]

The idea that we are now dealing with a single, massively complex system and that human actions have the potential to disrupt this system in discernible and lasting ways provided the impetus for the eventual proposal, first put forward by the scientist Paul Crutzen in 2000, that we have entered a new geological epoch: the Anthropocene. There is as yet no official declaration from scientists that we are in the new epoch, but the idea has spread remarkably quickly through the social sciences and humanities.

When we talk about entering a new epoch, we are speaking the language of geology, specifically stratigraphy or the study of the earth's sedimentary rock layers. Geologists understand the history of the planet as a series of ever-shorter and more fine-grained demarcations, represented in the **Geologic Time Scale**. The key way in which these demarcations are made is by noticing changes in the composition of rock from one stratum to the next. For example if at a certain place in the strata the composition of fossils changes dramatically this likely indicates a mass extinction event, the kind of thing that can radically alter the whole biosphere. Such an alteration may call for a new epoch.

The series begins with eons, proceeding next to eras, periods, epochs and ages. The later terms are nestled within the earlier ones. For example, we are just coming out of the Holocene epoch, which began about 11,700 years ago. The Holocene, in turn, is contained within the Quaternary period and itself contains a number of ages. So from the standpoint of stratigraphical analysis, to say that we have entered the Anthropocene is to claim that humans (the "anthropos" of the Anthropocene) are now laying down traces of their presence in the crust of the earth. Even if we were to become extinct within, say, the next 500 years, these traces – visible in the accumulation of plastics, fuel ash particles, carbon dioxide and methane concentrations, the radio carbon bomb spike and more – could in principle be detected by an alien geologist from the far future analyzing the stratum of earth rock dating from roughly the middle of the 20th century.

From the standpoint of climate change ethics, it is important not to get too distracted by the purely stratigraphical aspect of this phenomenon. Rather, we need to appreciate the ethical implications of the claim that "the earth system as a whole [is] being qualitatively transformed by human action."[9] Why? Because among other things, ethics is about responding appropriately to risks, and, as Sunstein notes, "risks are parts of systems."[10] We therefore need to be aware of how our actions reverberate throughout the larger systems in which they have become enmeshed. From our standpoint the key message of the Anthropocene is that humans have become responsible for the *whole Earth system*. To appreciate how momentous this is, think of it in the context of our historically evolving understanding about how we fit into the larger cosmic order.

Prior to the modern period (circa 1600) we thought of the earth as the center of the solar system. This was geocentrism, a synthesis of the views of the Greek philosopher Aristotle (384–322 BCE) and the Alexandrian astronomer Ptolemy (100–168 CE). It was culturally dominant in the ancient Greek and Roman worlds and throughout most of the Christian period in the West. The notion was especially amenable to the Christian Church because it accorded so well with the biblical emphasis on the special place of humans in the larger Creation. We were, on this conception, the most important part of the divinely created order and so our planet had to be literally at the center of things. All of this changed when Copernicus (1473–1543) discovered that the heavenly bodies revolve around the sun, and that heliocentrism is thus the correct astronomical theory.

These events might seem a long way from the concerns of environmentalists, but there is a sense in which contemporary environmental awareness is one of many late cultural offshoots of the "Copernican Revolution." For what Copernicus did, most fundamentally, is unseat humanity from its elevated position in the cosmos. The sort of environmental concern that emerges in the 1960s – and that is reflected to a large extent in the field of environmental ethics – is thus "Copernican" because it is aimed in the first place at putting humans in their place vis-à-vis the rest of the biosphere. It is premised on the notion that we humans are a part of a larger natural order and that the most pressing ethical task is to find our appropriate place in this larger order, not to simply dominate and exploit it. As with the original Copernican Revolution, it is thus an attempt to infuse our understanding of our place in the whole – whether the cosmos or the biosphere – with a measure of humility.

But wait! Doesn't the very idea of the Anthropocene fly in the face of this evolving self-understanding? Aren't we now saying that we humans are, in effect, the center of the Earth system? Isn't the Anthropocene therefore a "pre-Copernican" throwback? We need to be very careful here. To recognize that we have entered a new epoch defined by the human impact on the Earth system is not necessarily to adopt an attitude of arrogance about the place of humans in the whole. We'll come back to this point in what follows but for now it will suffice to underline a single basic claim. It is this: we cannot help but shape the Earth system now, so the only remaining question is whether we do so with purpose or haphazardly.

Climate change is a shining example of haphazard shaping. The effects we are having on the planet's flora and fauna are the unintended consequences of rampant industrialization powered by fossil fuels, but nobody intended this outcome. Let's see what's involved in more purposeful Earth system shaping.

Activist preservationism

Perhaps the most dramatic discovery our hypothetical alien geologist would make is the sharp alteration in the fossil record between our time and what came before. As we have seen (in Chapter 1), we are facing a biodiversity crisis so grave that it rivals the five previous mass extinction events in potential scope. Some have proposed responding to this crisis by actively intervening in ecosystems to save them and the species making them up.

Compare this stance to the one that dominated our thinking about species preservation previously, the notion at work in the national park systems of Canada and the U.S. for instance. Here, the idea was to create a space apart from the human sphere, a space in which plants and animals could be left alone to flourish on their own terms, protected from the most destructive forms of human influence. The idea was that the interests of species will be best served by our leaving the places they inhabit alone as much as we can.

In the new epoch, this *laissez-faire* model of preservation is obsolete. As Ronald Sandler has noted, climate change is intensifying the threats to biodiversity even as it undermines the manner in which we have traditionally dealt with such threats:

> Place-based preservation strategies depend upon the relative stability of background climatic and ecological conditions. Global climate change disrupts that stability. To the extent that it does so in a particular location, place-based preservation strategies for the at-risk species that are there are less viable. They cannot preserve the species' form of life in their ecological context.[11]

In response to this new reality, we have come to realize that we sometimes need to intervene directly in ecosystems to save their constituent members. Ecologists have expressed the commitment to reshaping the biosphere in this context through the following novel preservation strategies:

- Assisted migration: moving populations from one place to another.
- Rewilding: assisted colonization of multiple species to a new place in order to make it "wilder." This often involves re-introduction of predator or keystone species.

- Ecosystem engineering: restoring whole ecosystems to some previous historical baseline state.
- Conservation cloning: cloning a species in order to conserve it.
- De-extinction: cloning extinct species from extant DNA.
- Facilitated genetic adaptation: altering a species' genetic make-up to assist it in adapting to the effects of climate change.[12]

These are all examples of what we might call **activist preservationism (AP)**. We will examine one AP scheme – facilitated genetic adaptation – more carefully later in the chapter, but for now it is important simply to note what they all represent. Proposing them as options for preservation policy is at least an implicit recognition that we are indeed in the Anthropocene, and that we had better learn how to become more conscious and conscientious designers of the biosphere.

Now, although they are by definition aimed at preserving species, we cannot dismiss the possibility that AP strategies will also create harms to the biosphere. For example, if we assist a species in migration, perhaps placing it further north because its existing habitat has become too hot, it may out-compete native species for scarce resources. If this leads to the extirpation of the native species, we have effectively made the decision that the introduced species is more important than the native one. On what basis? Similar challenges and dilemmas arise for the other strategies. For example, if we get sufficiently good at de-extinction we will have to decide where to put these re-animated plants and animals. The biosphere is crowded, resources are scarce and ecosystems are relatively closed networks of energy transfer.

So with AP we are proposing to redesign large parts of the biosphere as a response to climate change but this will inevitably have its casualties. This fact challenges us to be specific about the values we are defending in the choices we make. However, even if there were no casualties of AP, in this sense, it does not follow that the strategies come with no moral cost. In an influential early treatment of this issue, Robert Elliot argues that we have reason to oppose the "faking" of nature involved in nature restoration projects even where there are no overt harms to other species. The analogy Elliot uses is that of a forged artwork. Suppose you were under the impression that the painting you own is an original Vermeer, when in fact it is an exact replica. Setting aside the issue that you probably paid too much for the forgery, in what sense have you been harmed if nobody, including you, ever finds out that your painting is a fake?

Elliot claims that the two pieces of art – the original and the forgery – having distinct provenances matters immensely. What you value about your painting is, among other things, what you take to be the history of its coming to be in a certain way, namely by the hand of Vermeer. If this is right then the forgery is, as a matter of fact, less valuable than the original. Similarly, "faking nature" by re-shaping it in the ways suggested involves altering the history of places and species in a way that might cheapen the value of what is created. If one of the things we value most about nature is how it came to be the way it is – expressed in a story about the long evolutionary pathways of its places and species – then replacing this with a new origin story represents a loss.[13]

If we take worries about faking nature seriously, our response might be to reject all forms of AP. The philosophical rationale for this approach is that it is morally better just to let nature be, whatever the costs of doing so. Elliot gives us one way of grounding this kind of claim, but his argument is mainly about the aesthetic values that are lost in faking nature. Is there a way of grounding our assessment of AP that is more centrally about morality?

Two moral doctrines

In fact there are two. The first is the **doctrine of double effect (DDE)**, the second the DDA, which we have already put to work in our discussion of Woollard's analysis of the non-identity problem. The DDE attempts to ground the claim that AP is permissible, while the DDA aims to produce the opposite result. As we will see, neither effort is wholly successful.

The doctrine of double effect (DDE)

The DDE has its roots in Catholic moral theory but there is nothing intrinsically theological about it. The idea is that there is a fundamental distinction between what an agent intends to do and what comes about as an unintended but foreseeable consequence of what she does. All else being equal, it may be permissible to bring about an unintended but foreseeable state of affairs, although it would be impermissible to intend directly to bring about that state of affairs. Is this a well-founded principle? It seems so. The DDE is sometimes invoked as a way of justifying civilian casualties in war. Whereas it is impermissible to intend to kill civilians (to make this the *aim* of military actions, whether as an end or a means), it may be permissible to kill civilians so long as this is a merely foreseen side effect of some other action.

Since some will argue that it is never permissible to kill civilians in war, think instead of one way of responding to the famous trolley problem. A trolley is coming down the tracks and will kill five people who are tied to the tracks just down the line. You can pull a switch that will divert the trolley onto a different track, thus saving the five people. Unfortunately, one person is tied to the track onto which you divert the train and she will be killed as a result of your action. Are you permitted to pull the switch? Many people say that you are because, whereas you can foresee that one person will die on account of your action, you do not intend that person's death. It is a foreseeable but unintended side effect of your action, an action moreover that is aimed at something good (saving five lives).

But is it not implausible in this case to say that we do *not* intend the otherwise prohibited action, the death we cause? The death just seems so *close* to the action we take that surely the only honest way to describe the situation is to say that we *intend* it. Shouldn't the DDE itself therefore prohibit the action? Let's consider a final example, one that is meant to help deal with this problem. Suppose you are with a group of people trapped in a room that is filling with deadly carbon monoxide. The largest person in your group is stuck in the only door, thus preventing everyone else's escape. It looks as though according to the DDE you should *not* dynamite the door since there is no way to interpret this action as anything but the intentional killing of the large person (this is the problem of closeness). But what if you could dynamite an opening *just beside* the large person, and in this way free yourself and your companions while also killing the large person? Here it looks like the DDE would allow the action because although it is close to the man in the door, the new hole is far enough away from him that it becomes plausible to say that his death is foreseen but unintended.

Now, we might say that AP is on a moral par with killing civilians in war or diverting the trolley to kill the one person. AP will cause foreseeable harms but in resorting to it we are not intending to produce these harms. But as we have just seen, there may be problems with describing as unintentional the actions involved in the trolley and civilian casualties cases. So it is the final example – blowing a hole in the wall *near* the man in the door – that seems most pertinent to AP. This is because for the most part the harms AP causes are close, but not *too* close, to the actions that cause them. If we relocate a threatened species, for example, it can take years for harmful knock-on effects to appear in the new habitat. AP is therefore permissible for the same reason that it is arguably permissible to blow a hole near the large person to save everyone else in the room. If we think the DDE is a sound doctrine, and that it fits AP on analogy with the man in the door, then AP looks like a justified environmental practice.

But is it a sound doctrine? The *intentions* of moral agents bear a heavy justificatory load in this doctrine and we might be suspicious about that. From the standpoint of an agent's moral responsibility for a harmful state of affairs, isn't the more important consideration whether or not she was part of a causal chain that helped bring about the state of affairs? It might be suggested that the ethically basic question is simply whether or not an agent caused, or helped to cause, a harmful state of affairs to obtain. For instance, with respect to any harmful state of affairs we can ask if the agent helped produce it or simply allowed it to happen. Answering this question in any particular case requires no appeal to the agent's intentions. If this type of consideration causes us to reject the DDE, then the latter will not ground a judgment of permissibility for AP. Is there a reason to jump directly to the other possibility, and declare AP *im*permissible?

The doctrine of doing and allowing (DDA)

This question brings us to the DDA, according to which it is worse to cause a harmful state of affairs than to allow it to happen. As with the DDE, the doctrine does appear to be a well-founded piece of commonsense morality, so we should take it seriously. As we saw in the previous chapter it is, for instance, at the heart of a commitment adopted by many opposing active euthanasia ("killing") while allowing for passive euthanasia ("letting die").

It is a fairly straightforward matter to see how the DDA can be applied to our issue. Climate change, as we encounter it now, is an ongoing causal sequence that will produce a certain harmful state of affairs. The decision to deploy certain AP strategies, by contrast, represents an active initiation of a causal sequence that will also produce a specific harmful state of affairs (among other things, including beneficial states of affairs). So AP is a doing while climate change is an allowing. If the choice is between AP and allowing unabated climate change to wreak havoc on non-human species and ecosystems, we are morally required to refrain from AP.

The argument is not obviously implausible. It does not tell us that we should cease combatting climate change altogether, for example. Presumably, we should engage in appropriate mitigation actions to lessen the harmful effects of climate change down the road. But we cannot rely on AP to help us save species in the event of a climatic emergency. Even so, there are at least two significant problems with the argument. First, why characterize climate change as an "allowing" rather than a "doing"? It is true that the current generation is not in the process of initiating climate change in the clear-cut way in which we might decide to initiate a program of AP. The roots of the climate crisis reach deep into the past and most of us have simply inherited a way of going about our lives that is, as it happens, leading to planetary calamity.

This can make it look as though we are, with respect to climate change, passive in the sense of that term relevant to the DDA. But this is surely false. Our decision to continue burning fossil fuels at current rates and to engage in unsustainable land use practices does bring about future states of affairs for which we appear to be morally responsible. After all, if we refrained from acting in these ways a different, and less harmful, future state of affairs would thereby likely be produced. If anything is clear from the failure to act meaningfully to combat climate change since 1988 it is that we are active agents in the production of harmful states of affairs. Of course, it is crucial to be precise about how this "we" is constituted. Not everyone is equally blameworthy for production of the relevant harms (as we discovered in Chapter 4).

Second, if generalized in such a way that it becomes a guiding principle of public policy the DDA is probably too restrictive. Consider an analogy put forward by Brian Berkey. A government is deciding whether or not to redistribute taxation to reduce poverty. It can (a) refuse to do so and allow the economy to take its "natural" course, the result of which is that a large number of people are impoverished; or (b) redistribute aggressively, the result of which is that fewer people are impoverished, while the richest people are economically harmed. Assume for the sake of argument that the harms are roughly equal in either case (though this is probably unrealistic). According to Berkey, the DDA, applied in the way we have been doing so far, would prohibit option (b) and counsel option (a).

Importantly, the government is not blameworthy for the higher level of poverty this would produce since, by hypothesis, it has merely allowed this to occur rather than doing it. Berkey's conclusion is compelling:

> These implications are, it seems to me, unacceptable. The state is no less responsible for the avoidable poverty that exists when it chooses a policy of non-redistribution than it is for similar poverty that exists as a result of its choice of a redistributive policy. Policy making ought to be guided by the aim of establishing background conditions that best promote the values underlying principles of justice, regardless of whether the policies that do so involve state action or inaction.[14]

What makes the two cases – AP and redistributive taxation – analogous is that although both are aimed at producing good consequences, they will also likely produce some harm. The DDA prohibits the state from ever being an *agent* of harm in such cases, even where the harm is outweighed by good consequences. That really does appear to be too restrictive.

Our consideration of the DDE and the DDA has left the moral status of AP somewhat in the air. While the DDE tries to show that AP is permissible and the DDA that it is impermissible, both positions have serious flaws. But whatever we think about these arguments, there are those who believe we humans now have moral *carte blanche* to redesign the atmosphere as we see fit. It is time to confront this set of attitudes.

Ecomodernism

Such enthusiasts come in different guises: the "ecomodernists," "ecopragmatists," or advocates of the "good Anthropocene." For simplicity, let's refer to them all as ecomodernists. What they have in common is the cheerful view that the Anthropocene heralds a new Enlightenment for humanity, a chance to imprint nature fully with human purposes, to recreate it technologically in the image of our best self-conception. It is an opportunity not a calamity. Erle Ellis, for example, has argued that humans have always been responsible "stewards of the biosphere," and that the Anthropocene finally gives us the chance to extend our essentially benevolent influence to the entire Earth system.[15]

Ecomodernism's critics, in turn, are worried that widespread adoption of the term "Anthropocene" will reinstate human arrogance towards the natural order. We can certainly appreciate this worry when confronted by the eco-modernist's smiling assessment of our current situation. Can such people really be so blind to all that is dark and problematic about a single species – one moreover of dubious moral competence, judging by the last hundred years or so of its history – now working the levers of the entire Earth system? In the interpretation of it offered by ecomodernism the Anthropocene looks like a cancellation or negation of the humility at the heart of the ethical approach to nature that has, as we saw earlier in the chapter, been developing for the past 50 years or so. Better to just ditch the whole idea of the Anthropocene if it invites this sort of hubris.

But this is to throw the baby out with the bathwater. For we can retain the idea that we have entered the Anthropocene without believing that there is anything intrinsically good about this. The ecomodernist belief that it *is* good is based on the assumption that we now have – or can at least aspire to have – control of the Earth system, so that we can make it over in accordance with our highest ideals. This confuses power and control. Although we now have more power than ever before – this is the central message of the Anthropocene – we have very little ability to predict or control the Earth system over whose workings we are exerting so much power. This is a crucial point.[16] Let's reflect on it a little more carefully.

Systems theorists have alerted us to the existence of "wickedly complex" systems. Wicked complexity refers to extreme interdependency among the elements of a system. Consider an example. Recent research has revealed that climate change will likely lead to a marked increase in eutrophication, the process by which oxygen-starved dead zones are created in large bodies of water. Here's how it works. CO_2 emissions lead to higher air temperatures; this increases evaporation, which alters precipitation patterns, causing, in some areas, much heavier rainfalls; in these areas the rate at which nitrogen is washed from agricultural fields into major waterways increases; the added nitrogen causes blooms of algae; the algae's decomposers consume the water's oxygen; finally, other oxygen-dependent species are potentially killed off. The problem is likely to be pronounced in the corn belt of the U.S., but also in India, China, and southeast Asia.[17]

The key here, and in the Anthropocene more generally, is the *entanglement* of human and biogeophysical systems. It can be very difficult to grasp the ethically salient connections, but they are there in abundance. For instance, the discovery regarding increased eutrophication means that the decision of someone living in Perth to buy corn-based products originating in Iowa or basmati rice grown in India is connected to so many other events in the Earth system, including, potentially, both the extirpation of some marine species half way around the world and the impoverishment of the humans that depend on this species for food. That is wicked complexity. It *cannot* be controlled, but it can be approached in a spirit of humility and ethical responsibility.

What, at bottom, is the difference between ecomodernists and advocates of AP? Both are proponents of intervening actively in nature through the use of various technologies. The difference is that AP does not necessarily express arrogance and hubris, whereas ecomodernism necessarily does. This point forces us to expand our understanding of the person we are calling "the advocate of AP." AP is a constellation of technology-enabled environmental practices, which as such might of course be pursued in the arrogant manner of the ecomodernist. The point here is that while an ecomodernist can also be an advocate of AP, the latter's more responsible advocates are much more apt to recognize the inherent limitations of the practices. By contrast, although they claim to recognize the scope of the challenges we face with a phenomenon like climate change, the ecomodernists are often absurdly optimistic about our capacity to meet these challenges so long as we leave technology and the market free to work their magic. There are two basic errors here.

The first is an inability to appreciate the sort of natural complexity that defines ecosystems. In this regard, the ecomodernists are dangerously ignorant of the science of ecology. The second is a tendency to forget about the extent to which the climate challenge is fundamentally political. According to Clive Hamilton, this second error is closely connected to the ecomodernist's unwarranted belief in the techno-fix (most of them are big boosters of the nuclear industry, for example):

> For the ecomoderns, the story of the past and the story of the future revolve around one thing: "Meaningful climate mitigation is fundamentally a technological challenge." It's an entire historiography in which the human relationship to the natural world depends essentially on human ingenuity and entrepreneurship. It is not kings, presidents, proletarians or generals who make history – but rather scientists, inventors and engineers, and it is they who will save us.[18]

Remove the regulatory shackles currently binding the engineers and the positive results will flow freely, assisted of course by an equally unfettered flow of capital. Because we live in a world of skewed opportunities and vulnerabilities, this is a politically naïve position. Because of it, ecomodernists have played right into the hands of climate change deniers, many of whom now style themselves ecomodernists. This convergence is not accidental: both groups – ecomodernists and climate deniers – view environmentalists as their primary opponents.

So, let's speak of the "responsible advocate of AP" in order to distinguish this person clearly from the ecomodernist. We can engage in AP out of a deep respect for natural processes. We can seek to keep our technological interventions to the minimum required to preserve biodiversity in some place (for example). We can back off if we judge that our technologies might be going too far. And, of course, we recognize that we can do all of this only against the backdrop of a politics deeply informed by considerations of justice. The ecomodernist is not constrained in any of these ways.

Coming back to a worry expressed earlier in the chapter, if we bear in mind the point that we cannot control the Earth system, we should not think that the Anthropocene necessarily takes us back to a pre-modern, pre-Copernican, understanding of our place in the whole. In other words, we should not balk at the purely scientific claim that we are now in the Anthropocene. This claim is merely descriptive. By itself it has no implications about what we should do in the face of this new reality, nor does it imply that there is something morally good about our new status in the Earth system. These are normative claims or questions and as such the science has little direct bearing on them. To announce the advent of the Anthropocene is not necessarily to celebrate its coming. We might instead bemoan and regret it, but also recognize that it brings with it new moral challenges.

Otherwise put, and against ecomodernist triumphalism, we should stress that many of our environmental policy choices in the age of climate change are going to be *tragic*. They will involve irreducible loss. We are probably stuck with being active interveners in the natural order on a scale significant enough to change evolutionary pathways. It is morally important to accept this task in a spirit of humility and respect for nature rather than with arrogance and hubris. Whichever attitude we ultimately adopt, however, all of this raises another key question: is "nature" as something independent of the human effectively dead?

The end of nature

Saving some species and ecosystems will place others at risk. That is bad enough. But in this section we will focus on an additional source of potentially tragic conflict, one between the value of wilderness preservation and that of species preservation. This is a conflict of values. It is easy to state in the abstract: protecting this or that species from the ravages of climate change obviously requires intervention into natural processes but this reduces or even eliminates the "otherness" of nature, its "wild" independence of the human. Does saving species entail losing wilderness in this sense of the term? To address this question we will focus on a single preservationist strategy: the genetic adaptation of species aimed at insulating the stock from certain climate change induced threats.

What exactly do we mean by the "wild"? The concept is intimately connected to that of "nature." Both terms have come to be understood as that which is independent of the human.[19] This formulation need not be taken to deny that humans are a part of nature, only that there is a whole sphere of happenings in the biosphere that has little if anything to do with us. The horseshoe crab has been living at the bottom of the ocean for some 300 million years. In that time, it has gone about its business entirely unaffected by our schemes. In this deflated sense of the term, there seems to be nothing to object to in the notion of nature as that which is independent of the human. But there's a problem here. After all, in acidifying and heating the oceans by loading the atmosphere with CO_2, have we not in fact cancelled the "otherness" of the horseshoe crab? Its habitat is now, in some measure, a human construct.

Generalizing from examples like this, many now speak of the end of nature, of wilderness as something that is effectively dead. Steven Vogel is the most articulate philosophical spokesman for this view. According to Vogel, we need to recognize that we live in a "postnatural" world and that this has implications for how we do environmental philosophy and ethics. There has been a tendency in Western culture generally to insist on a separation of the products of culture and the things of nature. Cultural products, in this view, are seen as superior to natural things. In one of its strains, environmental philosophy simply inverts this value judgment without abolishing the fundamental distinction that underlies it, the one between culture and nature. Contrary to the traditional view, nature now becomes the normative standard *for* the cultural. For example, the commonplace suggestion that industrialization and urbanization have cut us off from nature and that to regain what we have lost we need to reestablish our "connection" to the natural world relies on this understanding of the key terms. This idea is the basis of the notion that we now suffer from "nature deficit disorder."

Vogel rejects this understanding of nature. His reason for doing so is not just that, as a matter of empirical fact, nothing is really human-independent now because anthropogenic climate change has altered the planet's basic chemistry (as we saw with our humble horseshoe crab). Just as importantly, the "natural" has never been a proper normative standard for us. The form of argument sketched above – that nature can be used as a *standard* for critiquing certain aspects of human culture or behavior – overlooks the fact that nature is rather nasty (red in tooth and claw). It is also a typical move for cultural conservatives to make. Slavery, for example, has been defended on the basis that some races are said to be "naturally" inferior to others. The same sort of claim has been made to deny rights to homosexuals and women.

Vogel therefore thinks we would be better off without the concept of nature.[20] We can still do environmental philosophy and ethics but only if we reject the distinction between what is built and what is natural and instead conceptualize all of reality as a *built environment*. In this case, the only question left to ask is whether or not what we make has been well built or poorly built. Some of this is undeniably compelling. For reasons that should be obvious, Vogel presents a view of reality – and of philosophy and ethics – that is eminently well-suited to our self-understanding in the Anthropocene. The new epoch is defined by the breakdown of a sharp distinction between the things of culture and the things of nature. However, Vogel himself is quite vague about how we can go on employing the distinction between good and bad building that, he thinks, we still require.

What is it to make or build *well* in the postnatural Anthropocene? This is a large question and we don't need to answer it comprehensively, but here's a suggestion. So far we have been assuming that there's no real distinction between "nature" and the "wild." But what if we say instead that postnature might allow some place for wilderness? Assuming that wilderness preservation is a good thing, we will in that case have provided one example of a practice that can produce well-built environments. So what is wilderness? Clare Palmer provides a useful analysis of the concept, and also addresses the question about whether species preservation and wilderness protection are necessarily at odds in the age of climate change. Let's look briefly at her analysis.

Palmer examines one strategy of species preservation, genetic adaptation of animals to help them cope with the effects of climate change on their habitats. We have seen (in Chapter 1) that one of the ways in which animals are responding to increased temperatures is by moving north or upwards into alpine regions (where these are available). But species may not be able to move as quickly as isotherms (temperature zones) are. James Hansen has shown that the average speed of migration was about 4 miles per decade in the second half of the 20th century, but that isotherms have been moving at about 35 miles per decade in this period. He predicts that the speed of isotherm movement could double by the end of this century.[21]

In the face of this onslaught it will not always be possible to assist species to migrate elsewhere, to say nothing of the dim possibility that species might accomplish this without our assistance. But what if some form of "genetic rescue" were technically feasible for a population facing extirpation? What if they could be made more tolerant to heat, for example? Are there any ethical issues with this kind of manipulation? In particular should we object to such strategies on account of their interference with wilderness? Palmer thinks not, that in many cases we can preserve species from the ravages of climate change through genetic adaptation while leaving them relatively wild.

Focusing just on animals, there are three aspects of the concept of wildness with which Palmer is working here: (a) "dispositional wildness," which refers to non-tameness, usually cashed out in terms of fear of or aggressiveness towards humans; (b) "self-willed wildness," the notion that these animals are free from human control or manipulation; and (c) "constitutive wildness," referring to non-domestication. Now, genetic adaptation is clearly no threat to (a) or (c). The goal is neither to tame nor domesticate species. But it does seem to affect (b). That is, the genetic rescue of these animals "does compromise wildness understood as the absence of intentional human influence on the location, shape, and design of beings and places."[22] Even so, the impact is minimal because the animals are not being modified to suit human purposes. To the contrary, the point is simply to make them better able to do what they were already doing but would not have been able to continue doing given the climate-altered landscape they now inhabit.

The question whether this form of AP is morally permissible becomes more urgent if we insist on doing ethics in a non-ideal manner in this area, because in this case we must always compare our choices with feasible options. For the species we are considering, the only other option is extinction or extirpation. Surely, it is permissible to compromise to some extent the value we place on leaving wilderness untrammeled if in doing so we are saving species from this fate. Though the details and differences matter, this conclusion should be generalizable to all AP strategies. Indeed, it can serve as one test for the ethical permissibility of any AP proposal.

The insight provided by this example gives us a way to think critically about Vogel's postnaturalism. We can agree with him that when we do environmental ethics we should be thinking mostly in terms of how to build the world well, but add that *one* measure of such building is the extent to which we allow for wildness, in Palmer's sense of this term, to flourish. That way, we can minimize the conflict between two values that clearly matter to us: wilderness protection and species preservation. These are the kinds of conflicts climate change foists on us. They do not appear to allow for utopian or ideal resolution.

Chapter summary

We have now entered the Anthropocene, a fact which means that we must think of ourselves as responsible for the whole Earth system. This is the context in which we must think of what anthropogenic climate change is doing to nature. We began the chapter with some reflections on the value of species. After laying out the general features of the Anthropocene, we next examined the ethics of protecting biodiversity in the age of climate change, focusing on various strategies of AP. This was followed by a look at two ways of thinking about the permissibility (or lack of it) of AP, grounded in the DDE and DDA. Next, we subjected "eco-modernism to critical scrutiny, making a careful distinction between it and the more humble attitude allowed for by AP. This brought us, finally, to an assessment of the "end of nature thesis" now popular with some environmental philosophers.

Questions for discussion

1 What is the ethical significance of the claim that we have entered a new epoch, the Anthropocene?
2 Do you agree with the ecomodernists that the Anthropocene presents us with the opportunity to realize our dreams of planetary control?
3 Have we reached the end of nature? What exactly does this mean and is the claim warranted?
4 Explain the various ways we have of valuing nature, especially species diversity. Does any one of them have priority over the others? Why or why not?

5   Does the preservationist's dilemma force us to question the point or power of aesthetic valuation in our choices? Would you agree with the claim that such valuation is at best rhetorical?

Suggested reading

Clive Hamilton, *Defiant Earth: The Fate of Humans in the Anthropocene* (London: Polity, 2017). A clearly written synthesis of the science and social science of the Anthropocene. Very accessible.

Dale Moellendorf, *The Moral Challenge of Dangerous Climate Change: Values, Poverty, and Policy* (Cambridge, MA, 2014), chapter 2. A spirited defence of aesthetic valuation applied to the problem of biodiversity protection.

Clare Palmer, "Saving Species but Losing Wildness: Should We Genetically Adapt Wild Animal Species to Help Them Respond to Climate Change?" *Midwest Studies in Philosophy* XL, 2016, 234–251. Excellent analysis of the ethics of facilitated genetic adaptation.

Notes

1   Dale Jamieson, *Ethics and the Environment* (Cambridge: Cambridge University Press, 2008), 74.
2   Stephen J. Gould, "What is a Species?" *Discover Magazine* (December, 1992).
3   Byron Williston (ed.), *Environmental Ethics for Canadians*, second edition (Don Mills: Oxford University Press), 346–347.
4   Darrel Moellendorf, *The Moral Challenge of Dangerous Climate Change: Values, Poverty, and Policy* (New York:Cambridge University Press, 2014), 52–53.
5   Williston, *Environmental Ethics...*, 202.
6   Glenn Parsons, "Aesthetic Weight and the Preservationist's Dilemma," in Byron Williston (ed.) *Environmental Ethics...*, 195–201 (201).
7   Ronald L. Sandler, "Global Climate Change and Species Preservation," in Byron Williston (ed.) *Environmental Ethics...*, 358–365 (365).
8   Quoted in Ian Angus, *Facing the Anthropocene: Fossil Capitalism and the Crisis of the Earth System* (New York: Monthly Review Press, 2016), 30–31.
9   Angus, *Facing the Anthropocene...*, 33.
10 Cass Sunstein, *The Laws of Fear: Beyond the Precautionary Principle* (Cambridge: Cambridge University Press, 2015), 47.
11 Sandler, "Global Climate Change...," 359.
12 Sandler, "Global Climate Change...," 360–361.
13 Robert Elliot, "Faking Nature," in Robert Elliot (ed.) *Environmental Ethics* (Oxford: Oxford University Press, 1995), 76–88.
14 Brian Berkey. "State Action, State Policy, and the Doing/Allowing Distinction." *Ethics, Policy and the Environment* 17(2), 2014, 147–149 (149).
15 Quoted in Clive Hamilton, *Defiant Earth: The Fate of Humans in the Anthropocene* (London: Polity, 2017), 15.
16 Byron Williston, *The Anthropocene Project: Virtue in the Age of Climate Change* (Oxford: Oxford University Press, 2015), chapter 2.
17 E. Sinha, A.M. Michaluk, V. Balaji, et al., "Eutrophication will increase during the 21st century as a result of precipitation changes." *Science* 357 (6349), July 28, 2017, 405–408.
18 Clive Hamilton, "The Techno-fix is in: A Critique of 'An Ecomodernist Manifesto.'" April 28, 2015. At: http://clivehamilton.com/the-technofix-is-in-a-critique-of-an-ecomodernist-manifesto/. Accessed January 30, 2018.

19 See Steven Vogel, *Thinking Like a Mall: Environmental Philosophy after the End of Nature* (Cambridge, MA: MIT Press, 2015), 9.

20 Vogel, *Thinking Like a Mall...*, chapter 1.

21 James Hansen, *Storms of My Grandchildren* (New York: Bloomsbury, 2009), 146.

22 Clare Palmer, "Saving Species but Losing Wildness: Should We Genetically Adapt Wild Animal Species to Help Them Respond to Climate Change?" *Midwest Studies in Philosophy* XL, 2016, 234–251 (249).

7 Individual duties

Introduction

Everything we have said so far about justice – both international and intergenerational – was focused on what collectives should do about climate change. We have been asking, for example, what a just distribution of the remaining carbon budget *among countries* looks like. That leaves untouched a large domain of philosophical inquiry: individual duties of climate justice. In this chapter we will address this topic. We begin by locating it in the inescapable context of collective action problems. In an effort to understand the psychological dynamics that make those situations go awry so often, we look at the idea any individual might have that his or her contributions to the problem are "negligible." We will attempt to find a way around this very compelling thought, first by showing how to moralize the small consumption choices we make all the time; and second, by turning to a virtue-ethical analysis of the problem. This will bring us to a direct consideration of what individuals should do in our non-ideal situation. We examine two options: (a) working for meaningful institutional change; and (b) carbon offsetting.

The prisoner's dilemma

In Chapters 4 and 5 we saw how our failure to find a just solution to the problem of climate change – internationally and intergenerationally – can be understood on the model of the tragedy of the commons. A similar problem haunts individual behaviors, though here the **prisoner's dilemma** is a better trope. We can see why this is so by looking again at the structure of collective action problems in the abstract.

A collection of agents is engaged in some enterprise that requires the cooperation of all, or *nearly* all, members. Such cooperation involves *restraint* on the part of each. In the short term this can look like a pure cost to the agent: she gets less now than she would if she had acted purely out of self-interest. But she also recognizes that not everyone can act on the basis of self-interest because the result of *that* would be contrary to everyone's interest. It is therefore collectively rational for all members to abide by the rules in order to achieve the optimal outcome. But each agent also has a powerful individual incentive to defect from the cooperative effort, to leave the pack. This is because of the "nearly" qualifier just mentioned. Each agent can reason that he will achieve the best outcome for himself if he defects from the group while the others do not. That way, he will gain the benefits of both cooperation and of non-cooperation. This is the so-called free-rider problem.

However, worried that other members of the group will become free-riders, the cooperative effort is undermined resulting in the production of what economists call sub-optimal outcomes. This problem affects even those who are very worried about such outcomes. I might care a great deal about climate change and realize that if everyone, say, switched to electric vehicles a big part of the problem would be solved. But I'm unlikely to act in this way if I believe there are too many others who will want to carry on driving gas-guzzlers. Electric cars cost more, so wouldn't I be a "sucker" if I bought one while recognizing that not enough others will do the same to alter the climate problem positively? Nobody wants to be a sucker, so nobody makes the positive choice (or not enough do). The result of our collective (in)action, however, is exactly as it is in Jamieson's amended bike-theft example (examined in Chapter 2): lots of people in far away parts of time and space will be deprived of the conditions of a good life by it.

As Jamieson points out, one of the things we need to be able to do in order to come to grips with this problem is to "moralize" apparently innocent actions. As it stands, almost nobody in the developed world feels like they are doing anything wrong in living high-carbon lifestyles. Moreover, many consumption choices are not even linked by consumers themselves to the problem of climate change, though they are in fact feeding it. People might not see the connection between consumer "upgrades" like heated steering wheels in their cars or increased Internet speed at home and a worsening climate. The big question therefore is how to get people to constrain themselves in their seemingly innocent consumer choices for moral reasons, but Jamieson argues convincingly that this "process of moralization is not well understood."[1]

Actually there are two distinct problems here, two reasons for being skeptical about the prospects for successful moralization. The first is that with climate change it really *is* difficult to link individual actions to discernible changes in the climate, let alone to the harms these cause. This is because, as we have seen in Chapter 1, the climate system is so complex. It involves feedbacks, non-linearities and thresholds. Moreover, we have seen that emissions emerge from billions of point sources and can result in harms spread out over the whole global population as well as to people of the future. In between, the emissions get mixed into the carbon cycle in bewilderingly complex ways.

In light of these facts, here is how Jamieson characterizes the key issue about attributing responsibility for climate change harms to individuals:

I, along with many other people, toss an invisible smidgen of something into a blender. A man takes a drink of the resulting mixture. Am I responsible for the graininess of the texture, the chalkiness of the taste, the way it makes him feel after drinking it, his resulting desire for a Budweiser? You might think that I am a smidgen responsible, since a smidgen is the amount that I tossed into the blender. But I am tempted to say that I am not responsible even for a smidgen of the result because there are so many thresholds, non-linearities and scalar differences that intervene between my action and the outcomes.[2]

We might therefore refer to the first problem of moralization as an epistemic one. Blaming people for harm-causing actions depends on drawing a clear line between cause and effect but that is just what we apparently cannot do in the case of the harms of climate change.

The second problem is that, even if we could make the appropriate causal connections and so overcome the epistemic problem, getting people to care about the production of harmful outcomes goes beyond showing them that they are causally responsible for those outcomes. Call this the motivational problem. Here's a somewhat gruesome analogy to help support the point. Suppose a slave-owner were whipping a slave for some trivial misdemeanor. The slave-owner need not be a skeptic about the causal chain beginning with his actions and ending with the pain visited on the slave's body. He would also likely be entirely willing to call this a harm. Perhaps the slave will be unable to work, or even move very much, for several weeks because of the assault. That's a clear harm to both the slave and the slave-owner. But because he considers the slave his property, the slave-owner cannot think that what he is doing is wrong. He doesn't care about the harms he is causing except insofar as they are effective in bending the slave's will to his aims.

The problem, noted by Jamieson, is that for most people morality is not tightly tied to harm. On the one hand, people can get very worked up morally about harmless activities like flag-burning while, on the other hand, they can be unmoved by obviously harmful actions, as with our slave-owner. Jamieson refers to the recent work of psychologists Daniel Gilbert and Jonathan Haidt to show that commonsense morality draws mostly on considerations of fairness and reciprocity, in-group loyalty, as well as purity and sanctity to ground its moral assessments of actions and agents.[3] It seems as though people need to be *offended* by a particular action in order to consider it out of bounds morally, but an action being perceived as merely harm-causing does not entail that it will also be seen as offensive.

We should probably take this point with a grain of salt. Jamieson notes that the psychologists on whom he is leaning here recognize that considerations of harm *are* relevant to commonsense morality, even if they are not the most important consideration. In fact, however, it seems as though they are quite often paramount. The debate in the U.S. about gun control, for example, appears to be focused on the issue of harm-causation. Advocates of tighter restrictions on access to certain weapons point to the harms caused by relatively unlimited access. Those favoring the status quo, by contrast, believe, among other things, that citizens ought to have ready access to these weapons because, if this is denied to them, the government is likelier to harm them. It is true that considerations like these are usually surrounded by appeals to some of the forces Gilbert and Haidt cite – in-group loyalty, most obviously – but the appeal to harm, or potential harm, seems to be primary on both sides.

In addition, there is often a complex interplay between perceptions of harm on the one hand and all the other factors on the other. What we often see in debates like the one about gun control in the U.S. is one side accusing the other of exaggerating the harms that will flow from adoption of their policies. In other words, the forces cited by Gilbert and Haidt bias us in ways that enable misperceptions of the harms that are likely to be caused by specific actions. This is what happens with one kind of climate change denial, for instance. As we will see in the next chapter, in the U.S., many people have become convinced that aggressive action on climate change is some kind of socialist plot, something that threatens "the American way of life," and *because* of this they are inclined to downplay the harms climate change will cause. Here, a specific conception of group loyalty biases agents in ways that distort their beliefs *about harm*. That's a very important psychological move because it testifies to the importance even climate deniers place on harm.

It seems safe to say that both of these problems – the epistemic problem and the motivation problem – reinforce the sub-optimal outcomes of the prisoner's dilemma of consumer behavior faced by people in the developed world. They complicate the issue of moralization. I might refuse to buy an electric vehicle, install solar panels on my roof, buy locally grown produce, purchase offsets, or cut down on my air travel either because I genuinely cannot see what harms these refusals produce or because, though in some sense I see the harms, I don't fully appreciate them because I'm not "offended" by their occurrence. Either way, and as an antidote to these tendencies, we seem justified in focusing on the way our actions *are* genuinely harm-causing.

In particular, it seems intuitively plausible to say that one way to break out of the vicious logic of the prisoner's dilemma is to make those participating in it more keenly aware of the harms their failures might bring about. Put negatively, it makes sense to suppose that the production of sub-optimal outcomes in these scenarios will persist so long as agents are either unaware or insufficiently appreciative of the harms their actions cause. The paradigm example of two prisoners locked in separate interrogation rooms by the police might obscure this to some extent. Each of these imaginary agents seems willing to allow terrible harms to come to the other so long as his own neck is saved. But most of us aren't criminals, driven solely by avarice, so a clear-eyed view of the harms a free-riding course of action can cause to other members of our collective can make the temptation to adopt that course less compelling.

One thing to notice about the epistemic and motivational problems is that they both assume the reality of the relevant harms. It's just that in the one case we have difficulty locating them, while in the other we aren't much moved by them. But, more radically, we might suppose that there are simply no harms worth worrying about here. Walter Sinnott-Armstrong puts the problem this way:

> [We] should not think that we can do enough simply by buying fuel-efficient cars, insulating our houses, and setting up a windmill to make our own electricity. That is all wonderful. But it does little or nothing to stop global warming, and also does not fulfill our real moral obligations, which are to get governments to do their job to prevent the disaster of excessive global warming. It is better to enjoy your Sunday driving while working to change the law so as to make it illegal for you to enjoy your Sunday driving.[4]

There's much to endorse here. For instance, Sinnott-Armstrong is surely correct to stress the importance of getting governments to do the right thing. This should make us work hard to build institutions that take climate change justice seriously. We'll return to this point in this chapter's penultimate section. For now, let's focus on the idea that there's nothing wrong with the "Sunday drive," a handy symbol of unnecessary consumption. It's not wrong, for Sinnott-Armstrong, because nothing we do as individuals can actually alter climatic outcomes, for good or ill. This is sometimes called the "negligibility thesis."

The negligibility thesis

In describing the **negligibility thesis (NT)** metaphors and analogies abound. For example, one often encounters the analogy of multiple agents throwing a brick through a window. More than one of them is required to break it, but not all of them. Or, we are told that the situation with climate change is like the voter's paradox. This problem is the most well-developed, with a whole game theoretical literature devoted to it completely separate from the climate change issue.

The basic idea of the voter's paradox is that because there is a negligible chance that your single vote will swing an election one way or another it is irrational to vote. After all, there is a convenience cost associated with voting – waiting in a long queue at a polling station, for example – that outweighs the miniscule probability that your vote will actually matter in deciding the election's outcome. Best to just stay at home and watch the results on TV. Of course, every individual can think and act this way, and if enough of them do the influence on the election's outcome will not be negligible. This is the paradox: individual acts do and do not matter to the election's outcome.

The person who genuinely doubts that he has a duty to vote because of this argument is appealing implicitly to a definition of morality put forward by Frank Jackson: "the morality of an action depends on the difference it makes; it depends, that is, on what would be the case were the act performed and what would be the case were the act not performed."[5]

In particular, it is not possible to say that any individual's decision to refrain from voting is wrong because that decision makes no difference to the election's outcome. It's pretty easy to see how this can be applied to the individual acts that cause climate change. None of them by itself is going to make any difference to climatic outcomes, and there is, as we have seen, some convenience cost associated with acting in a less carbon-intensive manner.

But perhaps we can avoid all the problems of the NT by simply denying the premise that our individual actions will have no appreciable effect on climatic outcomes. This is the course taken by John Nolt, in an effort to counter the notion that "the harm caused by an individual's participation in a greenhouse-gas-intensive economy is negligible."[6] Under a business as usual scenario if we divide the total harm caused by America, for example, by the number of Americans, Nolt thinks that each American is responsible for the deaths of two future people. Broome, presumably employing the same kind of calculation, comes up with a more modest figure: each of us in the developed world is responsible for destroying "more than six months of healthy human life."[7]

Broome also gives the same point a monetary expression: "the monetary value of the harm you do over a lifetime ranges between $19,000 and $65,000, or between 65 cents and over $2 per day for every day you are alive."[8]

The difference between Nolt's and Broome's numbers is probably due to the fact that Nolt is talking about Americans and Broome about members of the developed world more generally. Since Americans, per capita, emit substantially more than most, they are responsible for more future death – or cost – than others. In any case, sticking with the death metric each of us in the developed world is, on these analyses, directly responsible for wiping out somewhere between 6 months and many years of future human life. No matter where any particular individual emitter belongs on this continuum of destruction she is thus responsible for very serious harm. Doesn't that answer the worry expressed by the NT?

Not really, and the clue as to why not is contained in the manner in which the numbers are obtained. As mentioned, the first step is to get some notion of the total harms – in either lives or money lost – that will result from a particular emissions trajectory (for example, RCP 8.5). Then you divide that total by the number of current emitters, assigning more or less to each of them based on the country to which they belong, in accordance with data about differential national emissions. But the NT shows that the total amount of harm with which you begin the calculation will be only negligibly affected by the subtraction of any single emitter's contribution. It's a mere drop that simply gets lost in the sea of other contributions. So if I decide to go carbon neutral, my actions by themselves make no difference to the total amount of climate change-induced suffering that will obtain in the world at some specified future date. How do we get around this problem?

Parfit argues that the kind of reasoning just rehearsed illustrates a "mistake in moral mathematics." Think of this with respect to the voter's paradox. The "mistake" is that the stakes are often very high in national elections, but the purely "rational" voter described just above fails to account for this in deciding what to do. Perhaps enough people reasoning as she does and staying home allows the far-right candidate to win a plurality of votes, causing a country's immediate political future to take a sinister turn in the direction of fascism. Think of the difference, Parfit urges, between an act that has a one-in-a-million chance of killing one person and an act that has the same odds of killing a million people. It might even be the same type of act, but what we might call its moral valence clearly alters in light of the different possible outcomes. We should focus on the severity of outcomes not just the odds of their coming to pass. If we do, Parfit argues, then where the stakes are very high we will see that "no chance, however small, should be ignored."[9]

Another way to put the point is that with climate change we are dealing with *threshold effects*, and that this fact changes the nature of the individual acts that go to make up the set of acts producing the harm. A threshold effect obtains when individual contributions to a problem are negligible but which together can produce a harm (or benefit). So far this is unhelpful. It simply gives a fancy label to the phenomenon already picked out by the NT. Jackson, presumably, would be unimpressed by the mere application of the label. He would still deny that the individual acts themselves can be praised or blamed morally in these kinds of cases. Parfit disagrees:

> [E]ven if an act harms no one, this act may be wrong because it is one of a set of acts that together harm other people. Similarly, even if some act benefits no one, it can be what someone ought to do, because it is one of a set of acts that together benefit other people.[10]

How do we adjudicate the matter between Jackson and Parfit? The key question is how it could be that a single act can be innocent in one context and not in another. Can the moral valence of a single consumer choice involving relatively high emissions be altered simply by the fact that a large enough mass of other agents are making similar choices? Perhaps so if we knew the precise size of the collective as well the relevant patterns of behavior of its other members, and were determined to modify our own behavior in light of this information.

But this kind of exercise will work only if we become much more aware of the extent to which our choices are made in and shaped by collective ideals and pressures. Focusing on individual consumer choices is a good idea for the obvious reason that the way we consume is a big part of the problem of GHG emissions. But it also highlights the difficulty we are having in framing the issue properly because it is counter-intuitive to see ourselves, in our consumption choices, as acting in a collective. The main problem here is that the collective in question – virtually everyone in the developed world – is about as *unstructured* as collectives can get. There is almost no coordinated activity among the members of the group, but we usually think of such coordination as an important feature of genuine collectives. This is why it is relatively straightforward to think of more structured collectives – like states or firms – as "agents" that can as such be responsible for what they do, whereas this is much harder to do with highly unstructured collectives like the consumer class.

But we must nevertheless attempt to do just this. For Parfit, this is *the* key to moralizing the small stuff. More specifically, we must think of ourselves as agents whose actions get their moral valence from three principal factors. Together, these factors define the *circumstances of moral action* in the age of climate change:

- A global population of 7 billion set to become 10 billion by 2050
- The looming threat of runaway climate change
- A finite and diminishing carbon budget that must be allocated justly

This is meant to apply mainly to consumers in the developed world, to give them reasons for constraint with respect to their carbon-intensive consumption choices. Any one of these agents is (a) emitting in a world of 7 billion or more other emitters, in a situation in which (b) our actions may trigger dangerous positive feedbacks in the climate system at any time and (c) the limited space remaining in the carbon budget must go chiefly to the developing world. There is literally nothing wrong with any carbon-intensive act in the absence of these three conditions, but with the conditions in place the very same act is morally blameworthy. So Sinnott-Armstrong is simply wrong about that Sunday drive.

Or is he? Maybe we are *still* mired in moral mathematics! The solution to the problem we are considering might still strike us as too calculative or rationalistic. Because it can never entirely dismiss the epistemic importance of certain *quantities* – the size of the relevant collective, the probability of negative outcomes, etc. – it does seem as though this approach will remain hostage to the thought that individual actions are negligible. One way to pursue this worry, and also lead us into the next section of the chapter, is to try and understand our negative reaction to being a member of a harm-causing collective in different terms. An agent reacting this way might not be calculating at all. Instead, she might simply find the idea of participation in such groups morally repugnant at some more basic, sub-rational level. In refraining from contributing to the effect she might not want to be a part of the group in question. She might be ashamed to be seen acting as these other people are, or she might feel morally tainted by the possibility that she will be judged "guilty by association" with such people. We should not dismiss this response as being "overly-emotional." Sometimes, emotions are sound guides to properly moral action.

Look again at the examples we have been using in this discussion. Many people *do* go out and vote in full knowledge of how the NT applies to this practice. Why do they do this? Presumably because they are afraid that if they fail to vote and the fascists win they will simply feel guilty or ashamed about this result. Is this irrational? It seems not. Or, take the example of the group of people throwing a brick through the window. No single brick will break the window, and each vandal knows this, but together the bricks do just that. If I refrain from throwing a brick simply because I find such vandalism repellent, am I being irrational?

Again, it seems not. To be sure, in these cases I am guided more by a "gut reaction" than a concrete belief but perhaps my gut is telling me something important here. Of course, we might respond to this suggestion by saying that if our gut reactions and emotions are to be trusted in such cases that is only because they are parasitic on our *calculations* about outcomes. If what we are worried about is justifying our actions, it's the calculations that are primary.

Let's consider one final example to help us push back against this challenge. Michael Sandel argues that we often respond in this fashion to price-gouging in times of resource scarcity:

> Outrage at price-gougers is more than mindless anger. It gestures at a moral argument worth taking seriously. Outrage is the special kind of anger you feel when you believe people are getting things they don't deserve. Outrage of this kind is anger at injustice.[11]

Similarly, we might think that those who engage in the sort of mob-behaviour that concerns us here are acting outrageously. Notice the important parallel between the Sunday driver and the price-gouger: both are acting, as we sometimes say, "within their rights." But this is compatible with saying that they are behaving outrageously because they have failed to take proper account of how their acts might be unjust. This kind of consideration leads us naturally to the virtues.

Turning to the virtues

Consider an individual's thought-process in the midst of a collective action problem like a prisoner's dilemma or tragedy of the commons. She is hyper-focused on the other agents with whom she is dealing. She is wondering what moves they will likely make in the "game" and is ready to make her own moves on the basis of theirs. She is flexible, her decisions being contingent upon how others behave or are likely to behave. In the classic case of the prisoner's dilemma examined above this is very easy to see, and it is also easy to appreciate how this way of deliberating gets both agents into trouble. Each is being interrogated by the cops, who get each of them to think that if the other prisoner beats him to a confession he will get the maximum sentence while the other will walk. This forces each prisoner to think in the first place about what the other prisoner will do. Fearing that the other will confess, he confesses which means, of course, that both confess. This is very bad for both.

Suppose, on the other hand, that the prisoners had gone into the situation thinking in the first place about the sorts of people they consider themselves to be. Maybe one of them considers herself unwaveringly loyal, for example: the sort of person for whom breaking a pact is literally unthinkable. An agent like this would not make her decisions contingent on what she takes to be the likely actions of other agents to whose fate she is bound in these situations. If both agents in the prisoner's dilemma thought of themselves this way, the sub-optimal outcome would be avoided since neither would confess.

Come back to the worry expressed towards the end of the previous section. In the very process of trying to moralize the small stuff the way we tried to do there, we might still be thinking too much about what other agents – all the other members of that huge, unstructured collective of co-consumers – are doing. Noticing this dynamic in the context of climate change Dale Jamieson argues that we should abandon moral mathematics altogether:

> Instead of looking to moral mathematics for practical solutions to large-scale collective action problems, we should focus instead on non-calculative generators of behaviour: character traits, dispositions, emotions ... When faced with global environmental change, our general policy should be to try to reduce our contribution regardless of the behaviour of others, and we are more likely to succeed in doing this by developing and inculcating the right virtues than by improving our calculative abilities.[12]

What exactly are these "non-calculative generators of behavior" and how can they help us become better at negotiating our way through collective action problems? The short answer to the first question is, "the virtues." Virtue ethics began with Aristotle. It was developed by his immediate philosophical successors in the Greco-Roman tradition and was the dominant form of moral theory in the Christian and Arab worlds for much of the period up until the 18th-century Enlightenment. It was also the dominant model in the Chinese tradition, forming the backbone of Confucian ethics.

With the subsequent rise of alternative moral theories – especially deontology and utilitarianism – the influence of virtue ethics waned in the West (though not in China), but it was reinvigorated in the last few decades of the 20th century and currently receives widespread attention from philosophers. Virtue ethics looks to dispositions or traits as the proper targets of moral assessment. It is concerned with the virtues and vices that make up individual character. So in praising people we might refer to them as courageous, kind, compassionate or frugal; in blaming them we might refer to them as cowardly, selfish, immoderate or unjust. In both cases, we are saying something about what we take to be a relatively stable, though not unchanging, foundation of behavior in the person.

That is an important feature of this type of assessment of others because it allows us to predict their future behaviour with some confidence. If you ask me whether or not my friend Sally is likely to donate money to your breast cancer campaign, I might answer by saying that I know Sally to be a very generous and kind person, making it likely that she will do so. This brings us to what is most important about the virtues. They impart, as Jamieson puts it, a measure of "non-contingency" to our behavior. That is, they provide us with an orientation to collective action situations that is exactly the opposite of what gets us into trouble in them. Sally enters her cooperative involvements with others with a self-definition as kind and generous, doing whatever the situation at hand demands of such a person. She does not allow her deliberations about what to do to become hijacked by worries about what the other agents with whom she is dealing are going to do. If this is broadly speaking what we need for the climate crisis, we need to ask, more specifically, what virtues will help with the task.

Virtues for the climate crisis

It might be helpful to divide such virtues into two broad categories. The first would have to do with our relations with other humans, the second with the rest of the biosphere. The distinction is for illustrative purposes only, of course, because human relations are not a sphere separate from our relations with the rest of the biosphere. But it serves a useful analytic purpose.

Human–human relations

Under the first heading, we are concerned chiefly with virtues that allow us to fulfill the demands of international and intergenerational climate justice. Here are a few prominent virtues that might help in this task.

Courage

Courage is the ability to manage fear. Aristotle argued that we should not try to transcend fear altogether, since this would invite recklessness. Nor, however, should we simply succumb to it, since this would result in cowardly behavior. The trick is to find what he called a "mean" between these two extremes. That sweet spot is courage. We need it because the pressure to live in accordance with the ways of business as usual is very strong in our culture. Even consuming more sustainably can be difficult, demanding courage. If all your peers are living in the lap of luxury, refusing to do so even though you have the means can come with social costs. This may seem trivial, but it is anything but. The virtue of courage can also show up in the context of environmental activism. It can take courage to expose yourself to the ridicule of others by speaking out against the fossil fuel regime or, more obviously, standing in the path of machines building oil pipelines.

Benevolence

To be benevolent is, literally, to be "good willed" or "of good will." It refers to the disposition to take the suffering and interests of others seriously, to seek as much as possible to alleviate their suffering and further their interests. The demands of international justice place a duty on us to take up this stance towards those who are most vulnerable to the ravages of climate change but did little or nothing to make it happen. The same applies to people of the future. We should add that benevolence can be a spur to act in accordance with all aspects of justice: procedural, distributive and corrective. Finally, notice that benevolence is very often parasitic on our conception of the things that count morally. We would not likely feel benevolent towards animals if we truly believed, with the 17th-century French philosopher René Descartes, that they are just super-fancy machines. This thought can make us wonder why we display so *little* benevolence towards people of the future. Is it because we think they are not morally considerable in virtue of being non-existent? If this is what we think, we should be prepared to defend this notion with reasons, not an easy task.

Hope

Hope is a dangerous virtue but probably a necessary one now. It is dangerous because it can degenerate so easily into wishful thinking. But it is conceptually distinct from this vice because by definition the hopeful person is aware of the probability of the hoped-for outcome. The wishful thinker ignores the relevant probabilities. It is necessary because it can be energizing. So long as the hoped-for outcome is not considered impossible, the hopeful agent will strive diligently to bring it into being. In an age when the temptation to despair is strong, withdrawal and political passivity become increasingly pronounced. In these times this virtue will be important. For example, the retired ecologist Guy McPherson has warned of the imminent extinction of humanity because of climate change. His views are not well-grounded in the science, but he seems to have engendered a groundswell of despair among the scientifically unwary. His message embodies a kind of moral darkness that may descend on us in the decades to come. So long as it does not degenerate into wishful thinking, hope is one antidote to the sort of scare-mongering engaged in by McPherson and his ilk.

Human-nature relations

This brings us to the virtues we require to help us live more sustainably on the planet. Here are a few of the most important.

Frugality

To be frugal is to live as simply as possible. This need not be seen as a justification of puritan restraint for its own sake or because one believes it to be what the divinity demands. Rather, it is the disposition to live conscientiously on a planet in ecological overshoot, in the recognition that the planet simply cannot sustain high-carbon lifestyles *en masse*. So, frugality here is understood as being intimately tied to ecological awareness. One crucial manifestation of it would be to stop consuming cattle products. The methane produced by the cattle industry is, as we have seen, out of control. This example illustrates the fact the being virtuous is not a call to perfection. The message is not "veganism or bust!" A genuinely frugal person can still enjoy life's many gustatory pleasures while taking a pass on the *filet mignon*.

Humility

To be humble is to seek to avoid that ancient vice, hubris. In the environmental domain, hubristic people believe that humans and their technologies are superior to the natural processes that govern the workings of the earth system. It is the belief that no matter what trouble we get ourselves into, ecologically speaking, our technologies will always light the way out. Many people see geoengineering, which we explore in Chapter 9, as the ultimate expression of hubris. And we have already seen, in Chapter 6, that it is an apt way of characterizing the ecomodernists' approach to life in the Anthropocene. To be humble, then, is to recognize that the human species is just a tiny part of the total story of life on this planet, that we are utterly dependent on healthy ecosystems, and that our ultimate goal should therefore be to fit into the biosphere – even as we "manage" it in fairly substantial ways – rather than dominate it.

Respect

It is at first jarring to see respect as a virtue under this heading, but respect for nature is probably a crucial virtue to cultivate now. To respect a thing is to allow it to go on in its own distinctive manner. This is the way we understand respect for other humans. We think for example that there is general duty to avoid coercing other people, bending them to our will, because such treatment involves a refusal to see them as things with their own ends and interests. We should, other things being equal, simply leave them alone. Here, we can see how the virtue of respect is tied to a more principle-based moral theory like deontology (recall, in this connection, the importance of autonomy, discussed in Chapter 4). Respect would be a good disposition to have in an age when our interference with other species is causing a mass extinction. Perhaps if we were more inclined to adopt an attitude of wonder at and reverence for other members of the biosphere, we'd be less inclined to usher them out of existence with such alacrity. The tendency to feel wonder and reverence often accompany a respectful disposition.

These then are just a few of the virtues the cultivation of which would likely make it easier for us to avoid sleepwalking into climate catastrophe. Four more points about all of this. First, the list is not exhaustive.[13] Many more virtues could be added: diligence, temperance, commitment, aesthetic sensibility, love, care, attunement, gratitude, and, as William Throop has suggested, "grit."[14] Second, the virtues are often mutually enforcing. This applies within each of the headings just discussed as well as between them. For example, being frugal in the sense required for a sound relation to the biosphere also helps an agent to be benevolent to those humans threatened by the effects of climate change. This is because being benevolent sometimes requires one to constrain oneself in one's consumption choices, something it is obviously easier to do if one is frugal. Third, we should stress the importance of moral education in virtue ethics. It can take a long time to cultivate the virtues, so if we think acquiring them is important we need to focus on the way they become inculcated in the young.

Finally, we should not confine ourselves to the Western tradition in thinking about the place of virtue in our lives. Many other moral and religious traditions have stressed the importance of this aspect of life. Obviously, we cannot catalogue all of those traditions here. But consider just one example, the Confucian tradition of virtue ethics. One of the possible problems with Western virtue ethics is that it still seems too oriented to the individual, and cannot therefore grasp the extent to which we need to think of ourselves as embedded in larger wholes. As Neville argues this is both why we need to turn to Confucian ethics and why it is misguided to translate the latter into Western terms:

> For the classic Confucians, ... understanding and engaging the metaphysical basis of value and order was essential. They always conceived the human to be set within the social which in turn is set within the cosmic ... Translating Confucianism into [Western] virtue ethics runs the risk of sheering off the metaphysical dimension and reducing Confucianism to the ethics of subjectivity. ... [W]ill the ancient integrity of classic Confucianism embracing ethics within a cosmic philosophy of value be compromised by the amazingly fruitful interpretation to Westerners of Confucianism as a person-oriented virtue ethics without metaphysics?[15]

Those of us working within the Western tradition of ethics should bear this in mind. It may be that, even with the turn to the virtues, we are still thinking about moral responsibility too subjectively – not metaphysically enough – and that this is precisely why we are mired in the sort of collective action problems characteristic of the climate crisis. We need to be open to the possibility that other traditions can show us a better path through this crisis.

This leaves one large question: what should individuals do to address the crisis? Having shown that we have some reasons for changing the way we are living, we surely need some guidance about what concrete steps we might take.

Building just institutions

We might argue that individual duties of climate change justice are best specified in the principles and regulatory arrangements of just institutions. This is an application of the more general view that *all* individual duties of justice are defined by and limited to the specifications of such institutions. This is known as the **institutional theory of justice (ITJ)**. ITJ is an attractive theory because it leaves a whole sphere of moral behavior largely untouched by the demands of such institutions. In liberal-democratic moral culture, individuals are given wide, though not unlimited, latitude to develop and organize their private lives around personal conceptions of the good which might have little or nothing to do with justice. This is not problematic so long as our institutions specify comprehensively the demands of justice that structure our relations with one another outside the private sphere.

The big problem with this approach to our problem is that we do not have just institutions for the climate crisis. ITJ as just sketched is therefore an ideal theory. So the question becomes this: what responsibilities of climate justice do individuals have in the non-ideal circumstances currently prevailing? Kok-Chor Tan has addressed this question in a helpful way, so we will work through his analysis carefully. As Tan sees it, there are at least three ways we could respond to a situation like the one we are in.

Deny that any duties of justice are binding on us

This is, roughly, the response of someone embracing the political philosophy of Thomas Hobbes. Hobbes, a 17th-century philosopher, believed that justice and injustice – right and wrong – exist only within an institutional framework, what he called "civil society." Take that framework away – which for him was the "state of nature" – and there are literally no responsibilities of justice remaining, though of course individuals could still consider themselves bound to look after the interests of particular other people in this situation. This is really an extreme or literal version of the ITJ. The problem with it is that it defies our intuitions. Most people do not believe that in non-ideal conditions we have no responsibilities of justice whatsoever.

This failure brings us to the second possible option.

Individuals must pick up all the slack of the missing institutions

This is, again roughly, the position of the utilitarian. It is also diametrically opposed to the previous position. Since just institutions do not exist, individuals must devote their lives to realizing the requirements of justice all on their own. As Tan points out, the problem with this position is that it is too demanding. The claims of justice would effectively swallow up all of our personal concerns. This is because the circumstances in which we currently exist with respect to dangerous emissions are *so* non-ideal. The developed world is so far from carrying out its emissions reduction responsibilities that, on this second approach, each individual must devote herself tirelessly to making up the difference.

Virtually every act in this agent's life would have to be assessed from the standpoint of the demands of climate justice. This, for Tan, is unacceptable.[16] Of course, we might respond to Tan by rejecting the ITJ in cases like this. In other words we might say that when the stakes are high, and compliance with the demands of justice is so low, individuals just *are* required to devote themselves wholeheartedly to morality in this fashion. It is unfortunate that little space is left for purely private pursuits but that is just the nature of the problem.

However, even if our individual duties are thought to be much more stringent in a situation of non-compliance than they would be in a situation of greater compliance, the real problem is that whatever individuals do in a situation of non-compliance is bound to be futile. This is because the approach is insufficiently collective. As Tan points out, a major source of emissions comes from the very structure of our "industrial and agricultural rules and practices."[17] If it suits me, I can become a vegan, get off the grid, and stand in the path of the bulldozers, but if the institutions under which I live favor widespread meat-eating, electricity generated by burning coal and unchecked industrial development, my acts will have little impact (we're back to the NT!). These are things that can be changed only through collective action aimed at the modification of our institutions. Individuals by themselves cannot affect this basic structure. This brings us to the third response.

Work to build just institutions

Tan argues that building institutions that comply with the demands of climate justice is the chief ethical task in our non-ideal situation:

> [S]ignificant emissions reductions cannot be achieved through personal action alone – such as recycling and reducing consumption – but ... require

collective action. Real change can be brought on only through infrastructural changes, revisions and institutional reforms. These infrastructural changes will require … a focus on institutions rather than on personal conduct.[18]

This is surely the right focus. It demands that individuals think less about their personal consumption choices and more about getting involved in the politics of climate change. Among other things, this means we have duties to work and vote for politicians who take the problem seriously by, for instance, advocating for the imposition of a meaningful carbon tax or cap and trade policy. Even so – to return to a problem broached in Chapter 2 – we must be mindful that our ethical theories, according to Gardiner, "have offered little guidance on the central question of the kinds of institutions that are needed to confront the problem, and the specific norms that should govern those institutions."[19]

From which it follows that there is a great deal of work to do on this front. We are now in a position to appreciate what was right about Sinnott-Armstrong's approach to Sunday driving. He argues, recall, that we should not worry about the drive itself but should vote for politicians that make behavior like this illegal or more costly. However, the main thrust of this chapter is to claim that we probably need *both* approaches. We need to work for changes at the institutional level as well as moralize the Sunday drive. Indeed, it is difficult to see how one will work without the other. Tan's approach to the issue allows for this dual focus though he is, as we have just seen, overwhelmingly focused on the institutional half of it. Having made the point about the need for institutional change, what concrete measures can individuals adopt to make them more responsible consumers?

Carbon offsetting

To focus the discussion, let's explore one approach to responsible consumption. The approach is **carbon offsetting**. Since you cannot eliminate your emissions altogether, the idea behind offsetting is that for every unit of carbon you emit you should see to it that an equivalent amount of carbon is not emitted. There is a thriving market in offsets. The way they work is that you pay an offsetting company and your money is used to fund projects, usually though not exclusively in the developing world, aimed at producing energy in green ways (construction of a biofuel plant for example).

One of the most important requirements that such projects must meet is that of "**additionality**." It must be the case that the project you are funding would not have gone ahead anyway, that its development is due entirely to funds received through offsetting. If the additionality requirement is not met with respect to some particular project then your funds are not helping to *prevent* the carbon that would otherwise have been emitted from being emitted. Broome sums up the case for offsetting thus:

Preventive offsetting is genuine offsetting, provided it leads to a real reduction of greenhouse gas. If you offset all your emissions by this means, you make sure that your presence in the world causes no greenhouse gas to be added to the atmosphere. You therefore do no harm to anyone through emissions.[20]

That is a bold claim: it entails that by offsetting you can effectively cancel the wrongness of your carbon emissions. By way of elaboration, let's notice two things about the practice of offsetting. The first that it can be somewhat difficult to ensure additionality. Fortunately, however, there are certifications that have been developed to help consumers make responsible choices here. Shopping for legitimate offset companies is now much like shopping for tuna that is dolphin-friendly or coffee that is fair trade. The options exist, you simply have to work a bit harder than usual to find them.

Second, offsetting is remarkably cheap. This is largely because the projects being funded are in the developing world where labor and the cost of raw materials are significantly cheaper than they are in the developed world. This is important because it means that many individuals in the developed world can probably afford to pay for both their direct and their indirect emissions. Direct emissions are those you are responsible for in your driving, flying, household heating and cooling, and so on. These can be tallied pretty accurately with carbon footprint calculators readily available on-line. Indirect emissions are more difficult to measure accurately because their sources are in things like the food we eat (much of which is imported) and the infrastructure we use (roads, buildings, etc.). The safest bet is to calculate your direct emissions and double or triple the amount you owe.[21] That should cover everything.

Of course by following this advice, you may overshoot what you owe but even with significant overshoot, we are talking about sums that are – let's be frank – objectively trivial for those whose household wealth puts them economically in the top 5% of the global population. Nor should we worry that the practice of offsetting somehow tries to makes wrong actions right. That is, we might think that offsetting is a bit like the medieval practice engaged in by the Catholic Church of selling indulgences to sinners so that they could have their time in purgatory reduced.[22] To many, like the rebel Luther, this normalized sin, perhaps even increasing it among those who thought they could pay their way out of it. The same would go for emissions-intensive behaviors. Those willing to buy offsets might not cut back on or may even increase their emissions, convinced that the practice of offsetting renders them permissible.

This may not be a significant worry. There is nothing intrinsically wrong with emitting carbon (unlike sinning, perhaps). It is wrong only insofar as it leads to dangerous interference in the climate system. *If* this effect can be negated through a practice like offsetting, then, for Broome, the wrong disappears altogether (as we have just seen). Not everyone will be satisfied with this answer. There are those who think that the real task is to reduce our collective carbon footprint radically. Practices like offsetting, they will insist, perpetuate a system of behaviors among individuals – long-haul flying, for example – that is not sustainable, partly because the vast majority of individuals doing these things do *not* offset their carbon emissions.

So everyone should probably offset *and* reduce *and* fight for institutional reform. The climate crisis surely requires this sort of multi-pronged approach on the part of every individual who is capable of it. Perhaps we can add that these are among the things the ideally virtuous agent will likely do as part of her understanding of what sort of person one should be in the age of climate change.

Chapter summary

This chapter has been about individual moral responsibility for climate change. We began by setting the problem of overconsumption in the context of prisoner's dilemma-type collective action problems. This led us to a discussion of the negligibility thesis, the thought any individual might have that his contribution to the problem of climate change is morally meaningless because it is so small. We tried to find a way around this thought, a way to moralize those small consumption choices. This brought us to consider a way of thinking about morality – the virtue-ethical approach – that departs significantly from standard moral theories. The task here was to find a way of thinking about our duties that avoided the "calculative" aspect of typical deliberation in collective action scenarios. After looking at a few of the key virtues we need to cultivate if we are to adopt this approach successfully, we examined the institutional approach to climate justice. Here, we concluded that, whatever other duties they have, individuals surely have a duty to change the institutions that govern and structure our collective existence. We concluded with a discussion of the practice of carbon offsetting, a duty that can be thought of as supplementary to that of changing our institutions.

Questions for discussion

1 Explain how prisoner's dilemmas typically result in sub-optimal outcomes and how this happens with respect to high-carbon consumption choices.

2 Is it possible to moralize individual consumption choices by showing that their moral valence changes under certain circumstances?

3 Does the turn to the virtues solve the problem of being too "calculative" in the context of collective action problems? If so, how? If not, why not?

4 Is the Western approach to the virtues too focused on the personal? Is something like the Confucian approach a good alternative?

5 What are the reasons, if any, for opposing the practice of carbon offsetting as a key way of fulfilling our individual duties of climate justice?

Suggested reading

Ronald Sandler, *Character and Environment: A Virtue-Oriented Approach to Environmental Ethics* (New York: Columbia University Press, 2007). The most comprehensive treatment of environmental virtue ethics. Not about climate change specifically, but very useful.

Byron Williston, *The Anthropocene Project: Virtue in the Age of Climate Change* (Oxford: Oxford University Press, 2015). The only book-length attempt to apply virtue ethics to the problem of climate change. The focus is on the virtues of justice, hope and truthfulness.

Kok-Choi Tan, "Individual Duties of Climate Justice under Non-Ideal Conditions," in Jeremy Moss (ed.), *Climate Change and Justice* (Cambridge: Cambridge University Press, 2015), 129–147. A thorough analysis of the institutional approach to individual justice.

Notes

1 Dale Jamieson, *Reason in a Dark Time: Why the Struggle against Climate Change Failed and What it Means for our Future* (Oxford: Oxford University Press, 2014), 176.
2 Jamieson, *Reason in a Dark Time...*, 164.
3 Jamieson, *Reason in a Dark Time...*, 168.
4 Walter Sinnott-Armstrong, "It's Not My Fault: Global Warming and Individual Moral Obligations," in Stephen Gardiner, Simon Caney, Henry Shue and Dale Jamieson (eds.), *Climate Ethics: Essential Readings* (Oxford: Oxford University Press, 2010), 332–346 (344).
5 Frank Jackson, "Which Effects?" in J. Dancy (ed.), *Reading Parfit* (Oxford: Blackwell, 1997), 42–53.
6 John Nolt, "How Harmful are the Average American's Greenhouse Gas Emissions?" *Ethics, Policy and the Environment* 14 (1), 2011, 3–10 (3).
7 John Broome, *Climate Matters* (New York: W.W. Norton, 2012), 74.
8 Broome, *Climate Matters...*, 75.
9 Derek Parfit, *Reasons and Persons* (Oxford: Oxford University Press, 1984), 75. Also the discussion in Steve Vanderheiden, *Atmospheric Justice: A Political Theory of Climate Change* (Oxford: Oxford University Press, 2008), 159–167.
10 Parfit, *Reasons and Persons...*, 70.
11 Michael J. Sandel, *Justice: What's the Right Thing to Do?* (New York: Farrar, Straus and Giroux, 2009), 7.
12 Dale Jamieson, "When Utilitarians Should Be Virtue Theorists," *Utilitas* 19 (2), 2007, 160–183 (167).
13 For a truly exhaustive list, see Ronald Sandler, *Character and Environment: A Virtue-Oriented Approach to Environmental Ethics* (New York: Columbia University Press, 2007), 82.
14 William Throop, Review of Byron Williston, *The Anthropocene Project: Virtue in the Age of Climate Change, Environmental Ethics* 39 (1), Spring, 2017, 105–108 (107).
15 Quoted in Eric L. Hutton, "On the 'Virtue-Turn' and the Problem of Categorizing Chinese Thought," *Dao* 14, 2014, 331–353 (338).
16 Kok-Chor Tan, "Individual Duties of Climate Justice under Non-Ideal Conditions," in Moss (ed.), *Climate Change and Justice*, 129–147 (136).
17 Tan, "Individual Duties...," 137.
18 Tan, "Individual Duties...," 144.
19 Stephen Gardiner and David Weisbach, *Debating Climate Ethics* (Oxford: Oxford University Press, 2016), 259.
20 Broome, *Climate Matters...*, 87.
21 Broome, *Climate Matters...*, 88–89.
22 Robert E. Goodin, "Selling Environmental Indulgences," in Gardiner, Caney, et al. (eds.), *Climate Ethics...*, 230–247.

8   Climate change denial

Introduction

Donald Trump once tweeted that climate change is a "total, and very expensive, hoax." Assume he believes this. He might be (accidentally) right about the high cost of climate change if we continue to do nothing about it, but what about the bit about climate change being a hoax? We can examine this belief itself and show – pretty easily, of course – that it is, in the language of epistemologists, "unjustified" because it is clearly contradicted by the facts. But does this go far enough as an *evaluation* of the belief? It seems not to. The assertion is so stupid that we may also want to ask, "who could believe such a thing?" Here, we are in the domain of virtue epistemology, the investigation of the character traits of believers. In this chapter, we look at climate change denial from this perspective. We begin with a sketch of virtue epistemology, moving next to a description of what the ideal epistemic agent believes about climate change. This brings us to climate change denial, which we examine in the subsequent three sections. The first two deal with a familiar form of denial – here, following Harry Frankfurt, analyzed as climate change "bullshit" – the third with a less familiar form that can show up among otherwise progressive people.

Virtue epistemology

Sometimes we are so appalled by what a person has done that our inclination is ask, "what sort of person would *do* a thing like that?"[1] We might answer our own question by asserting that this person must be especially greedy, selfish, unkind or lacking in compassion. To illustrate, let's return to Sandel's price-gouger, encountered in the previous chapter. Suppose a coastal community is suffering immensely after an unexpectedly high storm surge destroyed much of the local power grid. Think, for instance, of the people of Puerto Rico after Hurricane Maria struck in 2017. Now imagine that the proprietor of a small hardware store in San Juan raises prices on essential goods like battery powered generators, realizing that he has the city's inhabitants in a desperate situation and that they will therefore be forced to pay the prices he is demanding.

The case is interesting because the proprietor is, let's suppose, violating nobody's rights: he is legally allowed to gouge his customers. In cases like this it seems insufficient to criticize his actions alone. We feel compelled to say something negative about the person's underlying character as well. Hence the question above. As we saw in the previous chapter, when we make this sort of move in morality we are in the domain of virtue ethics. Sandel says that the price-gouger's actions are objectionable mainly because he fails to exhibit "civic virtue" when this is what we expect of him.[2]

Epistemology – the theory of knowledge – has always been normative at its core: it is about getting our beliefs right, getting them to match up with the way the world really is. Epistemologists tell us that we *should* try and do these things, that we *ought* to increase the ratio of true to false beliefs in our total set of beliefs. Traditionally, however, the target of this exercise has been the beliefs themselves. Philosophers ask whether or not a particular belief is "justified" given available evidence and prevailing standards of logical argumentation. This focus is fine with respect to many of our beliefs. For example, most progress in science can be understood this way. When a theory has been falsified by the discovery of new facts it is abandoned and the scientist will accordingly attempt to formulate a more appropriate theory, one that fits the facts better than the first. In the language of epistemology, the first belief has been shown to be unjustified and has been replaced by another that is, at least provisionally, justified.

Recently, epistemologists have begun to wonder about the normative connection between beliefs and character traits, making the latter rather than the former the main target of normative assessment. This is virtue epistemology. We require it because the language of justification sometimes does not seem to be normatively deep enough. For example, many Americans have asked, "what kind of person could *believe* that giving ordinary citizens legal permission to stockpile assault weapons is good public policy?" In the wake of a slaughter like the one that occurred in Parkland, Florida in February, 2018, an answer might suggest itself readily: only those who are especially callous, close-minded or too dim-witted to grasp the limited applicability of the Second Amendment of the U.S. Constitution to the contemporary world.

In examples like this we are of course interested in actions. We are worried about the gun-rights advocate voting for politicians who will not challenge the gun lobby. These politicians enable the proliferation of dangerous firearms among the populace and so are partly responsible for the problem. But we may also feel compelled to assess the character of the belief holder herself. It seems somehow inadequate to say only that her beliefs about guns are unjustified. The point applies just as strongly to what we consider especially praiseworthy epistemic achievements. Giordano Bruno (1548–1600) was burned at the stake for disseminating heretical cosmological theories about the place of the earth relative to the sun. Calling his Copernican worldview "justified" or "warranted," though correct, hardly seems to capture what we think about this feat of belief. Surely we want to add something about the courage or integrity of this believer.

So our intuitions seem to push us towards accepting the idea of epistemic virtues and vices. Virtue epistemologists have developed two competing theoretical models used to pick out these virtues and vices. The first is "reliabilism." The reliabilist thinks that the virtues are skills or faculties the correct employment of which results, other things being equal, in justified beliefs. So we can speak here of good vision or hearing, as well as memory and logical skill as virtues. For the reliabilist what really matters is the production of justified beliefs, so anything that can produce them in a reliable way should be called a virtue. The failure of the skills or faculties – poor vision, memory, etc. – are, in turn, the intellectual vices.[3] The second theoretical model is "responsibilism." The responsibilist believes that our moral assessment of believers should focus on the motives producing beliefs.[4]

The differences between reliabilism and responsibilism are diverse and complex, and quite beyond the scope of our inquiry. However, one difference is important to highlight because it bears on an issue that is relevant to this chapter. The issue has to do with the tendency we have to praise or blame agents for the beliefs they hold. It looks as though reliabilists will not give us a very robust account of this. Of course, it may be true that my intellectual failings are the product a poor memory, let's say, and that this is something I could have worked more diligently to improve. I should have been doing Sudoku puzzles instead of watching so much football all those years (or at least doing the puzzles while watching the football). Perhaps, but how do we explain this failing? Do we point to some other underdeveloped skill or faculty or do we say instead that I've been lazy? At some stage in the explanation for my intellectual shortcomings it may be quite tempting to point to something that looks like a motive or disposition rather than a mere skill or faculty.

This is usually what we intend when we use the language of "vice." Of course, the reliabilist can use the language of vice too, as we have seen. Poor memory is a vice for the reliabilist. But this usage looks to be metaphorical. Memory is a skill or capacity which as such exists on a spectrum of development. It makes little sense to understand capacities like this as legitimate targets of moral assessment. Virtue and vice, by contrast, are rooted in our characters and these *are* legitimate targets of moral assessment. Why? Because we have some control over them. We are responsible for them and therefore also for the behaviors and beliefs to which they give rise.

If this is right it means that in addition to being moral agents we are also epistemic agents. We have *some* control over the set of beliefs we hold at any time. We can revise and refine this set in accordance with appropriate evidentiary and logical standards. We can be blamed for epistemic failure and praised for epistemic success. However, the real value of responsibilist virtue epistemology is that it allows us to go beyond mere praise and blame. We can say exactly what it is about the underlying character that warrants these attitudes. We can celebrate an epistemic agent for being courageous and open-minded in espousing her beliefs; or we can criticize and shun her for being conformist and close-minded in her beliefs. Responsibilism looks like the right theoretical model.

There's a further feature of both versions of virtue epistemology that is especially important to highlight, though, again, I think the responsibilist can make better sense of it than can the reliabilist. Character assessments are important because they deepen or increase our understanding of ourselves and others as co-producers of knowledge. They draw us, as believers, into a normative circle of agents whose ultimate goal is to find out more and more about the world we inhabit together. They help us understand the sense in which the acquisition of knowledge is something social, something we do as a collective.

We are apt to think of knowledge as something acquired and owned by individuals, but this conception of knowledge misconstrues things quite badly. Our beliefs are built on the epistemic labor of others. This is especially the case with true beliefs and the point applies to intellectual mavericks as much as it does to ordinary believers. Newton – a genuine epistemic maverick – once remarked that if he seemed to see further than some it was only because he stood on the shoulders of giants. That expresses the social conception of knowledge that is especially congenial to virtue epistemology. If you are inclined to doubt this, ask yourself what the *point* of epistemic character assessment is supposed to be minus this social aspect.

We could say that we are inclined to worry about another agent's increasing the ratio of true to false beliefs in her total belief set because it is better *for her* if she does this. This is no doubt true but it is at best half the story. Think of a simple example. If a child expresses the belief to his parents and siblings that he should get to *both* slice the pie *and* choose the first piece, the parent might chide him for his greed. What more can we say here? Well, we might say the family is a collective, trying to develop fair practices of resource distribution among its members. The greedy child has a false belief about how this can best be achieved. But the key point is that if the lesson has been imparted successfully the whole group is better off for it, not just the greedy child. The collective stock of beliefs with respect to the problem of resource distribution among its members has been improved.

How can virtue epistemology help us understand climate change denial? In the aftermath of the devastating 2017 hurricane season in the Caribbean Pope Francis called climate change deniers "stupid." The statement fits the virtue-epistemological approach nicely. The Pope went on to say that deniers should ask scientists what is going on with the climate because the scientists "speak very clearly" on this issue.[5] Although his remark is not exactly subtle (at least for a Pope), Francis is clearly attacking the character of certain epistemic agents, arguing in effect that only stupid *people* deny the reality of climate change. So in the spirit of the pontiff, let's explore the question from this angle. Who are these stupid people and how exactly have they gone wrong in the all-important task of belief-formation?

How to believe in climate change

Actually, before attempting to get a philosophical grip on the phenomenon of climate change denial it might be a good idea to show what the virtuous epistemic agent looks like with respect to her beliefs about climate change. Here we remain in the territory of standard or traditional epistemology. It is somewhat difficult to get a start on this because there are innumerable beliefs one might have about this issue. But given what we have said so far in this book, it seems correct to boil things down to these three beliefs:

(B1): Climate change is happening now
(B2): Contemporary climate change is anthropogenic
(B3): Avoiding dangerous interference in the climate system requires aggressive mitigation measures in the short term

These three beliefs – let's call them the Trio – are pretty basic. We could expand on each of them to show that it contains many sub-beliefs and we could probably add a few more basic beliefs. But let's be parsimonious and stick with the Trio in this form.

An agent who has her epistemic house in order on this issue will believe all three elements of the Trio. It follows that there is more than one way to be a climate change denier. Most of the people who earn this label deny (B1) and/ or (B2). The deniers who get much less attention are those who accept (B1) and (B2) but refuse to accept (B3), or who accept it "in theory" but do not believe it requires *them* to do very much to address the problem. We'll analyze the first type of denier in the next two sections and the second type in the final section, but let's first assemble a picture of how an *ideal* epistemic agent approaches the Trio. This will give us someone concrete with whom to contrast deniers. We'll start with an obvious question: why should *anyone* who is not an expert in climate science believe the Trio?

As befits the social theory of knowledge defended just above it is important to notice that our belief-sets are permeated with items rooted in the testimony of others. If we read about a coup d'état in some far away country and believe it, we are doing so on the testimony of the journalist filing the report. When you think about it you will realize that many, perhaps most, of our beliefs – from the weather forecast to your child's assertion that she did indeed brush her teeth this morning – are formed this way. This makes the issue of *trust* central to epistemology. In visiting a particular website for your political news you are evidently trusting it more than you do some alternative. Why? You might say that your preferred source does not sensationalize the stories, that its journalists regularly win awards for the quality of their reporting, that the editor is considered an honest person and so on.

But what about the beliefs we have that are based on the testimony of scientific experts? Most of us do not understand all the scientific detail behind each element of the Trio. If we nevertheless believe it this is because we trust the scientists, but why should we? This is a special kind of testimonial belief, that involved in the transmission of knowledge from experts to non-experts. Surely, we must be able to point to some criteria that justify our accepting the testimony of experts about climate change. After all, it is always possible that we are being hoodwinked. The 18th-century philosopher Thomas Reid argues that beliefs based in testimony, including expert testimony, *can* be justified. He offers two tests such beliefs must pass in order to deserve the support of non-experts.[6]

The first is what he calls "concurrence" among various experts working on different aspects of a problem. One of the most striking things about climate change science is the degree to which the basic facts are corroborated from a number of distinct perspectives. For instance, a recent study compared the instrumental temperature record to data from over 170 temperature-sensitive paleo proxies, concluding that the concurrence among these sources indicates "a significant warming trend from 1880–1995."[7] Findings like this are important because they render implausible, or even absurd, the notion that scientists are somehow colluding to misrepresent the facts.

The second test of testimonial beliefs is what Reid calls the "number and disinterestedness of witnesses."[8] Let's analyze these two components separately. First, "number." Deniers sometimes pour scorn on the oft-repeated claim that 97% of climate scientists are in agreement on the basic facts, but the number is well-established. It comes from a 2009 survey of the scientific literature that looked at how many articles published in proper peer-reviewed journals expressed agreement with the claims that climate change is happening and is anthropogenic, i.e., (B1) and (B2) of the Trio.[9] Ninety-seven percent agreement on any topic is about as high as it gets in science. It puts climate change on an epistemic par with the theory of natural selection.

This brings us to the "disinterestedness" of scientists. To be disinterested is to be objective, to remove personal – "interested" – considerations from one's deliberations about the facts. The first point to note here has to do with the motives of scientists. The claim made by some deniers that scientists are falsifying data in order to obtain grant money from governmental and non-governmental funding agencies is laughable on its face. Most scientists are disinterested in the sense Reid intends: they are motivated by a desire to discover the truth about the natural world. This is, we might say, a good intrinsic to the practice of science, something any individual scientist might therefore aim to acquire. Like all of us, however, scientists also require goods extrinsic to their practice, like money. But from the fact that they require financial support to do research it does not follow that securing research money is their primary professional aim. To think otherwise is to confuse intrinsic and extrinsic goods.

However, we don't need to rely wholly on this understanding of the motives of the scientist to ground the belief in his or her disinterestedness because scientists have developed a process that brings us as close to a guarantee of objectivity as we are ever going to get. That process is peer-review. It is a commonplace feature of all academic research but it gets amped-up significantly in the products that interest us the most here: IPCC reports. The 2007 IPCC report (AR4) analyzed over 10,000 articles and reports, all of them already peer-reviewed. AR4 as a whole went through four separate levels of peer-review, receiving over 90,000 comments from over 2,500 scientists. Similar statistics apply to AR5. That is an extraordinarily thorough process of oversight. According to Paul Beggs, a geophysicist, it is "arguably the most rigorous and transparent peer-review process in the history of science."[10]

In sum, employing Reid's criteria, non-experts would appear to have solid reasons for believing what the experts have told them about (B1) and (B2). The same is true with respect to (B3), though here things are more complex because of the different ways in which "dangerous interference in the climate system" can be understood. Still, in spite of the fact that people have different perceptions of risk we should not overstate this point. The effects associated with an increase in global temperatures approaching 5°C are going to be bad for virtually all of us as well as most non-human members of the biosphere. This is something we *know* from the science alone. Moreover, it follows that the best way to avoid these effects is to reduce the flow of GHGs to the atmosphere very quickly, i.e., to engage in aggressive mitigation. That's all there is to (B3).

This leads us to a consideration of the virtues our ideal epistemic agent will likely possess. She will probably have to be quite courageous because there are deniers everywhere whom she will sometimes feel compelled to confront. These people can be quite nasty. Some of them, for instance, sent death threats to the climate scientist Michael Mann. But our agent will also need to have integrity. Integrity is about psychic "wholeness," in this case ensuring that one translates one's beliefs about the world, where appropriate, into action. Belief is not an end in itself. As the philosopher W.K. Clifford put it, "nor is that truly a belief at all which has not some influence upon the actions of him who holds it."[11] This may be a slight overstatement – my belief that my kitchen floor has 56 tiles might *never* manifest in any action on my part, including speech-acts – but Clifford was surely on to something. We will return to integrity in the final section of this chapter.

So in believing the Trio an ideally virtuous agent will likely display both courage and integrity. But there is at least one more virtue she will possess, namely open-mindedness. According to Nomy Arpaly, open-mindedness is especially important when two conditions prevail. The first is that something morally meaningful is at stake, in which case the person in question is uniquely attuned to the facts that matter. The second is when there is counter-evidence presented. Now climate change matters morally if anything does. But it is also true that it is really easy for most people to disregard climate change. They might say: most of the effects will be in the future, most of the people affected live elsewhere, the weather today is more or less normal, driving my car won't make a difference anyway, climate science is just complicated mathematics, etc.

All these strategies are ways of making the evidence for climate change less salient than it should be and, by implication, making the "evidence" against it more salient. But once we engage in this inversion of salience we also invite a forgetting of the moral importance of the issue, the pressing demands it is making on us. Arpaly argues that being open-minded helps us resist these powerful urges because it keeps our attention riveted on the morally important facts themselves. It is this attention-focusing aspect of the virtue that makes Arpaly's account so relevant to the climate change issue:

> Who then is the person who is morally praiseworthy for open-mindedness? She is the person whose moral concern insulates her from the pull of other concerns that would otherwise render her unresponsive to evidence, in contexts in which something morally significant might be at stake.[12]

Open-mindedness, courage and integrity thus help support belief in the Trio.

This list of virtues is not meant to be exhaustive, but it paints a sufficiently detailed picture of the ideal epistemic agent to serve as a helpful contrast to the denier, to whom we turn next.

Climate change bullshit

As might be expected, the most prominent forms of climate change denial are aimed at (B1) and (B2). Here, as compiled by Danny Chivers, are some of the things one often hears from deniers under each heading:

- Attacks on (B1)

  a CO_2 is not a greenhouse gas.
  b   When the climate changed in the deep past the warming came first. and the CO_2 rose later.
  c   Many scientists disagree with the consensus on climate change.
  d   The planet is not warming up.
  e   The planet cooled between 1940 and 1970.
  f   Scientists have manipulated the data.
  g   We can't trust the computer models on which IPCC projections rely.
  h   The glaciers are growing, not shrinking.
  i   It's all a hoax created by the Chinese.

- Attacks on (B2)

    a   Volcanoes produce more CO_2 than humans.
    b   Current warming is caused by sunspots.
    c   Current warming is caused by cosmic rays.
    d   Current warming is caused by … anything but us.

Some of these are just silly, others have the appearance of plausibility, but all have been conclusively refuted. So we won't bother to catalogue the arguments against those claims here.[13] We are more interested in the person who believes such things.

From this perspective, the claims just catalogued are not actually the most important part of the problem of climate change denial. The main problem is rather the way such claims can get translated into our perceptions of risk and cost. It is not difficult to understand how this might work. One hears claims like the ones just listed articulated in the media on a fairly regular basis and concludes that there is evidently a good deal of scientific confusion about climate change. Most people get their opinions about the world from the news media and, in a misguided effort to appear balanced and objective on this issue, the media *has* presented things as though there are two roughly equal sides to this story. But if that is the case, then surely we cannot be certain that the threat is imminent and this means that we should be careful about taking drastic steps to address it.

This line of reasoning is most pronounced in the developed world, among people who think they have the least to lose from climate change and the most to gain from being stingy about addressing it through robust mitigation efforts. In Canada, the U.K., Germany and Australia citizens tend to be divided along partisan lines on the key questions about climate change, but this kind of division is most stark in the U.S. For example, only 20% of Republicans think that climate change is a serious issue, whereas 68% of Democrats believe this. Half of Republicans support limiting GHGs, while 82% of Democrats support this measure. Only 12% of Republicans believe that climate change will harm them personally, while 42% of Democrats believe this. And finally, while 53% of Democrats believe that climate change is harming people now, only 24% of Republicans believe this.[14]

While it is tempting to focus on the differences between supporters of the two political parties revealed by these numbers, it is perhaps more shocking to observe that barely half of all Democrats – the most progressive portion of the American electorate – believe that climate change (a) will ever affect *them* in any meaningful way; and (b) is creating present harms. We should also point out that although 83% of Democrats support efforts to reduce GHGs, there is no indication that the number would be that high were the U.S. forced to do this on the scale required to address the problem meaningfully. In other words, the survey asked people only if they were willing to countenance *some* action in this area. It is plausible to suppose that the results would have been much less encouraging if the question had been more precise about how much the developed world should cut if, say, we took the PPP seriously.

How did this come to pass? How did so many people in the developed world come to believe, in effect, that the problem is either not real or is not worth addressing seriously? The short answer is that, at least in the U.S., there has been a well-funded, concerted and exhaustively documented effort to confuse ordinary people about this issue. Fossil fuel companies like Exxon-Mobil and billionaires like the Koch brothers have spent enormous sums of money to fund conservative think tanks (among other strategies) whose sole purpose is to spread disinformation about climate change and to bankroll politicians who will work tirelessly to oppose any measures aimed at regulating fossil fuels.

In her landmark study of the billionaires behind the rise of the Radical Right in America, Jane Mayer notes, for example, that from 2005 to 2008 Charles and David Koch – most of whose personal investments are in the fossil fuel industry – put about $25 million into various organizations aimed at combatting action on climate change. The main strategy employed here is what Mayer refers to as "weaponized philanthropy," the creation of non-profit and therefore largely tax-exempt organizations set up to challenge climate science. Mayer cites the research of the sociologist Robert Brulle on this issue:

> During the seven-year period [Brulle] studied, these foundations distributed $558 million in the form of 5,299 grants to ninety-one different nonprofit organizations. The money went to think tanks, advocacy groups, trade associations, other foundations, and academic and legal programs. Cumulatively, this private network waged a permanent campaign to undermine America's faith in climate science and to defeat any effort to regulate carbon emissions.[15]

Years ago, cigarette companies hired advertisers to convince the public that the science on the links between smoking and lung cancer was not settled. "Doubt," they proclaimed, was their "product." The fossil fuel industry hired the very same advertisers to peddle essentially the same message about climate change.[16] It worked.

How do we characterize the people behind this vast deception? Harry Frankfurt makes a useful distinction between the liar and the bullshitter. Both are deceivers, but Frankfurt argues that the bullshitter is worse than the liar. This is because the bullshitter has no interest whatsoever in the truth. His sole aim is to assert epistemic power over others by deceiving them. The liar, by contrast, displays a certain perverse respect for the truth, since he must track the truth in order to assert its opposite. To be an effective liar you must know the truth, but to be an effective bullshitter all you need to know is whatever is required to get you into a position of power. Frankfurt holds that the bull-shitter is deceiving us "not about the facts, nor even what he takes the facts to be," but, more darkly, about "his enterprise."[17] His enterprise is power and domination, and it is just this he seeks to cover up.

There is another important distinction between lying and bullshitting, not discussed by Frankfurt. It is that lying can sometimes be permissible because it is done to prevent greater harms or out of respect for the person lied to. Not everyone agrees with this. Kant, famously, argued that lying is always impermissible. But not many people agree with him about this. If someone is being chased by an axe-murderer and has hidden in your home, most people believe that it is permissible to lie to the axe-murderer about his would-be victim's whereabouts. Or again, if my aunt asks for my opinion about her new shoes, which I find ugly, I might tell her they are beautiful if I know that the truth would make her feel awful. Bullshitting is not like either of these cases. It is always disrespectful and, arguably, harm-causing.[18] It is an epistemic tool of unjust domination.

All those who have sowed doubt about climate change, or paid others to sow it for them, are producers of bullshit. Their victims, those who believe that the science is not settled, are consumers of bullshit. It is difficult to know what more to say about the producers, but here is one way of registering moral disapproval of their "enterprise." Discussing examples like O'Brien from Orwell's *1984*, Jason Baehr has coined the phrase, "epistemic malevolence" to describe those who seek to undermine the "epistemic well-being" of other agents.[19] By deliberately polluting the pool of socially vital information so that other agents find it very difficult to assess the facts accurately, the climate change bullshitter would appear to have an evil will (the literal meaning of "malevolent"). This might be the worst thing we can say about anybody, though it is, alas, unlikely to move the bullshitter himself.

Given the stakes – the potential for runaway climate change consequent on just the sort of political inertia for which they have been paying so handsomely – and the nakedly pecuniary motives that seem to be driving them, describing the producers of climate change bullshit as epistemically malevolent appears warranted. So, how can we fight back against them?

Dealing with bullshit: producers and consumers

The distinction between producers and consumers of climate change bullshit gives us a useful way to approach this question. But what exactly is the question? Well, as regards the producers it is whether or not we should *tolerate* their speech. The language of toleration in political philosophy has to do primarily with whether the authorities are justified in preventing people from expressing themselves in certain ways. In liberal democracies, freedom of expression is widely tolerated, for reasons laid down famously by John Stuart Mill. Mill argues that "there ought to exist the fullest liberty of professing and discussing, as a matter of ethical conviction, any doctrine, however immoral it may be considered." For Mill, the reason for this wide permission is that stifling freedom of expression is likely to lead to social conformity and moral stagnation, what he called "mental slavery."[20]

Of course, there are limits to this kind of toleration, limits defined by the harm principle, which we encountered in Chapter 2. According to the harm principle, recall, we are justified in interfering with the freedom of expression of others when, but only when, that expression is harming another member of the community. Otherwise, the policy is one of hands-off, no matter how morally repugnant we find the views being expressed. The paradigm example of speech that is justifiably prohibited by appeal to the harm principle is yelling "Fire!" in a crowded theatre when there is no fire. But speech that merely "offends" is not considered harmful in the same way (some philosophers have attempted to show that offensive speech should not be tolerated any more than harmful speech is, but we need not enter into that debate here).

Our initial question is whether or not the production of bullshit about climate change should be considered politically protected speech, according to the relatively narrow terms defined by the harm principle. Catriona McKinnon has argued recently that it should not be. Drawing on Jason Stanley's work on propaganda, McKinnon classifies what she calls "industrial climate denial" as a form of what Stanley terms "undermining demagoguery." This is: "A contribution to public discourse that is presented as an embodiment of a worthy political, economic or rational ideal, but is in the service of a goal that tends to undermine that very ideal."[21]

This seems to fit the case of climate change bullshit. For one of the things the producers of this form of denial have done over the years is present themselves as the defenders of "sound science" against what they call "junk science" (basically anything produced by the IPCC).

For example, in 1995 a few members of the U.S. Congress, working through the House Subcommittee on Energy and the Environment, set up hearings called "Scientific Integrity and the Public Trust." Here is how Vanderheiden characterizes this process: "Describing climate science as based on 'junk science,' … the central strategy of these hearings was to call into question the integrity of mainstream science, and thereby to discredit the empirical bases of the nation's environmental policies."[22]

Now, if the nation's environmental policies are put in place partly to protect its citizens from perceived threats, and if sound empirical analyses are required to do this properly (i.e., actually to address the threats), then it looks as though McKinnon is correct to say that by masquerading as sound science, climate change denial is undermining the very project it claims to be defending.

This is all very pressing given the potential for catastrophic climate change. It means that the enterprise in which climate bullshitters are engaged is very likely to lead to substantial social harms. With this in mind, McKinnon would have us alter the example of yelling "Fire!" in a crowded theatre so that it better fits the case at hand. With climate denial, she argues, it is more like a fire *has* started in a crowded theatre. While plenty of people recognize the danger, and begin warning others of it, a small group attempts to drown out these voices in an effort to convince people that there is no danger. The result is a paralyzing confusion. Since there is in fact a fire the result of this confusion is catastrophic, with many lives lost that could have been saved had the fire deniers been silenced coercively (or, if it is too late for that, punished after the event for their misdeed).[23]

McKinnon concludes from this analogy that we are permitted to silence – coercively, if necessary – industrial climate change denial. This is provocative, but we should register some suspicion of it as a practically workable approach to our problem. For one thing the silencing strategy is unlikely to work very *quickly* and even if it begins to bear fruit it will probably never fully eradicate the production of climate bullshit. This is because it is essentially a legal tool and legal challenges to expression can take a very long time to work their way through the courts. Even if legislators closed some of the loopholes that allow for the sort of "weaponized philanthropy" described by Mayer, others will surely open up. And those defending the production of bullshit will drag the legal process out for longer than we have to wait. We are, after all, talking about people with very deep pockets.

Or there could be something like "denial leakage" on analogy with carbon leakage. Prevented from expressing themselves in one jurisdiction deniers will simply relocate to a more permissive one. Of course, in the age of the Internet this talk of jurisdictional boundaries constraining the flow of information might not make much sense anyway. For as long as is relevant there will therefore likely be some bullshit about climate change in the air. This means that even as we attempt to silence its producers we need to think about how to deal with its consumers. What can we say about them?

Coercive silencing is surely out of the question with this group, at least on the grounds laid out just above. Bullshit's consumers are not intending to undermine public policy, hence they are not creating social harms in the same way or to the same degree as are the producers. So the consumers need to be moved entirely by persuasion, though as it stands currently those convinced of the Trio and those who think it is a liberal hoax designed to increase governmental control of the lives of ordinary citizens are talking past one another. In a recent analysis of this phenomenon, Simon Keller has presented a way for the "environmentalist" – basically, someone who accepts the Trio – to "empathize" with the climate change denier in an effort to spur meaningful dialogue between the two groups.

The key, says Keller, is to see both positions as examples of "ideology." Keller uses the concept of ideology to indicate something like a more or less coherent "worldview" (so it should not in this context be confused with our treatment of it in Chapter 4). On this understanding, the problem of climate change fits into the worldview that has been espoused by environmentalists for decades. This is because climate change reveals the following "truths":

- The global rich exploit the global poor.
- We need to be more frugal, consume less.
- We should respect nature.
- We should eat less meat.
- Governments should regulate polluting industries aggressively, perhaps through taxation.
- We should challenge state sovereignty and instead build more effective international institutions.[24]

What about the climate change "skeptic"? Keller says she likely has these beliefs, among others:

- Industrial activity benefits all of us and is a sign of progress.
- Consumption and innovation bring people out of poverty.
- Nature is a resource.
- A vegetarian diet is not appealing.
- Governments already tax us too much.
- We should be suspicious of international institutions.[25]

Both of these are belief "packages." Adopting either commits you to a specific stance on particular policy questions. Moreover, if you buy the skeptical package, then you will, other things being equal, also be very strongly inclined to believe what the producers of climate change bullshit are telling you: that climate science is overblown, that it represents an effort to establish more governmental control over our lives, that environmentalists are seeking "world government," that there are better scientific explanations for the weird weather we have been seeing than those offered by the IPCC, that climate science is part of a socialist scheme to suck money away from wealthy countries and channel it to poorer ones, that climate scientists are just in it for the grant money, that the Chinese are trying to fool everyone else. And so on.

Of course we can tell an analogous story about the environmentalist. As Keller puts it, from *inside* either belief package this is all "subjectively rational."[26] If this is right, then the solution to the impasse is to keep ideology out of the conversations we have about climate change. Keller argues that we can separate questions about whether or not climate change exists from questions about what to do about it if it does:

> If we were not presented with the science of climate change as part of a broader package – if descriptions of what is happening to the climate were not paired with exhortations to change our lifestyles, for example – then our independent assessment of elements of that broader package would not be so relevant to decisions about whether to trust the science.[27]

There are good reasons to endorse this strategy in principle. Ideological commitments are generally very deeply entrenched parts of an agent's moral-psychological makeup. They are rooted in powerful non-rational sources of group loyalty. Each element gains its motivational power precisely from being a member of this emotionally grounded package. So if we could pick out parts of these packages and construct our policy discussions around them we might make some progress. However, we should not be too optimistic about the chances of a strategy like this succeeding, for at least two reasons.

First, the way the package functions in practice – that is, in real conversations about climate change – is that any element, when raised out loud, triggers the others. For example, it is difficult to speak intelligently about the science of climate change without invoking the work of the IPCC, but the moment one does this in conversation with a denier she will invariably move to fears about world government or the corruption of climate scientists. Keller's argument here thus appears somewhat naïve. Second, it may not always be a good idea to separate discussion of the climate science from other elements of the packages we tend to bring to our discussions of it. To take Keller's example just above, what if habits of consumption in the developed world are the root of the problem, as seems plausible? In that case, taking them off the table in discussions of what is to be done about climate change guarantees that we will have the wrong sort of discussion.

In short, isolating individual beliefs about climate change from their ideological packages is either desirable but impractical or not desirable at all. Perhaps we will never eradicate altogether the production and consumption of climate change bullshit, though we can doubtless succeed in limiting it to some extent along the lines of the two strategies discussed in this section. In any case, there may be another source of "denial" worth exploring, one that hits closer to home than we might find comfortable.

The problem of integrity

In the previous two sections we have been discussing climate change denial as if it were something in which "we" more enlightened people would never indulge. We have been tapping into what the environmentalist George Marshall calls an "enemy narrative" about climate change. Marshall thinks this is misguided: "The missing truth, deliberately avoided in these enemy narratives, is that in high-carbon societies everyone contributes to the emissions that cause the problem and everyone has a strong reason to ignore the problems or to write their own alibi."[28] This is an important insight and Marshall is correct to underline it in the context of a discussion about climate change denial. But we must expand on his somewhat underdeveloped treatment of the issue.

There are various ways of writing one's own "alibi," various beliefs one might hold that have this function. To complete our picture of climate change denial, let's put this in terms of strategies aimed at undermining (B3):

- Attacks on (B3)

  a   Climate change will have net benefits.
  b   There are bigger problems for us to tackle than climate change.
  c   It's too late to mitigate, so we should focus entirely on adaptation instead.
  d   Anthropogenic climate change is primarily a population issue.
  e   I can do my moral part to address the problem without material sacrifice.[29]
  f   Technology will show us a way out of the crisis.
  g   We are hard-wired to ignore things like climate change.

Belief in one or more of these items is widespread among people who otherwise consider themselves progressive. This is a much more difficult problem than the one involving denial of (B1) and/or (B2). Rather than analyzing each belief separately, let's try to find a more general problem with all of them (though in a moment we will want to say something specific about the last item (g)).

In constructing our picture of what the ideal epistemic agent believes about climate change, we noted that she will likely need to possess the virtue of integrity, so let's begin by coming back to that virtue. Why is integrity important? Because it is one thing to accept the Trio, quite another to live up to its demands in one's behaviors and choices. Integrity is sometimes treated as a moral virtue, but specifically *epistemic* integrity is about the fit between an agent's belief set and her choices and behaviors. In this section, we are interested in agents who accept (B1) and (B2) and who *claim* to accept (B3) but also espouse at least one of the anti-(B3) beliefs listed above or some other belief that has the same effect on her choices and behaviors as the anti-(B3) ones do.

There is a precedent for speaking this way amongst researchers interested in this issue. For example, the sociologist Kari Marie Norgaard has written about a small Norwegian ski village she calls "Bygdaby" (the fictionalized name of a real village). She constructs a picture of how the people of the village think about climate change that reveals a great deal about the problem we are investigating. The people of Bygdaby consider themselves to be progressive, "liberals" in the American political vernacular. They are aware of and concerned to do something about the social, economic and environmental problems that generally trouble this sort of person. They are also relatively wealthy from the exploitation of North Sea oil and gas reserves. Norway is the eighth largest oil exporter and the third largest natural gas exporter in the world.

We have here the curious situation of people who, for the most part, understand the gravity of the climate crisis and are typically motivated to help alleviate problems that have anything to do with social justice, but whose high standard of living depends on perpetuating the main cause of the crisis. The people of Bygdaby, in short, are a good stand-in for a large sector of people in the developed world, especially those – like North-Americans – living in oil-producing and exporting liberal democratic countries. Norgaard provides a detailed account of the manner in which the people of Bygdaby avoid talking and thinking about the climate crisis, the way they control information about it so as to lessen its emotional impact on them.

In a telling passage she describes these tactics as a form of "denial":

> [A]t this time, people had a variety of methods available for normalizing or minimizing disturbing information. These methods can be called strategies of denial. It is significant that what I describe as "climate denial" felt to people in Bygdaby (and, indeed, to people around the world) like "everyday life." Nonresponse to climate change was produced through cultural practices of everyday life.[30]

It is important to emphasize that, like the citizens of Bygdaby, many of us consider ourselves to be just people. We demand that our governments live up to the ideals in the U.N. Declaration of Human Rights, for example. We are rightly appalled by government-sanctioned human rights abuses and will not countenance behavior like this from our own representatives.

So why are we not appalled by climate change? The question is rhetorical: we are not appalled because we have not squarely faced the truth about the issue. There is no getting around the fact that, if we are to avoid massive violations of human rights, we must change the way we are currently acting. We must cut our carbon emissions drastically in the short to medium term. Because we have moved so slowly the switch to a fossil-free economy is not going to be painless. The path from RCP 8.5 to RCP 2.6 is steep and rocky, an arduous climb. It may be that at some level many of us get this, which is why we seek out ways of not coming fully to grips with it in our actions (just like Norgaard's subjects). We want a solution to the climate crisis that involves *no* material sacrifice from us, *no* downward pressure on our standard of living.

This desire explains the attraction of most of the items on the anti-(B3) list. These beliefs can help us avoid painful or disruptive information about our lifestyles, so we are predisposed to take them more seriously than they deserve to be. For example, it is often said that we are not able to make the requisite changes because of our biology. Marshall, for example, subtitles his book, "Why our Brains Are Hard-Wired to Ignore Climate Change." The message is straightforward and ubiquitous in the popular literature on climate change: we evolved in small, tightly-knit groups and are therefore not equipped by the forces of natural selection to adopt the sort of long-range concerns climate change demands of us. We don't care about the spatially and temporally far-flung consequences of our actions, but the fault is in our genes.

If the claim is just that our biological inheritance makes the requisite thinking difficult for us there is no reason to dispute it. However, if it is taken as a form of biological determinism – and this is in effect how many people *do* take it, when they reference it to rationalize inaction – there are counter-examples to it. First Nations groups in Canada think explicitly of how their decisions will affect non-human members of the biosphere as well as human members of the "seventh generation." Human rights victories like the abolition of slavery and the suffragette movement are clear examples of pushing our moral boundaries well beyond the small groups in which we evolved. Adopting the proper level of moral concern for the entities affected by climate change is of a piece with these instances of moral expansion.

History shows that we *can* do this, which brings us back to the responsibi-list version of virtue epistemology. Doing the right thing requires having the right beliefs. These beliefs – the Trio – are out there, waiting to be adopted. It is in our power to do so and to act on them. But unless we prize the epistemic virtue of integrity we are unlikely to make all the appropriate connections.

Chapter summary

In this chapter we have explored the phenomenon of climate change denial from the standpoint of responsibilist virtue epistemology. We began with a description of the standpoint itself, moving next to a consideration of what the ideal epistemic agent believes about climate change. Here, we highlighted the importance of "the Trio" of beliefs such an agent must adopt and what virtues she will likely require in order to hold them steadfastly. This brought us to climate change denial. We examined the nature of "bullshit" about climate change, the production and dissemination of information designed deliberately by people in positions of economic and social power to confuse others about the fundamental facts of climate change. We also noticed an important distinction between producers and consumers of climate change bullshit. This brought us, finally, to a consideration of a different kind of denial, that involved in a deficiency of integrity among those who claim not to be deniers in the more obvious sense of this term.

Questions for discussion

1   Describe virtue epistemology. Is it helpful in some cases to go beyond an agent's beliefs to a moral consideration of the agent holding the beliefs? Why or why not?
2   Can you think of virtues – beyond courage, open-mindedness and integrity – that an ideal epistemic agent might possess for the climate crisis?
3   Is the characterization of some climate change deniers as bullshitters both accurate and helpful? Explain.
4   Should we tolerate the producers of climate change bullshit? Should we empathize with its consumers?
5   Are *you* a climate change denier?

Suggested reading

Byron Williston, *The Anthropocene Project: Virtue in the Age of Climate Change* (Oxford: Oxford University Press, 2015), chapter 5. The most extensive philosophical treatment of this issue in the literature.

Kari Marie Norgaard, *Living in Denial: Climate Change, Emotions and Everyday Life* (Cambridge, MA: The MIT Press, 2011). A detailed sociological portrait of climate change denial among the wealthy and progressive.

Catriona McKinnon, "Should we Tolerate Climate Change Denial?" *Midwest Studies in Philosophy* XL, 2016, 205–226. A well-argued defence of the claim that climate change denial should not be morally or politically "tolerated."

Notes

1 Thomas E. Hill Jr., "Ideals of Human Excellence and Preserving Natural Environments," *Environmental Ethics* 5 (3), 1983, 211–224.

2 Michael J. Sandel, *Justice: What's the Right Thing to Do?* (New York: Farrar, Straus and Giroux, 2009), 6.

3 Ernest Sosa, *Knowledge in Perspective* (Cambridge: Cambridge University Press, 1991).

4 Linda Zagzebski, *Virtues of the Mind* (Cambridge: Cambridge University Press, 1996).

5 Al-Jazeera, September 12, 2017. http://www.aljazeera.com/news/2017/09/pope-francis-slams-climate-change-doubters-stupid-170911172634528.html. Accessed October 23, 2017.

6 Thomas Reid, *Inquiry into the Human Mind*, ed. Timothy Duggan (Chicago: University of Chicago Press, 1970), 197. The following four paragraphs are drawn from Byron Williston, *The Anthropocene Project: Virtue in the Age of Climate Change* (Oxford: Oxford University Press, 2015), 117–119.

7 D.M. Armstrong, E.M. Mauk, E.R. Wahl, et al., "Global Warming in an Independent Record of the Past 130 Years," *Geophysical Research Letters* 40 (1), 2013, 189–193.

8 Reid, *An Inquiry…*, 197.

9 P.T. Doran and M. Kendall Zimmermann, "Examining the Scientific Consensus on Climate Change," *Transactions of the American Geophysical Union* 90, 2009, 22.

10 Quoted in Stacey Feldman, "Climate Scientists Defend IPCC Peer-Review as Most Rigorous in History," *Inside Climate News*, February 26, 2010, https://insideclimatenews.org/news/20100226/climate-scientists-defend-ipcc-peer-review-most-rigorous-history. Accessed October 25, 2017. See Williston, *The Anthropocene Project…*, 118.

11 W.K. Clifford, *The Ethics of Belief and Other Essays* (Amherst, NY: Prometheus Books, 1999), 73.

12 Nomy Arpaly, "Open-Mindedness as a Moral Virtue," *American Philosophical Quarterly* 48 (1), 2011, 75–85 (81).

13 If you want to track all this down, start with Chivers' excellent summary and go to his sources for more information. Danny Chivers, *Climate Change Denial* (Adelaide, SA: New Internationalist Publications, 2013).

14 PEW Research Center, "What the world thinks about climate change in 7 charts." http://www.pewresearch.org/fact-tank/2016/04/18/what-the-world-thinks-about-climate-change-in-7-charts/. Accessed October 25, 2017.

15 Jane Mayer, *Dark Money: The Hidden History of the Billionaires Behind the Rise of the Radical Right* (New York: Anchor Books, 2017), 253–254.

16 James Hoggan, *Climate Cover-Up: The Crusade to Deny Global Warming* (Vancouver: Greystone Books, 2009), 64–67. The following three paragraphs draw on Byron Williston, *The Anthropocene Project…*, 108–113.

17 Harry Frankfurt, "On Bullshit," *The Importance of What we Care About* (Cambridge: Cambridge University Press, 1988), 117–133 (130).

18 Byron Williston (ed.), *Environmental Ethics for Canadians*, second edition (Don Mills: Oxford University Press), 314–315.

19 Jason Baehr, *The Inquiring Mind: On Intellectual Virtues and Virtue Epistemology* (Oxford: Oxford University Press, 2011).

20 John Stuart Mill, *On Liberty*, in Andrew Bailey (ed.), *First Philosophy* (Peterborough: Broadview Press, 2011), 200–240 (218).

21 Jason Stanley, quoted in Catriona McKinnon, "Should we Tolerate Climate Change Denial?" *Midwest Studies in Philosophy* XL, 2016, 205–226 (210).

22 Steve Vanderheiden, *Atmospheric Justice: A Political Theory of Climate Change* (Oxford: Oxford University Press, 2008), 37.

23 McKinnon, "Should we Tolerate…?" 213.

24 Simon Keller, "Empathising with Skepticism about Climate Change," in Jeremy Moss (ed.), *Climate Change and Justice* (Cambridge: Cambridge University Press, 2015), 219–235 (222).

25 Keller, "Empathising…," 229.

26 Keller, "Empathising…," 229.

27 Keller, "Empathising…," 234.

28 George Marshall, *Don't Even Think About It: Why our Brains are Hard-Wired to Ignore Climate Change* (New York: Bloomsbury, 2014), 42.

29 Chivers, *Climate Change Denial*.

30 Kari Marie Norgaard, *Living in Denial: Climate Change, Emotions and Everyday Life* (Cambridge, MA: The MIT Press, 2011), 121. This, and the previous two paragraphs, draw on Byron Williston, *The Anthropocene Project…*, 121–122.

9 Geoengineering

Introduction

So far we have considered, among many other things, the steps we must take in order to avert the disaster of a 4–5°C rise in average global temperatures by 2100. The most important task is to decarbonize the global economy rapidly, thus mitigating future damages. This must, we have seen, be coupled with the aggressive pursuit of a variety of adaptation measures designed to help us cope with the challenges that are in store for us no matter what we do. But what if the focus on mitigation and adaptation is not sufficient to avoid climatic disaster? What if our political inertia on this issue is simply too entrenched to ground the reasonable belief that we will change our ways in time to avert disaster? In this chapter we will explore one increasingly prominent way of responding to this perceived situation: the turn to geoengineering. This term refers to a suite of technologies whose aim is to cool the planet artificially, ideally buying us time to adapt to the effects of climate change. As we will see, proposals to research and deploy geoengineering technologies raise profound ethical questions.

The turn to geoengineering

According to the influential Royal Society Report on the topic, **geoengineering** can be defined as "the deliberate large-scale manipulation of the planetary environment to counteract anthropogenic climate change."[1] The idea has gained considerable traction in policy circles recently. Indeed, in its most recent report the IPCC has, for the first time, provided a synthesis and assessment of the current literature on this topic.[2] There are two broad geoengineering categories. The first is **Carbon Dioxide Removal (CDR)**, the second **Solar Radiation Management (SRM)**.

The point of CDR schemes is to remove carbon dioxide from the atmosphere and store it in planetary reservoirs of some kind. CDR technologies include afforestation, soil carbon management, biochar, ocean fertilization and direct air capture. In each case, carbon is "pulled" from the atmosphere and sequestered in biomass (trees, algae, etc.) or underground geological pockets (depleted aquifers or oil reservoirs, etc.). CDR technologies have a slow impact on planetary temperatures, are relatively costly to implement and difficult to scale up.

SRM technologies are aimed at reducing the planet's temperature by lowering the quantity of solar energy absorbed by the earth. This is done by increasing the earth's albedo (reflectivity) in one way or another. Techniques include loading the stratosphere with sulphate aerosols, placing mirrors in space, seeding clouds to enhance their brightness, converting rooftops and other terrestrial spaces to a lighter color and genetically engineering plants with brighter leaves. In contrast to most CDR technologies, SRM technologies have the potential to affect planetary temperatures quickly, are relatively inexpensive and, in some cases, can be scaled-up significantly.

As the Royal Society's definition makes clear, geoengineering has arisen as a response to anthropogenic climate change. More particularly, many see it as a reasonable response to that threat given our evident inability to adopt appropriate mitigation measures. Since this failure could lead to climate disaster it makes sense to have some climatic "insurance," a planetary "Plan B" to help ameliorate the disaster. The most widely discussed option is a form of SRM, **stratospheric aerosol injection (SAI)**. SAI works by lofting large quantities of sulphates into the upper atmosphere, thus creating what the IPCC refers to as "a high-altitude reflective layer."[3] The idea is modeled on a natural phenomenon, the climatic effects of volcanic eruptions. In 1991 Mount Pinatubo in the Philippines erupted, spewing massive quantities of sulphates into the atmosphere. This had the effect of lowering global temperatures discernibly for several weeks after the eruption.

So the plan is, roughly, to mimic volcanoes in case of a climate change induced planetary emergency. Again, there is *some* agreement among scientists that deployment of SRM is technically feasible, that it would be an effective means of temperature reduction and that it would not be prohibitively expensive. Because so much of the literature on geoengineering, including the philosophical literature, focuses on this form of SRM (that is, SAI) we will do so in this chapter as well. Many of the conclusions arrived at will also apply to other forms of SRM.

According to the IPCC, because it would lower average global temperatures, successful deployment of SRM could have beneficial climatic side effects. It could, for instance, slow down sea-level rise significantly. This is because, as we saw in Chapter 1, climate change-induced sea-level rise is caused by enhanced glacial and ice sheet run-off as well as thermosteric water expansion. Both would likely be curtailed by a reduction in global mean temperature.[4] However, SRM comes with many risks and uncertainties. For example, models indicate that its deployment would affect the hydrological cycle in ways that could have negative impacts on humans and other species.

There are two ways this might happen. The first is through alteration in precipitation and evaporation patterns in regions, such as South Asia, that rely on the monsoon for agriculture. The second is by altering the rate of plant transpiration, which could impact the "recycling of water over continents, soil moisture and surface hydrology."[5]

But the most important point to note regarding risks is that the SRM-induced temperature reduction we are talking about merely *masks* the effects of all that carbon in the atmosphere. If it is not accompanied by mitigation in the form of reducing GHG emissions, SRM is not really solving the problem. It is only applying a Band-Aid to it. There are two points to emphasize about this. The first is that if GHG emissions continue to rise even as we deploy SRM, we can never stop deployment. But since continued deployment depends on high levels of international co-operation, there is no guarantee that we will achieve it in the face of potential geo-political friction. This is the "termination problem," discussed at some length below. If we cease deployment we invite swift climate catastrophe because all that carbon we have been emitting will be suddenly *unmasked*.

Second, SAI will not help decrease the problem of ocean acidification. The latter is, we have seen (in Chapter 1), a function of the amount of carbon dioxide transferred from the atmosphere to the oceans. But, by hypothesis, this amount will continue to rise even if we have masked the temperature effects of increased atmospheric carbon. So ocean biodiversity will remain severely threatened, something that would have severe knock-on effects throughout the biosphere.

The problem of political inertia about climate change is undeniable. We have done virtually nothing to head off this problem since we identified it clearly as such in 1988. There are few reasons to think that is going to change any time soon. This invites contemplation of radical technological proposals. We find ourselves at an impasse, and might therefore choose geoengineering as the "lesser of two evils." Here is the argument for this choice:

1   If we continue to emit carbon at current levels we will bring on climate disaster.
2   There is no evidence to suggest that we will stop emitting at these levels in the time required to avoid disaster.
3   So we need an insurance plan.
4   Geoengineering is the most viable insurance plan we have got.
5   Geoengineering is risky.
6   But it is less risky than unchecked climate change.
7   Therefore, we should expand research into geoengineering with a view to deploying it in case of a climate emergency.[6]

It is difficult to deny propositions (1) and (2), though it is still ethically important to fight the inertia so we may want to resist (2). Proposition (5) looks unassailable. Almost all scientists, as well as the IPCC, advocate extreme caution in our approach to these technologies, sometimes suggesting we should declare a moratorium on further research into them for decades to come.

However, propositions (3), (4) and (6) are not obviously correct. Moreover, they conceal value judgments and ethical complexities that we need to bring to light. Much of the rest of this chapter will seek to do this. For example, proposition (6) is subject to acute and unavoidable uncertainty, the more so the further into the future we are gazing. If any of these propositions is shown to be false, or improbable, the conclusion (7) will not follow. Let's begin with an analysis of the idea that geoengineering represents some kind of insurance policy.

Moral hazard and moral corruption

Perhaps the most ubiquitous claim one finds in these discussions is some version of proposition (3). But does framing geoengineering as an insurance policy invite reckless behavior on the part of the "insured"? This is the problem of "moral hazard." As we will see, it is tied intimately to worries about the "corrupt" moral reasoning allegedly involved in our whole approach to the phenomenon of climate change.

Moral hazard

The problem of moral hazard originated with the insurance industry. It describes what many take to be a pervasive behavioral pattern. When people have insurance on a good they will take bigger risks in their treatment of the good than they would without insurance. Most people, for example, will take extra precautions to fireproof their house if they do not have insurance on it. Having insurance on your car will cause you to drive less carefully than you would without it. And so on. Applied to our case, the claim is that if we believe we have a feasible Plan B for the climate in the form of some geoengineering scheme we will be less likely to engage in serious efforts at mitigation and adaptation. Because we have convinced ourselves that we are technologically protected, we might not only do nothing to curb GHG emissions but even increase them. But although the moral hazard problem seems straightforward, recent philosophical work on it has revealed it to be anything but.

In a careful discussion of the issue, Ben Hale has argued that the concept of moral hazard is too vague to do much philosophical work. For Hale, the moral hazard problem is invoked to pick out three distinct reasons for concern about our behavior: its bad consequences, its abdication of epistemic responsibility and its encouragement of moral vice. Consequentialist reasons invoke the likelihood that the insured individual will behave in ways that increase losses. Abdication of epistemic responsibility points to the tendency to ignore or dismiss reasons for caution. The problem of vice is that insurance produces dispositions in the insured that are morally objectionable: over-indulgence, greed, hubris and so on. Hale's main point is that the appeals we find to the problem of moral hazard with respect to geoengineering all make implicit use of one or more of these reasons for concern. We need to clarify which is being assumed in each invocation of the moral hazard problem and decide if these reasons are compelling in that case.[7] Let's take a closer look at these three reasons for concern.

Take first the consequentialist reason. As mentioned already, it has been suggested that insurance produces negative outcomes because those who are insured behave more recklessly. This seems to make intuitive sense applied to examples like driving. But even here we might raise some questions. Do you really drive more recklessly than you would were you not insured? As Hale notes, it seems as though there are reasons for caution on the road – most obviously, the near universal desire to avoid death or injury – that are entirely independent of the driver's knowledge that he is insured. The same line of reasoning presumably applies to anti-lock brakes, airbags, eye wash stations in chemical labs, having fire extinguishers handy, smoke alarms in good working condition and so on. The most important question to ask with respect to any of these technologies, says Hale, is not whether they lead to more reckless behavior but whether or not they lead to more death or injury. And there is little evidence to support the claim that they do.[8]

This brings us to the second reason for concern, the one about abdication of epistemic responsibility. It is of course possible that some set of behaviors, tied to the adoption of a technology, will produce negative outcomes but that we tend to underestimate – or ignore altogether – the probability of the bad outcomes occurring. This is a real concern with SRM, but Hale argues that it looks as though it can be overcome by clarifying what this technology is and is not capable of providing by way of protection. As we have seen, it can at best keep global average temperatures lower than they would be without it and prevent some sea level rise. But it will not prevent or slow down ocean acidification and it will have negative knock-on effects in the biosphere of uncertain severity.

Once we realize this, it should be obvious that SRM without mitigation and adaptation will probably produce bad outcomes. In a recent update to its report the Royal Society emphasizes this point, arguing for what they call a "portfolio" approach to geoengineering:

> Cutting global greenhouse gas emissions must remain our highest priority. Parties to the UN Framework Convention on Climate Change should make increased efforts toward mitigating and adapting to climate change, and in particular to agreeing to global emissions reductions of at least 50 per cent by 2050 and more thereafter. Nothing now known about geoengineering options gives any reason to diminish these efforts.[9]

The solution to the moral hazard problem in this form is, then, simply to ensure that people are better informed about the limitations of geoengineering technologies. The main problem with framing our response this way, however, is that this model of science communication – formally known as the "knowledge deficit hypothesis" – has been discredited by social scientists. People need more than the bare facts if they are to be moved to change their ways or their beliefs.

Analysis of this issue would take us too far afield. In any case, nobody is suggesting that the communication of facts by scientists should be abandoned, only that it is not by itself sufficient to get the relevant points across to the wider public. Suppose we take the recommendation of the Royal Society just quoted to entail that it is impermissible to pursue SRM without *also* engaging aggressively in mitigation and adaptation (they don't use this sort of language themselves). The question then is why we might advocate for research into SRM in the knowledge that we are doing so little to mitigate and adapt.

This describes current reality, but it looks as though we can get away with it only if we are deceiving ourselves about the nature of SRM. And maybe we are doing *this* because we are beneficiaries of the current state of affairs – the one involving high GHG emissions – which we therefore want to perpetuate for as long as possible. This would make us greedy and our greed would be an important part of the explanation of why we are prone to moral hazard on this issue. This brings us to Hale's third and final reason for concern: that our approach to geoengineering is somehow vicious. Because it fits this description so well and has also become so influential in climate ethics, let's look briefly at Gardiner's analysis of geoengineering.

Moral corruption

Gardiner has argued that our tendency to frame the geoengineering challenge as a "lesser evil" argument betrays a fundamental "moral corruption" in us. In one form or another the lesser evil argument is ubiquitous here (we relied on it in the 7-proposition argument, just above). Its advocates say that we should conduct research into and perhaps deploy SRM to deal with a potential climate emergency because the effects of the climate emergency would be so much worse than whatever negative outcomes would be produced by SRM deployment. Gardiner's argument is complex so I want to expand upon just one of its key features: the claim that in employing lesser evil arguments we give ourselves the moral luxury of supposing we face a real dilemma.[10]

To see how this works, think of agents in genuine moral dilemmas. Abstractly, these take the following paradigmatic form. An agent must perform action A or action B. She believes that both A and B are morally wrong, but that B is more morally wrong than A. So she chooses the lesser evil, action A. For example, imagine I find myself financially destitute but I'm the sole provider for my family and my child requires expensive emergency medical treatment. My only options are (a) to sell our home, which has been in the family for generations and which I promised my father on his deathbed I would never sell; or (b) to take a lucrative job with a company that is known to manufacture land mines, though I believe the use of these weapons is reprehensible.

Assuming these two courses exhaust the options available to me, it makes sense to say I should probably choose (a) because it is the lesser of two evils. Whereas option (a) involves promise-breaking, which is usually bad, being an accessory to the spread of land mines is clearly much worse since it will contribute to harming some people very gravely. There are a number of things we can say about agents in this kind of situation. For example, although I have by definition done something wrong in choosing (a), and wrong by my own lights, it is difficult to blame me for my decision. Even so, Gardiner argues that we might think it appropriate for me to be "marred" by that decision, to feel guilty for breaking the promise. We would react with dismay to someone who simply shrugs off all such negative feelings in cases like this.

However, this paradigm situation could be altered in a way that would affect our assessment of the agent. For instance, we might discover that the agent had culpably *put himself* into a dilemma. Since in this case he would be blameworthy for the existence of the dilemma itself we would be much less inclined to let him off the hook for the bad outcomes of his choice than we would if he had been forced into the dilemma by someone else (or by the world itself). In the above example, you would presumably assess me differently were you to discover that it was my gambling habit that put me into such dire financial straits. And this looks to be the appropriate way to think about the geoengineering case. SRM might be the lesser evil in case of a climate emergency but it cannot be forgotten that we have created the emergency through our culpable neglect of the problem of climate change.

The reason this is important is because it exacerbates the wrongness of what we do. The agent who has put herself into a moral dilemma has done something more morally wrong than the agent who simply finds herself in one, even if both choose the same action in order to get beyond the dilemma. It follows that it is morally important for us to strive to avoid situations of moral dilemma if we can. We are not yet in a situation of moral dilemma with respect to climate change and geoengineering but we tend to interpret our situation as though we are. That is, it may still be possible to avoid the emergency, or at least diminish it, through aggressive mitigation and adaptation. But, says Gardiner, because we have succumbed to "moral corruption," we have prematurely cast ourselves as dilemmatic choosers.

In truth, we are in the process of *putting ourselves* into a moral dilemma. The distinction is absolutely crucial from the moral point of view. Gardiner's overarching claim is that because we greedily desire to perpetuate our high-carbon lifestyles, but also realize dimly that this is leading to catastrophe, we are looking for a means of moral assuagement. Geoengineering thought of as the lesser evil fits the bill perfectly. It means we can refrain altogether from making significant material sacrifices while congratulating ourselves for being strong enough to make the "tough" choice in the form of a techno-fix. Of course, it does not follow that we should never pursue SRM. At some point we may well find ourselves in the relevant dilemma, whichever way we got there. Gardiner's point is only that if we do get there it will be our own fault and that this fact should mar us deeply if we choose to geoengineer.

This still leaves us with the task of determining whether or not it is permissible to engineer the climate. In the very first discussion of the ethics of geoengineering by a philosopher, Dale Jamieson argues that, quite apart from questions of technical feasibility and economics, we need to ask of any geoengineering scheme whether "implementing the project would not seriously and system-atically violate any important, well-founded ethical principles or considera-tions."[11] Any proposal that cannot meet this condition should be considered impermissible.

One of the most important results of our discussion in previous chapters is that the principle or conviction that is perhaps most well-founded in our thinking about climate change – and more generally too – is that of justice. Despite the efforts of some – neo-liberal economists mostly, as well as the politicians who follow their lead – to dismiss considerations of justice, they will simply not go away that easily. So, it might be fruitful to apply Jamieson's test of geoengineering permissibility to this concept. Is geoengineering a just response to climate change?

Just governance

Chapters 4 and 5 have already examined the question of climate justice at both the international and intergenerational levels. In this section we will rely on some of the results of those chapters, but there are also problems of justice that are unique to the phenomenon of geoengineering. To help maintain our focus, we will address concerns about justice through a particular lens: the legitimate governance of geoengineering technologies. The reason for this focus is that geoengineering is a much narrower phenomenon than climate change. Because it involves choices about how political institutions will handle a relatively well-defined set of technologies it makes sense to consider it as a problem of governance. As we will see, the governance lens illuminates important issues of domination, distribution of likely harms, consent and compensation as they arise in thinking through the challenges of geoengineering.

First, let's see why governance is thought to be such an important concern in this area. In 2010, there was a major international conference on geoengi-neering held at Asilomar, California. Five principles were adopted by the delegates, one of which has specifically to do with governance:

Governments must clarify responsibilities for, and, when necessary, create new mechanisms for the governance and oversight of large-scale climate engineering research activities that have the potential or intent to significantly modify the environment or affect society. These mechanisms should build upon and expand existing structures and norms for governing scientific research and, in the event of damaging outcomes, establish who would bear the cost and the degree of liability and proof that are required.[12]

As this principle implies, we need sub-national, national and international institutions capable of dealing with all this complexity. But we won't know how to structure the institutions without a clearer picture of whose rights and interests are at stake with respect to the policy proposals we are contemplating.

Of special concern in this context are power imbalances existing either among countries (or groups of countries) in the present or between the present and the future. Where such imbalances exist the relatively disempowered are vulnerable in a number of ways and are therefore in danger of having their rights violated. This is the broad possibility on which we should concentrate in talking about the justice of SRM. Let's separate our analysis into four areas of concern about power imbalances and the vulnerabilities to which they give rise: distributive justice, intergenerational justice, procedural justice and corrective justice.[13]

Distributive justice

Distributive justice concerns how to distribute, or allocate, benefits and burdens within some politically circumscribed group. With respect to geoengineering, we are most concerned with who bears the burdens of the harms caused by deployment. There are three important sources of vulnerability to be considered here: geographical, military and economic.[14]

First, some people will be forced to bear disproportionate burdens simply because of where they live. For example, if monsoons are disrupted, agricultural output in some parts of South Asia could drop. Populations having difficulty feeding themselves because of this may be forced to migrate in order to find food. Generally speaking the costs and risks of migration – whether within a state or across an international border – are very high. Whatever else it is, migration should therefore be thought of as an extreme burden for those who are forced to undertake it. This is morally arbitrary and therefore unjust. It would be akin to depriving someone of equal access to education just because of the morally arbitrary fact that she has darker skin than members of the majority population of a political community. At the very least, people subject to harms like this must be compensated for them, a point addressed just below.

Second, because SRM can be "weaponized" some populations face specifically military vulnerability. This could both express and exacerbate situations of existing international power disparity. Somewhat paradoxically, the threat here could be either of deployment or prevention of deployment of SRM. With respect to the threat of deployment imagine the United States had been granted special authority to deploy SRM through the U.N. Security Council. If it wanted to coerce India into accepting the terms of a lopsided trade deal it could threaten deployment of SRM, in full knowledge of the potential for monsoon disruption this would lead to. As for the threat of prevention, suppose a coalition of Baltic States were suffering from heat waves, which a reflective shield would likely ameliorate. Russia, fearing a drought-induced collapse of its wheat crop from this deployment, might threaten the coalition with military attack if it went ahead with the deployment. Existing imbalances in military strength among countries can thus force unjust burdens on the relatively weak.

The final area of concern under the heading of distributive justice is economic vulnerability. Imagine that SRM deployment would allow global temperature rise to stay below 2°C, and that this would benefit nearly everyone on the planet because far fewer people would be subject to the ravages of heat waves and sea-level rise. However, if carbon emissions continue to rise throughout the SRM deployment and this causes a spike in ocean acidification, global fisheries could be damaged.

Now, approximately 2.5 billion people derive at least 20% of their animal protein from fish. Thriving fisheries are located all over the world but tend to be concentrated in the global south. The result is that a disproportionate number of people in countries from this part of the world – Sri-Lanka, Philippines, Mauritania, Bangladesh, Morocco, Mozambique, etc. – are vulnerable to a shock in the global fish stock of the sort that could be caused by unchecked ocean acidification.

Richer countries that also rely on their fisheries – Japan, Norway, the U.K., Canada, etc. – will feel the shock too. But these are among the most diversified economies in the world. Diversification is an important measure of economic stability, and therefore also of wealth, because where significant diversification obtains damage to one sector of an economy can be made up for by enhanced performance in another. It is therefore likely that Japan or Norway could cope economically with a temporary shock to its fishery whereas this would devastate the Philippines or Morocco. Moreover, even if the disruption were not temporary, developed countries are generally much further along in the use of aquaculture and genetic modification technologies, so they could in principle adapt to the new reality with relative ease by employing these technologies.

In short, in the imagined scenario developing countries will be forced to bear costs that could be overwhelming, whereas developed countries can likely avoid this. Because this state of affairs is a product of economic – as well as geographical – luck it seems unjust on its face. Generalizing from this case we see that the economic disparity between the rich and poor countries of the world can affect their vulnerabilities to geoengineering in a way that reflects their vulnerabilities to climate change itself.

Intergenerational justice

We have seen in Chapter 5 that the problem of intergenerational climate justice is in some ways an intensification of the dynamics underlying international climate justice. Wherever there are power imbalances and a consequent skewing of vulnerabilities, appeals to justice are important. But there is no more pronounced power imbalance than the one between present and future generations. The latter have literally no power over us even though some of the decisions we make will affect their rights and interests in fundamental ways. This is, as we have seen, why Gardiner employs the very strong moral language of tyranny to characterize the stance of present people to people of the future.

This is related to SRM due to the "termination problem." If SRM is not accompanied by mitigation and carbon emissions continue to rise, the reflective shield will have to be maintained in perpetuity. This will demand ongoing international agreements about burden-sharing, technology transfers and so on. The usual stuff of international diplomacy, to be sure, but in this case the potential cost of disagreement is exceedingly high. It is very risky to hold the global climate hostage to the vagaries of garden-variety geopolitical bargaining. By deciding to deploy SRM now, we saddle future generations with all the problems of perpetuating it, even though they played no part in the decision to deploy it.

That might be considered tyrannical on its face, but this judgment is probably too hasty. Suppose the main problems here could be overcome. That is, suppose (a) the reflective shield worked sufficiently well that temperatures and sea-levels were prevented from rising dangerously; and (b) international institutions were created that were able to maintain the system in perpetuity. In this case SRM would provide significant net benefits to the future relative to the world they would inherit without it. In that case would we be doing something wrong in forcing them to perpetuate the system?

Patrick Taylor Smith thinks we would be and that this is because we would be exercising undue power over them, i.e., dominating them:

> It is irrelevant that this new power could be used to benefit those subject to it, and it would be equally irrelevant even if the negative side effects of its deployment were relatively *de minimus*; dominating power is not immune from moral criticism simply because it might be used well or because it might not be all that harmful.[15]

For Smith, SRM is like "humane" slavery. We can imagine a slaveholder who treated his slaves just like family, but of course the problem is that his authority over them is still absolute and is exercised arbitrarily. It is intrinsically unjust because the threat of abuse hangs over the head of the slave even as she is otherwise being treated "well." Similarly, SRM without mitigation is intrinsically unjust because it places future people under the threat of termination and the climate catastrophe that would follow.

This is a powerful analysis. For one thing, it does not rule out SRM altogether. Were SRM accompanied by aggressive mitigation and adaptation – the portfolio approach recommended by the Royal Society – the threat would effectively be removed at some point in the future. It follows that we would not stand in a relationship of dominance, let alone tyranny, to that generation for which the threat was removed and that SRM deployment in the present might therefore be permissible. Still, there are at least two grounds for suspicion here.

First, the residency time of carbon in the atmosphere can be very long, so even if we were to undertake decarbonization immediately the threat identified would persist well beyond the current generation. What do we say about the generations intervening between the deployers and those no longer under the threat? Suppose we are generation A and they are generation D. Generations B and C will still have to live under the threat and so our relationship to them is one of domination, on Smith's understanding of the notion. It does not look as though we can justify violating the rights of generations B and C in this manner. At the very least, more work is needed to show how this *might* be justified, since it is arbitrary to say that we are permitted to dominate some people (those belonging to B and C) but not others (those belonging to D and beyond).

Second, we might wonder if an argument like Smith's proves too much. Imagine a national health care system that was very costly to maintain but that shielded a significant number of people from health care costs that would otherwise sink them financially. Imagine in addition that no measures are taken at the governmental level to combat the main sources of declining health in society: obesity, smoking, etc. If we are the generation that decides to implement a program like this in response to a crisis are we dominating future generations, those "forced" to maintain the program? On Smith's understanding we would appear to be if the consequence of dismantling the program in the future is that many people die or become morbid. This would be the threat under which we have placed future people because of (a) our refusal to tackle the root causes of poor health; and (b) our creation of an expensive health care program that must be maintained in perpetuity.

But we might argue that these considerations alone do not justify refraining from creating the program if it is needed to manage a health care crisis, *even if we take no measures to address root causes*. By parity of reasoning, it might be permissible to have SRM ready for deployment in case of a climate emergency even if we take no significant measures to mitigate and adapt.

Procedural justice

Procedural justice is about equity in the *processes* employed to facilitate decisions about how benefits and burdens are distributed. It has to do with constructing institutionally embedded rules that govern the negotiations of interested parties – including, somehow, future generations – about anything from the allocation of scarce resources to the specification of research priorities. To qualify as genuinely fair, such procedures must be transparent and it must be reasonable for all interested parties to consent to them. There are two issues to consider under the heading of procedural justice as it relates to geoengineering: securing broad consent for deployment and defining research priorities.

The issue of securing consent arises because one of the key worries with this technology is that of unilateral deployment. That is, because SRM is relatively cheap a country that believed deployment was necessary to protect its own vital interests could undertake it without cooperating or even consulting with other interested parties. Moreover, it could attempt to justify doing so by appeal to self-defence. China, for example, might decide that too many of its citizens are dying in heat waves and respond accordingly. But this could have negative knock-on effects for other countries that were not consulted about the deployment. It might, for instance, exacerbate drought conditions in the Sahel region of Africa. Even a non-state actor such as a corporation might decide to launch some geoengineering scheme as a way to make money on the "voluntary offset market."

These possibilities point to the need for institutional mechanisms that regulate the behavior of all parties to optimize outcomes for all. Jamieson doubts that we will be able to come up with ethically appropriate mechanisms to decide on SRM deployment:

> Even if we assume that nations are the proper decision-makers for attempts to change the global climate, [this] leaves open the question of the threshold of agreement that is required (majority? consensus?) and the institutional location of the decision-making process. It is sometimes suggested that the UN Security Council would be the most appropriate institution for authorizing intentional climate change, but the moral authority of the Security Council is itself in question and it is not clear that under the UN Charter it has competence over such matters.[16]

However, we should not consider the problem insurmountable. One reason for some optimism is that poorer countries have some leverage over rich ones precisely *because* of the possibility of relatively easy, unilateral deployment.

Assuming that this is something rich countries want regulated they will at least have to sit down somewhere and negotiate in good faith with everyone else. Contrast the power that nuclear-armed countries have over those without nuclear arms. Because the costs of nuclear armament are so high, non-armed countries generally have no credible leverage over armed countries on this issue. That is one reason why the current global nuclear arms arrangement – which is really a geopolitical power *imbalance* – has remained more or less static since the end of the Second World War.

This brings us to the second issue of procedural justice. Everything we have been talking about so far has to do with the potential deployment of SRM. But there is a prior question that is relevant to concerns about justice: what is the best way to do research into the possibilities? This might sound like a question with an obvious answer: let the scientists do the research. But this simple answer conceals significant moral complexity. As is the case with much high tech research, most of the research currently being done on geoengineering is happening in the developed world. This could understandably make developing countries nervous about whose interests are being looked after in this research. Additionally, there is the significant problem of "lock in" or "path dependency." When governments or private corporations sink significant money into researching a particular technology, there is an increased chance of that technology ultimately being deployed. This has led some to worry that enhanced research into geoengineering is a fast track to deployment.[17]

These points raise many questions. Will those technologies that primarily benefit rich countries be emphasized in research programs? In seeking out "public-private" ventures in an effort to raise capital for geoengineering research and development will governments become beholden to the interests of profit-driven firms? Will embarking on a research program of this magnitude undermine the effort to mitigate climate change through reductions in carbon emissions? And finally, how do we incorporate the vital interests of future people into our decision-making procedures so that the institutions governing geoengineering research and deployment are genuinely intergenerational in scope? Such questions indicate clearly that any research program embarked upon must be defined and constrained ahead of time by multiple justice-based considerations.

Corrective justice

Corrective justice is about compensating the victims of actions (or omissions) that have harmed them. With respect to SRM, corrective justice requires that we are able to identify beneficiaries and victims of these technologies. On the assumption prevalent in the literature that SRM will create "winners" and "losers," this should not in principle be difficult to do.

Those of us in the present who, let's say, decide to deploy SRM will clearly benefit from the deployment (if it works). Not only will we be protected from the ravages of excess heat or sea-level rise but we will also be forced to pay less than we would were we to engage strenuously in mitigation and adaptation. The same considerations apply to some members of the future, namely those who are still protected from the heat and sea-level rise by SRM and who also do not have to spend an inordinate amount of money to keep the whole thing going. The victims would be those members of the present or future who suffered net losses due to deployment, for example those whose livelihoods were affected negatively by changes in the hydrological cycle.

Considerations of corrective justice would require those identified as beneficiaries to compensate those identified as having been harmed. However, things are not as simple as this portrayal of them suggests. As Toby Svoboda and Peter Irvine have argued, there are considerable difficulties on two fronts. The first concerns establishing a causal connection between the harms we have identified and SRM. Call this the technical issue. The second is about what ethical principles should guide our decisions about compensation. Call this the ethical issue.[18]

The technical issue is similar to the challenge of attributing a particular weather event to climate change. In fact Svoboda and Irvine assimilate the difficulty inherent in SRM detection to the difficulty inherent in climate change detection. In either case we need to rely on computer modeling. Suppose there is an interruption of the Indian monsoon for two years running, beginning just one year after SRM deployment. The basic approach is to create two simulations with slightly different inputs. The first includes all known causal factors including SRM. The second is the same as the first minus the SRM input. If the first model scenario captures the observed phenomena better than the second, then the interruption of the monsoon can be attributed, at least in part, to SRM.[19]

The problem is that it is difficult in principle to be sure that any model captures all relevant causes. There could be some cause that was not a part of the model even though it played a large role in bringing about the consequence. If we are demanding that some people pay compensation to others, this sort of uncertainty can be quite problematic morally because it can lead us to misidentify those responsible for payment, the real "polluters." There is much more to be said about this issue. The attribution problem has received a lot of attention from researchers of late. The result is that steady progress is being made in our ability to attribute specific weather events to anthropogenic climate change.

These results will clearly be relevant to establishing causal links between SRM deployment and subsequent harms. So although the worry raised by Svoboda and Irvine is worth paying attention to, it should not be considered the end of the debate. In other words, we should not overstate the difficulty of the technical issue. The task is to go with the pronouncements of our best science regarding attribution, and let the chips fall where they may. If we later discover that a party had been asked unjustly to provide compensation, it will, one hopes, always be possible to re-compensate them for their losses.

This brings us to the ethical issue. Svoboda and Irvine argue that the most obviously applicable theoretical tool we have here, the polluter pays principle (PPP), is not up to the challenge. As we have seen in Chapter 4, the PPP tells us that those who are historically responsible for harm-causing pollution should pay to clean it up, other things being equal. Svboda and Irvine claim that there are at least two problems with the PPP as applied to SRM:

- It is not clear whether individuals or collectives are responsible for SRM.
- The PPP is unfair to countries that deploy SRM for purposes of self-defence.[20]

These are important points but they do not undermine the applicability of the PPP to this issue. The first problem is much more relevant to climate change than to geoengineering. With climate change there are billions of point sources, varying in size from individual agents to states. This is one of the factors making responsibility so difficult to determine in this case. But if geoengineering is undertaken it will be because of the decision of an entity that is, by contrast, eminently identifiable as a collective: a state, a coalition of states, or a corporation. Individuals play little role here except, perhaps, as citizens of states or shareholders of corporations that may be responsible for deployment. In that case, the bearer of primary responsibility, the collective, would presumably pass on compensation costs to citizens and shareholders.

The second problem arises because a state might engage in SRM literally to save itself, for instance if it were threatened with imminent and catastrophic flooding due to sea-level rise. Would this state be on the hook to compensate the victims of the deployment? If so, this seems unjust. R.K. Garcia responds as follows: "The problem with this argument is that it fails to acknowledge the scope restriction built into the PPP. The PPP does not range over all agents *causally* responsible for pollution. It ranges over all agents *morally* responsible for pollution."[21]

Here, the state is not culpable for the harms consequent on its actions because it is forced to engage in such actions as a matter of survival. This seems to be a correct application of a principle of self-defense most of us recognize. We should add, however, that whether or not the state in question ought to compensate the victims of its actions will also depend on (a) its ability to pay and (b) its historical responsibility for climate change.

This concludes our consideration of SRM and justice, but we should note two more points before moving on. First, it is worth underlining a key point of this analysis, namely that the justice-related threat of SRM is not so much that it will *create* situations of international and intergenerational injustice as that it will *exacerbate* existing power imbalances. Shue's notion of compound injustice – encountered in Chapter 4 – is helpful here: "Compound injustice occurs when an initial injustice paves the way for a second, as when colonial exploitation weakens the colonized nation to such an extent that the colonizer can impose unequal treaties upon it even after it gains independence."[22]

In the kinds of scenarios we have been examining in this section, SRM deployment is probably best viewed as a potential third or even fourth level of compound injustice. Thus an original injustice between two countries – colonization, to take Shue's example – might be compounded by post-colonization trade arrangements that are unjust, which might in turn be compounded by the injustice of climate change. If the effects of SRM are even worse for the disempowered country than those of climate change itself, the original injustice will be compounded on yet another level by SRM. That is a special reason for caution with respect to these technologies.

Second, we have to this point been trying to determine whether or not SRM deployment, or even research into it, *breaches* any well-founded principles of justice. However, we might instead conceive of SRM as a means to the pursuit of justice. Holly Jean Buck, for instance, has argued that geoengineering, properly conceived and executed, "could be scaled up in ways that alleviate structural aspects of human development problems such as inequality, energy, poverty, food security, and land access."[23] That is, to the extent that these problems are, in significant part, attributable to climatic conditions, and we have the means to alter these conditions technologically in ways that ameliorate the problems, we should do so. Buck interprets the event that has given rise to the possibility of geoengineering – that is, climate change – as an *opportunity* for moral progress rather than a crisis we should bemoan. Geoengineering is the tool for seizing the opportunity.

Others have put forward a similar view. Here, for example, is Oliver Morton, talking specifically about SAI:

> The ultimate challenge is not just to picture what an earthsystem subject to some deliberate level of design might be like. It is to picture a world in which you would feel happy about such a design being realized. It is about finding happiness and exercising compassion on a planetary scale ... The goal is to help you imagine a world attractive enough that many would welcome it, but robust and provisional enough that its creation does not require everyone to agree on every aspect of it; a world that requires neither uniformity of outlook nor the suppression of dissent, but offers ways for justice and sympathy to spread out through the human world and into the earthsystem beyond.[24]

Such sentiments remind us of the discussion of ecomodernism in Chapter 6. There, recall, we pointed out that ecomodernism has a peculiar blind spot insofar as it tends to ignore the political dimensions of our environmental problems. While in no way abandoning that analysis, we can now state the problem more crisply. Ecomodernism is a form of magical thinking. As Morton would have it, universal justice will emerge all by itself from the unfettered application of technology, in this case SAI. Our discussion of geoengineering in this chapter allows us to appreciate the profound error in this way of thinking. Unless considerations of justice act as a *prior constraint* on research into and deployment of these technologies they will almost certainly extend and even exacerbate the current system of skewed vulnerabilities and opportunities.

This is a fitting point on which to end this chapter and the book. The prospect of geoengineering shows how far down the path of moral compromise we have travelled in the age of climate change. The lesser of two evils argument for geoengineering illustrates this nicely. What we are proposing to do with these technologies is alter the entire biosphere technologically so that we might survive a few decades or centuries more. This is a moment of grave and unprecedented existential uncertainty in our collective career. I think we must admit that we do not really know where we are going, that we are tampering recklessly with forces we do not comprehend and that a question mark therefore hangs over the future of our species. At the very least we need to be asking pointed questions about the values that are most important to us and the trade-offs we are willing to make just to survive. In its ancient and often forgotten role as the conscience of the species, philosophy has therefore never been more important.

So in closing I want to re-iterate and expand on something I said in the Introduction, namely that taking our ethical responsibilities seriously in this area is the only justifiable way forward. Climate change is upon us because we have failed ethically, that much is undeniable. But I would not have written this book if I thought the failure was complete, that we are now hopelessly adrift, that brute chance is our only possible savior. If we believe there's a reason to carry on at all, to fight for political change – and many of us still do! – that is surely because we can still find purchase in our hearts and minds for the notion that we are all fundamentally part of a single community of living things, a community spanning nations, species and generations. That is some reason to hope that we might yet discover a morally decent path through the gathering darkness.

Chapter summary

This chapter has considered an intriguing but also deeply morally problematic way of responding to the climate crisis. The prospect of geoengineering raises fundamental questions about justice, moral corruption and international cooperation, among others. We began by examining why the prospect has emerged, showing how it is meant to counter the threat of climate catastrophe. Next, we discussed the problem of moral hazard, the worry that belief in a techno-fix for climate change will cause us to give up on mitigation and adaptation. We also saw how this problem is illuminated using Gardiner's concept of moral corruption. Since to this point the discussion left open the central question of geoengineering's moral permissibility, we explored this by reference to the multifaceted concept of justice.

Questions for discussion

1 Some have defended a "portfolio" approach to geoengineering, according to which it is permissible but only if accompanied by mitigation and adaptation. Is this approach promising?
2 Is the moral hazard argument sound as applied to geoengineering? Should such an argument focus on consequences, epistemic responsibility or vice (or some combination of them)?
3 Which of the four justice-based approaches – distributive, procedural, intergenerational and corrective – provides the best basis for a critique of geoengineering?
4 Is the very idea of geoengineering morally outlandish? Explain.
5 What does the prospect of geoengineering tell us about ourselves? Are the ecomodernists perhaps correct to say that we should look forward to this prospect?

Suggested reading

Christopher J. Preston (ed.), *Engineering the Climate: The Ethics of Solar Radiation Management* (Lanham: Lexington Books, 2012). The first collection of essays on this topic, including some destined to become classics in the field. Very broad-ranging.

Dale Jamieson, "Ethics and Intentional Climate Change," *Climatic Change* 33, 1996, 323–336. The first paper on the topic and still one of the best. Jamieson outlines key criteria for the permissibility of geoengineering.

Stephen Gardiner, *A Perfect Moral Storm: The Ethical Tragedy of Climate Change* (Oxford: Oxford University Press, 2011), chapter 10. Gardiner's analysis in this chapter is rich and complex. The discussion of the role of moral corruption in our thinking about geoengineering is seminal.

Christopher J. Preston, *Climate Justice and Geoengineering: Ethics and Policy in the Anthropocene* (Lanham: Roman and Littlefield, 2016). This is the second volume on the topic edited by Christopher Preston. It is more focused than the first volume, containing some superb analyses of geoengineering and justice.

Notes

1 John Shepard, Ken Caldeira, Peter Cox, Joanna Haigh, David Keith, Brian Launder, Georgina Mace, Gordon MacKerron, John Pyle, Steve Rayner, Catherine Redgwell and Andrew Watson, *Geoengineering the Climate: Science, Governance and Uncertainty* (London: Royal Society, 2009), 1.
2 Intergovernmental Panel on Climate Change (IPCC). 2014. Assessment Report 5 (AR5), WG II, chapter 6, *Assessing Transformation Pathways*, 485–489.
3 IPCC, *Assessing Transformation Pathways*, chapter 6, 486.
4 IPCC, *Assessing Transformation Pathways*, chapter 6, 487.
5 IPCC, *Assessing Transformation Pathways*, chapter 6, 487.
6 Stephen Gardiner, *A Perfect Moral Storm: The Ethical Tragedy of Climate Change* (Oxford: Oxford University Press, 2011), 353. This is an adaptation of Gardiner's presentation of the lesser evil argument.

7   Ben Hale, "The World that Would Have Been: Moral Hazard Arguments against Geoengineering," in Christopher J. Preston (ed.), *Engineering the Climate: The Ethics of Solar Radiation Management* (Lanham: Lexington Books, 2012), 113–131.

8   Hale, "The World that Would Have Been…," 130.

9   J.G. Shepard, "Geoengineering the Climate: An Overview and Update," *Philosophical Transactions of the Royal Society* 370, 2012, 4166–4175 (4173).

10   Stephen Gardiner, *A Perfect Moral Storm: The Ethical Tragedy of Climate Change* (Oxford: Oxford University Press, 2011), 379–394.

11   Dale Jamieson, "Ethics and Intentional Climate Change," *Climatic Change* 33, 1996, 323–336 (326).

12   Asilomar Scientific Organizing Committee, *Recommendations on Principles for Research into Climate Engineering Techniques* (Washington: Climate Institute, 2014). http://www.geoengineeringwatch.org/documents/AsilomarConferenceReport.pdf.

13   This follows the approach of Toby Svboda, Klaus Keller, Marlos Goes and Nancy Tuana, "Sulfate Aerosol Geoengineering: The Question of Justice," *Public Affairs Quarterly* 25 (3), 2011, 157–179.

14   A similar analysis is in Christopher J. Preston, "Solar Radiation Management and Vulnerable Populations: The Moral Deficit and its Prospects," in Preston (ed.), *Engineering the Climate*, 77–94 (83).

15   Patrick Taylor Smith, "Domination and the Ethics of Solar Radiation Management," in Preston (ed.), *Engineering the Climate*, 43–61 (50).

16   Dale Jamieson, *Reason in A Dark Time: Why the Struggle against Climate Change Failed and What It Means for Our Future* (Oxford: Oxford University Press, 2014), 223.

17   On this issue, see Stephen Gardiner "Is 'Arming the Future' with Geoengineering Really the Lesser Evil?: Some Doubts about Intentionally Manipulating the Climate System," in Stephen M. Gardiner, Simon Caney, Dale Jamieson and Henry Shue (eds.), *Climate Ethics: Essential Readings* (Oxford: Oxford University Press, 2010), 284–315..

18   Toby Svboda and Peter Irvine, "Ethical and Technical Challenges in Compensating for Harm Due to Solar Radiation Management," *Ethics, Policy and the Environment* 17 (2), 2014, 157–174.

19   Svboda and Irvine, "Ethical and Technical Challenges…," 161.

20   The discussion here tracks R.K. Garcia's analysis of Svboda and Irvine. See R.K. Garcia,"Towards a Just Solar Radiation Management Compensation System: A Defense of the Polluter Pays Principle," *Ethics, Policy and the Environment* 17 (2), 2014, 178–182.

21   Garcia, "Towards a Just Solar Radiation Management System…," 182.

22   Henry Shue, *Climate Justice: Vulnerability and Protection* (Oxford: Oxford University Press, 2014), 4.

23   Holly Jean Buck, "Climate Remediation to Address Social Development Challenges," in Preston (ed.), *Engineering the Climate*, 133–148 (133).

24   Oliver Morton, *The Planet Remade: How Geoengineering Could Change the World* (Princeton: Princeton University Press, 2015), 31.

Glossary

Ability to pay principle (APP)   A principle of distributive justice applied to environmental problems. If a party is able to reduce or prevent harm then, other things equal, it may have to pay to do so. Usually applicable in a situation of non-compliance, i.e., when those who should be paying are not.

Abrupt climate change   Dramatic shifts in climatic regimes over relatively short periods of time (centuries or even decades).

Acidification   The process by which ocean water's pH is reduced through the introduction of unusually high amounts of CO_2 into the water. Affects negatively the ability of many marine organisms to build shells.

Activist preservationism (AP)   The idea, especially relevant to the Anthropocene, that in order to preserve species effectively we may need to actively manage their habitats or even alter them technologically. Examples de-extinction; rewilding.

Additionality   With respect to carbon offsetting, it must be the case that the carbon that is prevented from being emitted would have been emitted had the offsetting measure not been adopted.

Anthropocene   A new geological epoch in which humans are the most powerful single causal force in the earth system. Although the body in charge of assigning these designations – the International Commission on Stratigraphy – has yet to make it official, the term has become ubiquitous across academic disciplines and in the culture at large.

Anthropogenic   Human-caused.

Beneficiary pays principle (BPP)   A principle of corrective justice applied to environmental problems. Even if a party is not to blame for an historically produced injustice, it can be liable for payment if it benefited from the economic structures the injustice has produced.

Business as usual   The economic and political status quo surrounding climate change behaviors.

Carbon cycle   The various ways carbon moves through the earth system. For example, atmospheric carbon can move from the atmosphere to the bodies of plants (through photosynthesis), and from there into rock formations once the plants die and fossilize.

Carbon Dioxide Removal (CDR)   A form of geoengineering whereby carbon sinks are enhanced. Example spreading iron filings in the ocean to increase marine photosynthesis.

Carbon offsetting   Seeing to it that for every unit of carbon emitted an equivalent amount is prevented from being emitted.

Common But Differentiated Responsibilities (CBDR)   A principle enunciated at the Rio Earth Summit in 1992. It recognized that although all countries have obligations to fight climate change these obligations are not the same for every country. In particular, those bearing most historical responsibility for the problem might be required to do more.

Consequentialism   A moral theory according to which the moral worth of an act is a function of the outcomes it produces.

Contractarianism   A moral theory which holds that an action is right to the extent that it is the product of an agreement among ideally well-informed and unbiased agents.

Corrective justice   That aspect of the theory of justice concerned with compensating victims of past injustice.

Cost-Benefit Analysis (CBA)   A tool used by economists to determine which policy measures should be chosen. The costs of each proposal are weighed against its benefits (usually in monetary terms). The rational choice is the one with highest net benefits or lowest net costs.

Demographic transition   The move from high birth and death rates to low birth and death rates. Most societies experience the transition moving from pre-industrial to late-industrial development.

Deontology   The moral doctrine that all humans are fundamentally equal and their status as rationally autonomous agents ought to be respected by all other moral agents. The philosophical foundation of human rights.

Difference principle   A principle of distributive justice introduced by John Rawls. Some economic inequality is permissible in society if and only if those on the bottom of the economic ladder are better off than they would be under a system of strict economic equality.

Discounting   A tool used by economists to determine the present value of expected future costs or benefits.

Distributive justice   That aspect of the theory of justice concerned with how benefits and burdens are distributed among a group.

Doctrine of Doing and Allowing (DDA)   It is morally worse to be the agent of harm than it is to allow that same harm to happen on its own (or through someone else's actions).

Doctrine of Double Effect (DDE)   It is morally permissible to cause harm so long as the harm was a foreseen but unintended consequence of one's action.

Geoengineering   A suite of technologies designed to cool the planet as a response to dangerous heating, either by enhancing carbon sinks or increasing the earth's capacity to reflect incoming solar radiation.

Geologic Time Scale   A system of dating the ages of the earth based on changes in rock strata.

Great Acceleration   That period, beginning about 1945, in which the human impact on the planet's biogeophysical systems expands exponentially.

Greenhouse gases (GHGs)   Gases that have the ability to trap heat in the lower atmosphere by absorbing the energy that would otherwise be re-radiated back to space. This warms the planet. The key GHGs are carbon dioxide, water vapor and methane.

Harm principle   First introduced by John Stuart Mill in the 19th century. The principle specifies that governments may not interfere with individual activities except insofar as those activities harm, or are likely to harm, other members of the political community.

Institutional Theory of Justice (ITJ)   Individual duties of justice are specified in and limited to what relevant institutions allow.

Instrumental temperature record   The record of global temperatures obtained by the use of thermometers. It dates back to about 1880.

Intergenerational arms race   A term coined by Stephen Gardiner, it refers to a state of affairs in which each generation is forced to burn fossil fuels to cope with climate chaos, thus making the problem even worse for each succeeding generation. The problem thus compounds down the generations.

Intergovernmental Panel on Climate Change (IPCC)   The body established in 1988 by the World Meteorological Association and the United Nations Environment Program to monitor the development of global climate change. The IPCC has issued five reports and is currently in the process of producing a sixth.

Just savings principle   Introduced by John Rawls as a way of accounting for our duties to future generations. We are required to maintain for them the institutions of justice as well as the material conditions supporting such institutions.

Kyoto Protocol   An international agreement about binding emissions reduction targets reached in 1997. It entered into force in 2005.

Moral cosmopolitanism   The moral doctrine that we are all citizens of the world, and that the ties we have to all of humanity are more important morally than those we have to our individual countries.

Nationally Determined Contributions (NDCs)   Part of the pledge and review system set up in the 2015 Paris Agreement. The NDCs are the emissions reduction targets each country develops on its own, to be inspected by other countries on a regular basis, then revised accordingly.

Negative feedback   Any effect of a causal system that turns back on that system in a way that diminishes the power of the cause.

Negative rights   Those rights citizens have not to be interfered with by their governments. For example, free speech and assembly.

Negligibility Thesis (NT)   The notion that individual contributions to some process or outcome are irrelevant to that process or outcome. For example, individual voting and the election of a specific candidate; individual carbon emissions and climate change.

Non-identity problem (NIP)   First introduced by Derek Parfit, the idea that future people cannot rightly blame us for polluting their world because their identity is contingent on our having made that choice. We have not wronged them since the only option *for them* is non-existence.

Paleoclimatology   The scientific study of the planet's deep climatic history.

Paris Agreement   The agreement reached at COP 21 in Paris in 2015 committing the world to staying at 1.5°C relative to the pre-industrial baseline.

Polluter Pays Principle (PPP)   A principle of corrective justice applied to environmental problems. In short: you broke it, you fix it.

Positive feedback   Any effect of a causal system that turns back on that system to enhance the power of the cause.

Positive rights   Those rights citizens have to be supplied with certain goods by their governments. For example, free health care.

Precautionary principle   The idea that we should not wait for full scientific certainty about some phenomenon to act on it if the consequences of not acting are potentially severe.

Pre-industrial baseline   A point of reference, circa 1750, for current and future temperature valuations. So, for example, the Paris Agreement would have us strive to keep the rise in global temperature to 1.5°C above the baseline.

Prisoner's dilemma   A game-theoretical construct in which two prisoners, separately interrogated by the police, produce a sub-optimal outcome for themselves by reneging on their prior agreement to stay silent.

Procedural justice   That aspect of the theory of justice concerned with the processes governing our decisions about how benefits and burdens are distributed among a group.

Proxy data   A way of gathering information about one phenomenon by inferring it from another. For example, temperatures not available through the instrumental record can be inferred from carbon dioxide levels revealed in ice cores.

Representative Concentration Pathways (RCPs)   A device employed in the fifth IPCC assessment report to create future warming scenarios. There are four such scenarios, each named for the amount of warming expected on that pathway by 2100.

Runaway climate change   A situation in which so many of the climate system's positive feedbacks have been tripped that accelerated warming is inevitable and unstoppable.

Sixth mass extinction   In the history of life on earth there have been five mass extinction events, events in which between 50% and 95% of all species were wiped out. Humans are now in the process of causing the sixth such event. Climate change is a significant causal factor in this unfolding event.

Solar Radiation Management (SRM)   A form of geoengineering aimed at increasing the capacity of the planet to reflect incoming sunlight. For example, mirrors in space.

Stratospheric Aerosol Injection (SAI)   Currently the most prominent form of SRM. The scheme is to inject sulphates (sulphur dioxide) into the stratosphere to reflect incoming sunlight.

United Nations Framework Convention on Climate Change (FCCC)   Established in 1992, this is the document that lays out the terms of the global effort to understand and address climate change.

Utilitarianism   A moral theory according to which an act is good insofar as it maximizes the net happiness or welfare of all those it affects. A form of consequentialism.

Virtue ethics   A moral theory holding that the moral quality of actions is a function of the character of the agent who performs them.

Index